INTANGIBLES IN COUNSELING

C. Gratton Kemp
Ohio State University

Houghton Mifflin Company · Boston
New York · Atlanta · Geneva, Ill. · Dallas · Palo Alto

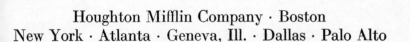

to Peggy

To Peggy

CONTENTS

CONTENTS

EDITOR'S INTRODUCTION

During the past decade there has been increasing discussion of philosophy and values in connection with counseling. The *nature of human behavior* is the province of psychology—how human beings behave, think, and feel, and what makes them behave the way they do. But *why behavior,* what its meaning is, why man exists, what is "good" existence—this is philosophy. As a counselor becomes increasingly engrossed with helping people, not merely understanding them, he deals not only with client behavior as such but with the meaning of the behavior to the client and its presumed usefulness in his life.

At this point, certainly, the counselor-psychologist enters the realm of philosophy, of meanings, of purposes and values. The psychologist as a scientist may eschew values (or perhaps he only deludes himself that he can do so), but the psychologically prepared counselor, the practitioner, cannot. He enters the life of man in all of its dimensions. Meanings and purpose are not the least of these.

Psychology's concern with philosophical assumptions has been one of the striking developments of the last decade. The American Psychological Association established a Division of Philosophical Psychology about 1963 and several of its annual meetings have included symposia on such topics as religion and psychotherapy, and value assumptions in different areas of psychology. Several journals including the *Journal of Counseling Psychology* and the *Personnel and Guidance Journal* have reflected a consistent concern with philosophy, religion, and values as significant counseling realities. All of this would have been unthinkable before 1950. Up to that time psychology had been engaged in running away from philosophy! Some psychologists still do, of course.

But the APA Division established next after the Division of Philosophical Psychology was the Division for the Experimental Analysis of Behavior. So it is still hard for a psychologist-counselor to maintain respectability as a student of a science and to admit concern with ontology (nature of reality), epistomology (nature of knowledge, of truth), and axiology (nature of values). Yet it is impossible for a *counselor*-psychologist, who attempts to see people as they live, *not* to be concerned with their dimensions of existence. The practitioner cannot divide his concern for behavior in an arbitrary fashion—

"observable behavior, yes," "meanings and values, no." He deals with a person as an indivisible whole—self-perceptions, feelings of limitations, conscience, anxieties, search for purpose, and all.

And so this book. In addition to the normal behavior concerns of the psychologist the author deals with what a person feels, hopes, dreams, imagines, searches for. Topics not commonly included in a psychologist's treatment of a counselor's job are found in this *counselor's* concern with a counselor's realities. We may not know what love, will, freedom, gropings for the meaning of existence, and decision ambivalences are in any empirical sense, but we know that they exist in the life of a person. These may be perceived as "soft" concepts when they are considered in the abstract, but they are seen as hard realities by the client who faces the counselor.

The author is a psychologist-philosopher, a practitioner with a deep sense of commitment to a person's worth. The reader may encounter concepts never touched upon in any ordinary course in his counselor preparation, but this does not mean that the counselor should be gingerly in dealing with them. Concern with the degree of freedom one has in his life, with the pressures of conscience, with the impact of change upon early religious concepts and commitments —these concerns exist in the lives of clients and influence their behavior, whether we choose to recognize them or not. Often we choose not to, because they represent ambivalences in our own lives. This, however, does not excuse us from grappling with them in the counseling relationship, or from the responsibility of attempting to clarify our own thinking regarding them.

To see these dimensions of life as realities for each client (not always to understand them) is to be a more mature and sophisticated counselor. It is quite possible that every counselor in the near future will be expected to be familiar with philosophical assumptions as well as psychological ones.

C. Gilbert Wrenn

PREFACE

The degree to which counseling succeeds is finally dependent upon the response of the counselee. This response is integrally related to philosophical questions that are little understood or discussed — the intangibles. These factors do not yield to measurement and many of them have therefore received only minor attention. But the person engaged in helping another must consider them unless he is willing to be partial, unintelligent and unrealistic in the helping relationship.

No counselor would deny either the existence or the importance of the intangibles. But the time and attention of counselors has been given to the study of those factors in the counseling relationship about which present research yields fairly exact information. No doubt they consider this a wiser use of their time and energies and perhaps more certain of yielding the desired results.

The less than minimum attention given to intangibles is understandable to a degree. The source of the information concerning them generally lies within the tenets of other, often unfamiliar, disciplines. The counselor's study attitudes and the methods of gaining information developed in the exact sciences do not increase his willingness to seek, or ease in gaining, understanding from such disciplines as philosophy, religion, history or literature. He may become impatient with the style, the nebulousness and complexity, and the absence of research bases in securing the necessary insights. Nevertheless, he is aware and concerned that his self-understanding and his understanding of the counselee could be improved if he had greater knowledge of this dimension in the counseling relationship. He confronts the difficult and time-consuming task of becoming knowledgeable about its nature and understanding of its functioning. The nature of this task in the past has been such that it has been relegated to a somewhat inconsequential place in the counselor's preparation and continuing study.

During recent years this situation has gradually changed. Within this time there has been progression in the scope and depth of interest. In the first stage it was brought to the attention of school counselors by writers that intangibles are an integral part of the counseling relationship. In the second stage the counselor was asked to ponder the idea that his own beliefs, motivations, and expectancies played a significant role in the process and outcomes of counseling. ". . . what is most personal and unique in each one of us is probably the very element which would, if it were shared or expressed, speak most deeply to others." [1] In the third stage he is asked to consider that the counselee's beliefs, his inner choice, his will, his capacity for relatedness, and other intangibles exercise a significant influence on process and results in the counseling relationship.

This book gives specific emphasis to the renewed and deepening interest in these integral elements in counseling. It is designed to provide help along three dimensions to counselors and others engaged in interpersonal relationships. It provides a wealth of background material for the understanding of each intangible. This material is drawn from several disciplines — psychology, philosophy, religion, sociology, and others. It relates the insights concerning the intangible directly to the counseling situation through illustrations and counseling protocol. Thirdly, it is open ended in its approach, involving the reader in further analysis and thought and providing direction through pertinent questions at the close of each chapter.

The following premises provide a consistent basis for understanding the content of the book: (1) Psychology on the one hand and philosophy and religion on the other each have a significant, helpful approach and information concerning intangibles. (2) The cultural setting bears a direct relationship to the characteristic functioning of intangibles. (3) The intangibles have an integral functioning relationship to the total self and are inseparable from other aspects of the self except for purposes of observation and description.

The book is equally devoted to the presentation and usefulness of both empirical and non-empirical findings as they find expression in the sciences, especially psychology, and in the non-scientific fields of philosophy and religion. In each chapter, ideas from both approaches are correlated and counseling is examined in relation to this correlation.

Three strands of thinking run throughout the book: man's lack of a valuing center, his uncritical manipulation of others, and his recognition of only horizontal values. To those who do not counsel, the book is a challenge to respect oneself as a person and, in the full understanding of this new found personhood, to respect others equally as persons. To counselors, it is a challenge to broaden the perspective of the counseling framework; to give proper place and considera-

[1] Carl R. Rogers, On Becoming a Person (Boston: Houghton Mifflin Company, 1961), p. 26.

tion to insights from both the scientific and the philosophical disciplines; to move from a partial to a wholistic concept, from the perception of an individual to the perception of a person.

This book is planned for counselors, especially those in schools, universities and seminaries. However, counselors in individual practice, in industry, in the church, in clinics and in youth groups will also gain clarification of their roles as well as new insights and understandings. Those engaged in giving leadership to youth and college age people will find the book a helpful source in understanding the values, problems and adjustments of these age groups. Those in colleges and universities who have responsibilities in the preparation of school counselors will find this book highly useful and a valued addition to present sources. Students have indicated the helpfulness of this material over a number of years.

The author is indebted to great teachers in philosophy, religion, education and psychology. His thinking has also been nurtured by graduate students who have discussed these ideas over the past several years. He has been encouraged to think deeply concerning a number of the issues in workshop and camp experiences of religious leaders and university students. To all of these groups he is grateful for his opportunity to share in these searching participative communities.

He is indebted in a special way to Dr. C. Gilbert Wrenn, whose own broad perspective and wisdom concerning life, together with his unusual ability to be objective and candid in a helpful manner, is much appreciated. His patient and continued criticism has done much to increase the clarity and usefulness of this book.

My wife, Agnes Lackie Kemp, to whom this book is dedicated, was a partner with me in all its stages. For our many discussions, her ability to ask critical questions and to clarify ideas, and her steady encouragement I am especially thankful.

C.G.K.

INTANGIBLES IN COUNSELING

THE
HUMAN
CONDITION

I

1

CONCEPTS OF MAN

Regardless of his theoretical assumptions and the quality of his skill, each counselor is finally confronted with what he believes about man. Does he believe that the counselee, when helped to understand his behavior and its causes, will change in a constructive direction? Does he believe that if the counselee expresses his feelings, relives his repressions and recognizes his true motivations, new directions will emerge, leading to desirable outcomes? Does he believe that the counselee himself can discern what to do, and with help will recognize and use this ability? Does he believe that basically man desires to improve his condition and will do so if psychological and other barriers are removed?

In thus examining what he believes, the counselor finds it difficult to make a satisfactory analysis. Why? Because man has always been a problem to himself. He asks many questions but attains only limited assurance about the answers. He recognizes in himself the same basic needs that animals have. He asks, should he think of himself as a superior animal, different only in degree from other animal life? If so, what is the character of his superiority? Is it his rational faculties, or his imagination, feeling and will, or some combination of these?

If man is only a superior animal, how does he account for his concerns, and recognition of happiness, guilt, love and despair? Even the questions he asks and the answers to which he subscribes hint at qualities difficult to subsume under the category of *homo faber*— a tool-making animal.

Some of the dilemmas in trying to understand man's nature become apparent in the consideration of his problems. At times he thinks of himself as evil, but then he is confronted with the question whether if he were truly evil he would be able to recognize this? At other times he views himself as essentially good, but finds it difficult to account for evil. Then he confronts the choice between blaming society and accepting responsibility for the results of his own actions. He asks if life is worth living, and recognizes that the ability to ask such a question implies a capacity beyond his rationality. He looks about him and ponders the fact that some men take their lives physically, and others submerge themselves in materialism. Such actions indicate that man is more than vitality. He has a freedom beyond his basic structure.

THE PRESENT SITUATION

Finding a satisfactory ground for his attitudes, beliefs, and values concerning himself becomes more difficult for the counselor as the modern amalgam of thought becomes increasingly complex. Often he hopefully acts as if the counselee lived in the simple world of his own childhood, a sort of world in which ambiguity was only a hidden word in the dictionary. But he is incorrect about the counselee, as he is about his idealization of the past.

Neither do his counselees know what to believe. The following description of a modest survey hints at the dilemma. A group of 152 graduate students from various educational and socio-economic backgrounds, ranging in age from 22 to 48 years, participated anonymously. Each was asked to write 20 statements beginning, "Man is . . ." Two judges made a content analysis of the responses.

The most convincing characteristic of the responses was the frequency with which each respondee held conflicting, and even contradictory, beliefs. It was common to read in the same paper, "Man is only the highest part of nature," and "Man is made in the image of God." Or, "Man is only a thinking animal," and "Man is a spirit, an immortal mind and soul." The following statements illustrate the contrast and complexity of viewpoints: "Man is a thinking, rational being with tremendous innate resources for feeling and vitality which need only to be tapped." "Man is unique because of his drive to actualize himself but often the way he thinks gets in his way." "Man is the animal which by working with others can build a utopia if he can stay out of war." "Man is the part of creation which could do great things if he could control his passions." Some papers had a few statements within a religious framework. "Man is a spirit temporarily housed in a mortal body." "Man is a child of God. God is his Father whose guidance he seeks." "Man is rational but he also depends on God for help." "Man is creative soul."

Although the sample is inadequate for the purpose of reaching valid conclusions, certain trends are discernable. There is not a consistent pattern of ideas about man. Contradictions seem to exist unrecognized. All of the subjects have a sense of man's great potential, and conclude that he makes the best of it through the use of his mind and/or his great energy, vitality and drive. It appears that most feel there is something unknown, a mystery, about man. At best the ideas are a confused mixture of opinions containing many threads of philosophical and religious thinking; at worst, a conglomeration concerning which any conclusions are almost impossible.

HISTORICAL CONCEPTS OF MAN

To comprehend the viewpoints concerning the nature of man it is necessary to examine, at least briefly, the historical antecedents of the present complexity. Modern viewpoints have their origin in two ancient and contrasting concepts, the Greek or classical view and the Biblical view of man.

The Classical View

The various strains of the classical view of man, whether Platonic, Aristotelian, or Stoic, share in common the conviction that man is to be understood from the standpoint of the uniqueness of his rational faculties and that "mind" is sharply distinguished from the body.

The mind or *nous* in the thought of Aristotle was the means of pure intellectual activity, a universal and immortal principle which entered man from without. Only the "passive" element of *nous,* as distinguished from the "active," was involved in and subject to the individuality of a particular physical organism. He described mind thus, "No mind knows itself by participation in the known; it becomes known by touching and knowing, so that the same thing is mind and object of mind." [1]

"Mind" was considered the organ of *logos,* the unifying and ordering principle. As such, "mind" was sharply separated from the body. The rational part of man was identified with the divine, for reason, as the creative principle, was considered identical with God. In the thinking of the Greeks man had particularity but not true individuality since the *nous,* the creative part, had no integral relationship with the rest of man.

[1] Aristotle, *Physics,* trans. by W. D. Ross (Oxford: Clarendon Press, 1908), p. 20.

The body-mind dualism led the Greeks to consider the body evil and the mind essentially good. These two viewpoints, "mind" as the creative principle, the immortal part of man separated from Universal Mind, and the body-mind dualism have heavily influenced the doctrine of man down to the present day.

These were not the only speculations of the Greeks concerning man. The Stoics differed slightly but significantly from Aristotle and Plato on the subject. The Stoics were uncertain whether reason should guide man to emulate nature as he discovers it outside his reason, or whether man's reason is in truth a spark of divine reason which should set him in opposition to the impulses of nature.

More important for future generations are two other strands: the primitive beginnings of naturalism and materialism. Democritus and Epicurus viewed man as wholly a part of nature. They reduced "mind" from its highest significance as immanental reason to mechanical necessity and tried to comprehend man in terms of mechanism.

Although the Greeks had great confidence in the virtue of the wise man, they did not expect that many men would be wise. Basically they were inclined toward melancholy as they considered the brevity of life and the mortality of man. The pessimism of the philosophers and that of the Greek tragedians had different origins. In the tragedies, Zeus, the god of the ultimate principle of law and order, is jealous of Dionysus, the god of human passion. But whereas the philosophers saw human passions as the mere impulses of the body, the dramatists saw these passions as something more. Therefore, they present the principle of law and order, represented by Zeus, defied by human vitalities which are creative and destructive. The purpose of the dramatists was to urge a proper restraint. Their plays demonstrate that the spirit of man expresses itself in his vital energies as well as in the harmonizing force of mind. For Greek tragedians the rational principle of order was ultimate and therefore the ending was tragic since Zeus remained God. However, the problem presented by the tragedies was apparently not recognized by those who later reviewed classicism.

The Biblical View

Let us now turn to the Biblical view of man as it is distinguished from the classical doctrine of man. Each view is based on different assumptions, the Greek view on metaphysical suppositions and the Biblical view on the presuppositions of Biblical faith. In Biblical faith, "God is both vitality and form and the source of all existence. He creates the world. This world is not God; but it is not evil because it is not god. Being God's creation, it is good." [2]

According to this view man is a unity of nature, mind and spirit. This monism is derived from the view of God as the creator, and from faith in the goodness of creation. The second distinguishing belief is the concept that man is made in "the image of God" and as such is primarily understood from the standpoint of God; that is, man does not fully understand himself through the use of either reason or feeling. Thus, this view grants man a capacity which in the Biblical viewpoint explains his uniqueness — the capacity for self-transcendence through which it is possible to live consciously below or above the level of reason. Man knows the world insofar as he does because he stands outside both himself and the world. Thus he never fully knows himself, and he believes that he is understood from beyond himself, that he is known and loved of God. In the confidence and joy of this relationship, man in response seeks to understand the purposes of God for his life.

Whereas the Greek tragedians considered the struggle of life to be between Zeus and Dionysus, reason and spirit, in the Biblical view the conflict is at the center of human personality, in the will. Thus man's failure in the Biblical sense is not because of his lack of ability (reason and vitality in any combination) but because of the wrong use of his freedom. Man's finiteness can be, and is, affirmed in this view as in the view of the Greeks. However, in the Biblical framework the unity of body and spirit can be emphasized in relation to God the creator and redeemer, who created both, whereas in the Greek view a strategic balance must be attained with reference to the emphasis on either.

A synthesis of the classical and Biblical interpretations was achieved in medieval Catholicism. This amalgam emphasized obedience of the individual to the universal rules of natural law. In addition, the religious institution became the safeguard of the individual in the relationship of the soul to God.

The Modern View

The modern period began by destroying this synthesis. The Renaissance emphasized the classical element and the Reformation abstracted the Biblical element. The Renaissance was a revival of

[2] Reinhold Niebuhr, *The Nature and Destiny of Man* (New York: Charles Scribner's Sons, 1946), p. 12.

classicism, with tremendous emphasis on individuality, especially the liberty and freedom of the individual. Although this emphasis upon individual autonomy was in part a reaction to Catholic authoritarianism, the source of emphasis on the individual is contained not in classicism but in Christianity.

The fusion of the Greek emphasis on rationalism and the Christian emphasis on the importance of the individual led to a new interpretation of man. The focus of this interpretation became the mystical ideas of the infinite potentialities of the human spirit. Such a focus results in the contemplation of God who fulfills each human individuality but omits the Protestant idea of the individual's sole responsibility to God who is both judge and redeemer.

The Reformation took a more sober view of man than did the Renaissance. Whereas the Renaissance was hopeful that man once redeemed by "grace" might reach great heights, the Reformation saw man as continuously in need of "grace" and the fact of sin as perennial and serious, without any possibility that man's self-contradiction would end and history would be fulfilled.

Reformation thought also placed high value on the individual and individuality. It focused, however, not on the individual's capacity to know the truth but upon his responsibility to God, from whom came forgiveness. Protestantism, following the Reformation, gave less significance to the concept of "natural law." Instead, the individual faced the responsibility of seeking to do God's will amidst all the complexities of human existence.

The Renaissance and Reformation views each had a revolutionary impact. But the outcomes proved to be not entirely, or perhaps even chiefly, a function of a philosophical revolution. Rather these views were examined against the background of great scientific, economic and cultural advances. As man discovered that his economic power depended upon his individual initiative and resourcefulness he began to see human history as a realm of human decisions alone rather than also as a realm of destiny. Efficiency became his chief concern. Science contributed to man's actual mastery of natural forces, which strengthened and confirmed his belief in human self-sufficiency. As man amazed himself his power and pride grew apace, subtly merged with the Christian idea of the significance of the individual in the sight of God. Man's great progress in the natural world reinforced his high estimation of himself and encouraged an easy conscience. The creatureliness of man and his responsibility to, and dependence upon, God retreated into the background. The Reformation conceptions became increasingly unpopular.

The virtual triumph of the early Renaissance viewpoint was succeeded by the seventeenth century stoicism of Descartes and Spinoza, later by the more radical Democritan naturalism, and finally by Epicurean materialism.

THE PRESENT VIEW OF MAN

The complexity of the present view of man centers around the problem of the relationship of form and vitality. Each naturalistic view attempts to interpret the whole man in terms of what each considers to be his essence.

One of the chief antinomies concerning man is that between idealism and romanticism. In idealism the essential man is the rational man. His reason is the source of both form (critical thought) and vitality (imagination, emotions and will). Also, reason is considered to be the order and form which transmutes vitality into genuine creativeness. This might define creativity too narrowly as only the product of a cultivated mind. The viewpoint of romanticism is more complex. The romantic naturalists interpret man primarily as vitality, and deny that either reason or mechanical nature explains his true essence. This interpretation of man has had significant influence; it seems to take into consideration, more than other naturalistic interpretations, both the particularity of man's physical existence and the unique self-knowledge of his spiritual life. This romanticism does because it is curiously compounded of Rousseauistic primitivism and Christian pietism. From Rousseau romanticism derives its emphasis on the non-rational forces, emotions, imagination and will. From pietism it takes the sense of the individual's unmediated relation to God. This in turn is secularized so that not only is the individual directly related to God but he becomes self-justifying and autonomous. This distortion is the result of a slight but significant change from Luther's original Protestant principle of the priesthood of all believers. Whereas Luther's principle emphasized the unique relation of faith and responsibility to God, the pietists emphasized the possibility of a direct and unmediated experience of unity between the believer and God.

Romanticism is more likely to be confused with the Christian faith than either of the other naturalistic philosophies. This is due in part to its understanding of the wide gulf which lies between the natural impulse and that of pride and power — in the language of Rousseau, between "the natural feeling which leads every animal to look to its own preservation, and the factitious feeling which arises in the state of society which leads every individual to make more of himself than any other." [3] On the other hand, the romantics' relativism in religion and politics is indicative of how far they have departed from the Christian faith. Romanticism understands the fact of goodness in creation both in its particularity and individuality but lacks perspective beyond creation.

The Biblical view of man adds to form and vitality the quality of spirit. Furthermore, spirit is considered an integral component of both form and vitality. This view of man is a unified concept of nature, mind and spirit. The whole man participates in all his actions, and man can be understood only from this unified perspective. "Spirit" is a special gift which, if used, helps man to know a quality of life impossible without it. This capacity, called by various names such as "inner choice" (Jungian psychologist Frances Wickes) or the "holy spirit" (the Bible), is rejected by both the rationalists and the romanticists. To the rationalists reason is supreme and man does not need the guidance of the "spirit." They find no place for the Biblical concept of creature and sinner. The romanticists reject the concept of "spirit" since to them man is autonomous and made in his own image, not in the image of God. As Swinburne expressed dramatically, "Glory to man in the highest for man is the master of things."

THE COUNSELOR AND THE NATURE OF MAN

Fred is well trained and considered one of the best counselors in the city. When he reviews his record he recognizes that he has been working on the assumption that each counselee can be understood from the standpoint of the uniqueness of his rational faculties. Once in a while he catches himself acting as if this ordering and unifying process of mind encompasses the complete entity of the counselee.

In this respect he was perplexed concerning the impasse he had reached with Jean. The referral note he had received did not seem to carry any unusual implications. It simply read: "Jean is one of our brilliant students. She is now in her senior year and dropping out of school to work in a factory on an assembly line making clocks. See what you can do. She's not the kind we want to lose."

Fred had smiled; he would help her to straighten out. He had helped others. As soon as she saw the foolishness of terminating her

[3] Jean Jacques Rousseau, *Social Contract* (New York: Wise, 1901), p. 197.

education in favor of a factory job when she could prepare for something much better, she would come around.

But she did not. After ten interviews he had to admit that he was getting nowhere. He had listened and he had presented alternatives. She had discussed, explored in depth, he thought, and with good sense. From his point of view, and he thought, now, from hers, the plausible, intelligent and sensible course would be to continue in school. She earned good grades, participated in extracurricular activities, and appeared to have satisfying social relationships in the community.

Fred wondered where he had failed. Did he not recognize the real problem? Had he formulated conclusions too hastily? Had he not helped her sufficiently to analyze the problem? Why was he not succeeding as well as he usually did? Were there considerations which should have been included and had not been?

Still puzzled, he made a phone call and arranged a time when he could get together with his counselor colleagues, Bob and Jim, to discuss his work. He had found such discussions about mutual problems in counseling stimulating and useful.

After Fred had communicated his concern to the others, Bob responded, "Well, as you have known for a long time, Fred, I don't go about it in quite the same way as you do. I don't believe that just because a certain idea makes good sense the counselee will carry it out."

"How would you proceed?" asked Fred with a slight and well concealed impatience.

"I don't know exactly," replied Bob, "but I would like her to discuss her feelings about the whole matter. I would hope that if I could understand and help her to clarify them, whether they are feelings of withdrawal, aggression, fear, disillusionment or the desire for freedom and independence, she would come to understand her behavior, begin to look at things more positively, and become interested in some constructive action."

"But she would have to use her rational abilities," rejoined Fred, "and the constructive action you would expect to be rational, practical and sensible?"

"Yes, indeed," answered Bob, "but I believe the counselee does not use his thinking abilities in planning constructively for the future until he has worked through his feelings which have become roadblocks to his progress."

It is clear that Fred and Bob are basically far apart in what they believe about the way the counselee moves toward health. Actually, they confront the old problem of the relationship of form and vitality. To Fred the essential man is the rational man, and his reason is the source of both form and vitality. Bob sees the counselee in terms of vitality and his counseling therefore emphasizes non-rational forces, the emotions, imagination and will. This vitality is the guiding, dependable, direction-giving force of the organism, but it is impeded by repressions and defenses from carrying out its function. Many counselors take a similar view. For them this position originating in "romanticism" provides a better understanding of man in terms of both the particularity of his physical existence and his natural impulses to pride and power.

However, Jim was not completely satisfied with the assumptions of either of his colleagues. He explained it this way: "I can't think of appealing to the critical, analytical powers of the counselee or of expecting constructive change when I help him to get rid of his defenses. I think of the counselee in one piece. I don't think he can be explained. I know that, for the most part, I work on a cause and effect idea, but I don't believe the counselee has to perform in that way. In fact, one reason why we have trouble understanding is just that at times there seems to be no way of accounting for what takes place. I know, I try, as you do, but I am not really satisfied that my hypotheses get me very far. I have known a counselee to act at times as if he didn't have any reason, that is, you might say, below the level of reason, and at other times above the level of reason, accomplishing something that we would have agreed was impossible.

"I think I am saying that we ourselves fail, for the same reason, not only because of our ability, that is, our reason and vitality in any combination, but because of the use we make of our freedom. So I wonder not only about the counselee's ability to understand and discuss his defenses but also whether he will use this freedom to understand himself and to reorient his life."

IMPLICATIONS

The character of the counselor's belief is a basic and integral part of the counseling relationship and is built on what he believes about the nature of man. To be intelligent regarding his counseling relationship, the counselor must clarify and make explicit to himself what he believes about the counselee. This will not be an easy task. Perhaps he has never actually confronted the fact that his counseling method has a direct relationship to his beliefs regarding the nature of man. Although schooled in the theories of personality basic to the various methods of counseling, he may not have made any attempt to see the functional relationship between these and his own beliefs about man's nature. He may find that a particular theory assumes more than he believes, or assumes something that he does not believe. What the counselor believes or disbelieves "comes through" to the counselee. The greater the congruence between the theory he has assimilated and what he really believes about man, the greater is the efficiency to be expected in the counseling process. The therapist's view of human nature does have consequences in his therapy.

As we have seen earlier, in accordance with the modern trend those of romantic leanings place faith in the vitality (feeling, imagination and will) of man. Rogers writes, "Man's behavior is exquisitely rational, moving with subtle and ordered complexity toward the goals his organism is endeavoring to achieve." He recognizes that man does not live in this fashion for the reason "that our defenses keep us from being aware of this rationality so that unconsciously we are moving in one direction while organismically we are moving in another." The man who is living "the good life" will "be increasingly a participant in the rationality of his organism." Thus the conclusion is that through the removal of defenses and reliance upon this "rationality of the organism," man will "live in increasing harmony with himself and others." [4] The counselor should ask, "Have I discovered this to be so, or do I find that man breaks and remakes the harmonies of nature?"

The counselor should analyze his counseling behavior to see whether he is assuming that under certain conditions man will move toward constructive goals, and if so, consistently or inconsistently. If the latter, how does he explain this? Does he assume that the process is at fault or that the counselee is asserting his human freedom? If the latter, is he willing to recognize that he has shifted from the romantic naturalist and scientific position to a position which allows extra-scientific findings?

Does the counselor discover that he relies upon the rationality of the counselee to recognize, evaluate, direct and control his natural impulses? If so, then he believes that man is a superior animal who, to realize his potential most fully, must use his mind to bring his creative energy under control. This position assumes that man can rely upon the ability of his mind in the accomplishment. Francis Bacon took this position, but he was uneasy lest the "unquietness

---

[4] Carl R. Rogers, "A Note on the Nature of Man," *Journal of Counseling Psychology*, 1957 (a), Vol. 4, p. 202.

of the spirit" would "interfere most mischievously in the discovery of causes." [5] If the counselor takes this position he attempts, like Bacon, to explain the whole of man by emphasis on one part. By so doing he either rejects the idea of man's freedom or identifies freedom with reason. In the latter case, he assumes that man's freedom is secure in the mind's urge toward coherence and synthesis, and he should recognize that he places implicit faith in the counselee's powers of critical thought.

As the counselor examines his beliefs, he may be convinced of his dependence upon the counselee's using, to equal degrees, both his rationality and his vitality, that is, both his ability for rational thought and his ability to use his imagination, feeling and will. He may decide that in making some decisions the mind will lead, while in making others the rationality (wisdom) of the organism will do so. Such beliefs may direct him, with reference to certain counselees, to perform in such a manner that the counselee will be strongly encouraged to use the results of critical thought as the basis for action. In other situations and with other counselees he may use a different strategy, in which he encourages the counselee to rely upon what he "feels," upon what his organism—his imagination, feeling and will —suggests as a course of action. This counselor believes, then, that in some instances the source of guidance is "form" (critical thought) and in others it is "vitality" (imagination, feeling and will).

The counselor may not be sure whether he believes more strongly in mind or in vitality. When he examines what takes place he may be inclined to say that it is a combination in which all the constructive forces within the individual are energized. At this point he has to ask what energizes these forces. He may believe that it is his loving concern for the counselee. This concern encourages within the counselee the ascendancy of the constructive forces. But there are times when his deepest loving concern does not seem to help. He may conclude that his loving concern was not real, not sincere, because of some split within him, some lack of unification due to guilt or separateness. However, this is not always the case, and therefore the cause must rest more with the counselee. The counselor reviews his procedures and his attitudes, and fails to find cause for failure.

At this point he might reflect upon the question whether this energizing force is a quality of the mind or a quality of the organism. He might approach the conclusion that the energizing force is a qual-

[5] Francis Bacon, *Novum Organum*, trans. by James Spedding, in Benjamin Rand, *Modern Classical Philosophers* (Boston: Houghton Mifflin Company, 1924).

ity of spirit — of the mystery of the individual whose activity is not necessarily contained within the tenets of scientific method — and that this quality is an integral part of both mind and vitality.

Such a conclusion he finds difficult to recognize and more difficult to accept. However well it may seem to explain the counseling relationship, especially the incomprehensible extremes of success and failure, he recognizes that this position cannot be scientifically demonstrated or measured; it is outside the tools of logical proof. Thus he is in the position of entertaining belief in something which is non-empirical. He is in the questionable realm of faith.

He may brush this possibility aside immediately and return to the safe ground of scientific evidence. He dichotomizes man into mind (rationality) and body (vitality), and subsumes spirit under either mind or vitality, depending upon the character of his beliefs and disbeliefs about man. Thus spirit loses identity in its own right. Mowrer warns us that "man cannot be fully understood either within the bounds of natural necessity or rational prudence. Long ago we were reminded that man did not live by bread alone, and it is none too early for us to turn our attention to the identification and better understanding of this 'something more.' " [6]

The counselor whose searching reveals to him that man has the potential for self-transcendence and human freedom entertains the possibility of a more comprehensive view of the counselee and greater perspective for the understanding of his counseling efforts and himself. Some elements in this comprehensive understanding could reasonably be considered to be the following:

1. The counselor keeps his equilibrium and remains humble. He does not become discouraged when he fails (or seems to fail); he re-examines himself and his process but recognizes that man's freedom may be used destructively as well as constructively. He does not become proud when he succeeds (or seems to succeed). He recognizes that man's freedom is his freedom to assert his powers against overwhelming odds.

2. He sees himself more realistically. He works in relation to, and in accordance with, processes some of which may not necessarily follow empirically developed scientific laws.

3. He has a developing and growing respect for the counselee

[6] O. H. Mowrer, "Some Philosophical Problems in Psychological Counseling," *Journal of Counseling Psychology,* 1957, Vol. 4, p. 4.

with reference to what he can explain and also concerning that which he can never quite fathom or predict.

4. He has a deepening respect for himself, for what he can observe and evaluate and change and for the part of himself which is influential, all purposeful and not explained completely within the bounds of rational thought, or the wisdom of the organism.[7]

QUESTIONS

1. What are indications that man is more than a superior animal?
2. Why is the concept of human freedom important to the counselor?
3. What are the crucial differences between the scientific viewpoint of man and the religious viewpoint?
4. Why is the philosophy of Democritus and Epicurus helpful in understanding today's values?

FOR FURTHER READING

Simon Doniger (ed.). *The Nature of Man in Theological and Psychological Perspective* (New York: Harper & Row, Publishers, Inc., 1962).

This book presents the points of view of theology and psychology on the nature of man. Section One is concerned with "Views of Man's Nature," Section Two with "Good and Evil in Man," and Section Three with "Man's Problems and Potentialities." The concluding chapter is devoted to an analysis of the relationship between theology and the behavioral sciences. Most useful is an analysis of the assumptions which once stood as roadblocks in the way of cooperation between the disciplines.

The book is planned to include approximately equal numbers of contributions from theologians, philosophers and educators, on the one end, and psychologists, psychiatrists and psychoanalysts, on the other.

Reinhold Niebuhr. *The Nature and Destiny of Man, A Christian Interpretation* (New York: Charles Scribner's Sons, 1946).

[7] C. Gratton Kemp, "Another Note on Counseling and the Nature of Man," *Journal of Counseling Psychology*, April 1961, based on pp. 187–188.

The two volumes, *Human Nature* and *Human Destiny,* are now bound under one cover. *Human Nature* examines and evaluates naturalistic interpretations of man, presents the Biblical view of man and contrasts and compares the naturalistic and Biblical viewpoints of man. *Human Destiny* considers the Christian doctrines of the fulfillment of human life and history. These doctrines are examined and contrasted with other doctrines of salvation, and the salient points in each are illuminated.

Erich Fromm. *The Heart of Man* (New York: Harper & Row, Publishers, Inc., 1964).

This is a psychological analysis in depth of the nature of good and evil in man. Fromm's thesis is that when man loses his capacity for independence, love and reason, he necessarily develops the forces of destructiveness which lead to his dehumanization. He considers love of death pathological and love of life normal. He emphasizes that man may escape from his greatest prison — the destructive aspect of himself. His analysis is clarified by many helpful illustrations.

2

THE SELF

Janet will graduate from nursing school in three months. She enjoys nursing and looks forward to entering the profession. She and Sam, whose father is the town's lumber king, have planned to marry when she graduates in June. Recently she attended a meeting at which she heard a medical doctor on furlough speak of the need for nurses in Rhodesia. She immediately felt inspired to go, but as the days go by she has become uncertain.

Her uncertainty increases after she discusses the question with Sam. The thought of postponing her marriage (or giving it up, which Sam has hinted would result) and going to Rhodesia, where a sixty-hour week and small pay are accepted, when she could have her own comfortable home and care for sick people here, causes her to hesitate.

In this dilemma, she goes to the counselor who helped her in high school. The counselor is soon in possession of the facts, which Janet freely relates to him. To him it is clear that when she could pursue her nursing career here and marry Sam, whom she loves, it would be very poor judgment to go to Rhodesia. He is surprised when after three sessions Janet, having apparently examined these conditions carefully, is still unsure what to do. At this juncture the counselor realizes that her indecision is rooted in considerations other than those which they have discussed. He is uneasy as he contemplates that an intelligent and successful young woman might be trying to make an important decision on some basis which supersedes sound reason. He finds himself wondering if there is some source of decision-making that is not necessarily contained within the process of logic. Is there something more than or different from reason that is part of the self and that might take over and decide on another basis, using reason as a guide but not as the only authority?

THE SCIENTIFIC VIEWPOINT

The various scientific disciplines have each been interested to some extent in the nature of the self. As might be expected, those sciences most concerned with the dynamics of the individual have given this problem considerable attention.

Gardner Murphy,[1] applying scientific methods in studying the self, asks, "Should the student of personality, at the present stage of research, posit a non-empirical entity, distinct from both organism and its perceptual response to forms and symbols, which are called a 'self'?" His decision is that "a tentative negative answer to this question seems advisable." However, he suggests that another answer may be given when "the present stage of inquiry" is more advanced. If there is a free and responsible self, can it be understood by empirical methods or perhaps only by introspection and dramatic dialogue? The latter would mean that although the self is not distinct from its "organism" or "perceptual" responses, it is not the same either.

Freud, who was aware of the introspective testimony to the reality of free will, regarded it as "subjective feeling." As such, he considered it subject to scientific study as part of a cause-and-effect sequence. The neo-Freudians[2] emphasize the dependence of the self on others for security and self-esteem, and consider the self the product of the immediate social environment.

B. F. Skinner[3] proposes methods for "conditioning" a person to "socially approved" ends. This he believes possible, since he considers the individual capable of critical thought but not of freedom to act above or below the level of the product of his thinking. Thus the possibility of effecting fairly permanent change follows directly from his theoretical assumptions.

Modern anthropology is also engaged in efforts to understand the total self. Kluckhohn and Murray conclude that "personality must be located in nature, within some field where there is together-

---

[1] Gardner Murphy, *Personality, a Biosocial Approach* (New York: Harper & Row, Publishers, Inc., 1947), p. 490.
[2] Harry Stack Sullivan, *Conceptions of Modern Psychiatry* (William Alanson White Psychiatric Foundation, 1947), p. 126.
[3] B. F. Skinner, *Walden Two* (New York: The Macmillan Co., 1962).

ness of all these processes or of representations of these processes. Thus we can state that personality is the organization of all the integrative processes in the brain." [4] Another anthropologist considers man "a dependent and culture the independent variable." [5] He assumes that the principle of cause and effect that explains physical phenomena should explain cultural phenomena equally well, and is surprised when the accusation of "fatalism" springs forth.

If cause-and-effect relationships can explain all that there is to know about the self, then improvement in human relations can be expected to result from scientific advancement. Even such a problem as understanding the integration of egotism and creativity, which manifests itself on all levels of behavior, can be understood and controlled. Egotism is a fairly universal concomitant of creative efforts, but it is commonly known that there is a point at which egocentricity ceases to be a harmless condition and becomes a harmful vice. The presence of egotism in motives and action has been attributed to the imposition of moral codes foreign to human nature. Dewey explains that "a few have administered and given rules; and the mass have with reluctance and in a passable fashion, obeyed." [6] He considers necessary a better understanding of human nature and scientific channeling of "drives." Dewey is certain that scientific knowledge will provide more competent rules to which men will more willingly conform because these will be in accord with the potentialities of human nature. As indicated by these illustrations, science interprets this quality of egotism in the self as the product of acculturation.

These important insights, although valuable, do not always satisfy counselors. Counselors experience situations in which they are unable to find satisfactory explanations for the counselee's behavior. Some counselors believe that the counselee has an additional capacity, which although not in opposition to the thought process is not necessarily contained within its principles. It is when the counselee makes use of this capacity that he tends to become less predictable to the counselor on the basis of cause-and-effect relationships. Psychologists place varying amounts of emphasis on this ca-

[4] Clyde Kluckhohn and Henry A. Murray, *Personality in Nature; Society and Culture* (New York: Alfred A. Knopf, Inc., 1948), p. 463.

[5] Leslie White, *Science of Culture, A Study of Man and Civilization* (New York: Farrar, Straus & Giroux, 1949), p. 343.

[6] John Dewey, *Human Nature and Conduct* (New York: Holt, Rinehart & Winston, Inc., 1922), pp. 2–3.

pacity, and describe it in various ways. In *The Inner World of Choice,*
Frances Wickes writes, "All decision and choice rests primarily upon
our openness to the transforming spirit." [7]

THE PHILOSOPHICAL VIEWPOINT

Most philosophies hold that the individual is unique in that he has
the capacity to transcend himself. This capacity does not oppose the
thought process, but is a further potential. It is unlike critical thought
in that one can get along well on the biological or "horizontal" level
without using it. However, if we do not avail ourselves of this capacity we do not realize our potential.

Realizing this potential is difficult. It requires a willingness, a
courage, an expectancy, a readiness to receive; it requires that one
struggle through the meaning of situations, come to an awareness of
the reality of his life; seek the purpose and direction of his life,
listen, and receive.

Certain counselors experience an understanding which rises to
consciousness out of the depth of the self. This understanding brings
with it the conviction that it is true; it lives within me. Through
examination of our socialized selves and our openness to the creative
spirit, we know. It exists. Although many counselors yearn for assurance that life holds more significance than the daily round of
mundane experience, many scholars and counselors fear that it would
discredit them to suggest that empirical science is not comprehensive.
So they remain prisoners of a world in which only that which is
measured and measurable can participate. The application of their
acknowledged tools of inquiry (rational, scientific and practical) provide for them a predetermined, obvious conclusion. It is their only
dimension for comprehension.

But as students of the self, we never completely escape the realization that there is more to the self than we have satisfactorily fathomed.
Most counselors would often welcome the indication that the counselee
is acting from a source of inner freedom. The counselor knows that he
is finally dependent upon the freedom of the counselee to make "the
inner choice."

Usually the counselee's guides to action are logic, practicality, and
imagination. By the use or misuse of these capacities, he may succeed or fail. In either case, he views what has happened to him as
the result of good or poor judgment and also as the result of circum-

[7] Frances G. Wickes, *The Inner World of Choice* (New York:
Harper & Row, Publishers, Inc., 1963), p. 2.

stances. If he considers his failure great, then he judges it not to be truly representative of him but to reside in that part of him which is not his whole self—the part of him that is caught in a set of circumstances. How frequently the counselor has heard a counselee say, "That is not like me. I don't know why I ever did it."

The counselor too is aware that he is most in touch with himself when he relates to this "inner choice" or ultimate being. In fact, the evidence is all about him that he could become the pawn of social forces and realistic pressures. Why is it that Arthur Miller's *The Death of a Salesman* returns continually to the screen and playhouse? Is it not because it speaks of something we sense, the loss of contact with the "inner choice"? The salesman did not avail himself of the capacity to transcend himself and social forces and discover the reality of the self. At the graveside, the younger brother remarks, "He had a good idea to come out first," and the older brother responds, "He never really knew who he was."

The counselor and counselee each discern a mystery and a meaning which is not completely demonstrable by a rational response. Furthermore, they surmise that the cause and effect relationships that they are using indicate a mystery of creativity beyond themselves. This is so because although a previous situation is an intelligible cause for the succeeding situation, it is not sufficient cause, as we would like to think.

It was Hume who first decreased confidence in the intelligibility of the world, and this apparently prompted Kant to write his critique of idealism. For the first time, confidence in reason was distinguished from a noumenal reality, *Ding an sich,* the mystery beyond the rationally intelligible phenomenal world. Leaders in several disciplines including philosophy, physics, and psychology are questioning the adequacy of the rational universal system as a basis for explaining the self. Existentialism recognizes the freedom of the individual and differentiates the deeper levels of self from reason. Sartre writes, "Thus there is no human nature because there is no God to conceive it. Man simply is. Not that he simply is what he conceives to be. But he is what he wills . . . He is what he wills to be after that leap toward existence." [8]

Another illustration of the dissatisfaction regarding rational relationships as the explanation of the self is the attention which the problem of determinism and freedom has lately received. Immer-

[8] Jean Paul Sartre, *Existentialism and Humanism* (New York: Philosophical Library, Inc., 1947) p. 56.

gluck describes it in these terms: "There is, on the one hand, modern psychology's commitment to the scientific method which has paid off not only in an impressive accruement of knowledge but which has also put on firm basis the causal and deterministic nexus of behavior; while on the other hand there remains the nagging conviction that somehow man must also be personally free. How to resolve this antimony?" [9]

Modern physics has stimulated serious concern with regard to the implications of its newer conceptualizations for the concept of human freedom. This concern took concrete form in Heisenberg's principle of uncertainty as a "proof" for the existence of at least some measure of free will in man.

Counseling psychologists are also taking full cognizance of the problem of fully understanding the self. Rogers, in a symposium, recognizes this but sees no resolution of it. As a scientist he holds to strict cause and effect sequence—"Nothing occurs outside of that"—but he maintains just as fervently that it is impossible for him "as a human being" to hold this view and resigns himself to accept this inconsistency as a "genuine paradox." [10] E. G. Boring suggests that strict causality be considered as a kind of "truncated model" to which freedom may be added.[11] S. Koch approves the "relegitimation of metaphysics," [12] which he apparently considers has taken place in some views of modern psychology. William James phrased the problem thus — that if you try to explain anything in complete scientific or religious terms you negate both explanations. This, unfortunately, does not supply any explanation.

Whatever his position, the counselor shares his dilemma and search with others. Many are seeking to answer the question, is the human "person" a body, psychological functions, or something else and something more? This something else and something more is, for Ponsoye, *love* in the metaphysical sense of the term; [13] for Stocker,

[9] Ludwig Immergluck, "Determinism—Freedom in Contemporary Psychology," *American Psychologist,* 1961, Vol. 19, pp. 270–281.
[10] Carl Rogers, "Cultural Evolution as Viewed by Psychologists," *Daedalus,* 1961, Vol. 90, pp. 574–575.
[11] E. G. Boring, "When Is Human Behavior Predetermined?" *Scientific Monitor,* 1957, Vol. 84, pp. 189–196.
[12] Sigmund Koch, "Psychological Science Versus the Science-Humanism Antimony: Intimations of a Significant Science of Man," *American Psychologist,* 1961, Vol. 16, pp. 629–639.
[13] Pierre Ponsoye, *L'Esprit, Force Biologique Fondamentale* (Montpellier: Causse, Graille et Castebau, 1942), p. 25.

the *heart* in Pascal's sense of the word;[14] for deRougemont, *spirit.* De Rougemont writes: "We're men through our body, our psyche, our mind, our unconscious, and our spirit . . . there are no sharp boundaries." [15]

Both counselor and counselee are often painfully aware that neither can find the meaning of life in himself or the world. They cannot identify with causality, for they know that they have a freedom transcending the causal links of nature. Neither do they find meaning in rationality, since they also transcend their own rational processes.

CONCLUSIONS

The problem of the freedom of the self is receiving increasing attention from thinkers in many disciplines. Allowing the possibility that the self has a freedom beyond and in addition to its rational processes opens the door to wide vistas of increasing importance to the counselor and to all who are engaged in relating to others in depth.

More counselors to an increasing degree are struggling with the meaning of the self. Some conclude that the self is only "a thinking thing." Others are unable to accept the conclusion that the rational man is the whole man and may arrive at the decision that nature, mind and spirit are integrally part of the self and part of every significant decision.

All counselors, it is hoped, will become able to respect the counselee whose views regarding the self differ from their own. As each counselor becomes more knowledgeable concerning his own views, it is to be expected that he will also become more sensitive to the indications of the counselee's struggle for meaning and will encourage in him the freedom to search for that in which he can believe.

QUESTIONS

1. Why should the counselor be concerned with the nature of the self?
2. What aspects of the self receive various interpretations?

[14] Arnold Stocker, D*esarroi de l'Hume Moderne* (Geneva: Editions du Mont-Blanc, Coll., "Action et Pensée, 1946, p. 43.
[15] Jean de Rougement, *Vie du Corps et Vie de l'Esprit* (Lyons: Paul Derain, 1945), p. 41.

3. What problem presents itself if the self cannot be explained fully by cause and effect relationships?

FOR FURTHER READING

Sidney M. Jourard. *Personal Adjustment,* Second Edition (New York: The Macmillan Co., 1963).

The author describes and analyzes those conditions which contribute to the development of a healthy self. His treatment is broad and clear, focusing in turn upon the several aspects of the relationship of the self to itself, others and the environment. Most closely related in focus to the discussion above are the chapters, "The Self-Structure in Healthy Personality," "Defense Versus Growth of Self," and "Conscience and Guilt in Healthy Personality."

Reinhold Niebuhr. *The Self and the Dramas of History* (New York: Charles Scribner's Sons, 1955).

This unusual book explores in depth the internal dialogue of the self, the self and its dramas in relation to faith and ontology, and resources for the self in its community and world-wide relationships. The author asserts the reality of the transcendent self and examines this human uniqueness in relation to other assumptions. He emphasizes the misunderstandings and shortcomings that can result from a one-dimensional viewpoint of man.

Frances G. Wickes. *The Inner World of Choice* (New York: Harper & Row, Publishers, Inc., 1963).

The author involves the reader in examining the inner life of the self. The book is illustrated with fascinating case histories, concrete incidents and sketches of dreams. One is challenged to take further steps along the road to self-awareness and to fulfilling oneself as a creative human being. Written at the request of her teacher, Carl G. Jung, it is a clear and perceptive account of the implications of his psychology for understanding the self and its relationship to the world.

3

CONSCIENCE

Conscience is directly or indirectly implicated in all relationships that give scope for ethical investigation. It is concerned with right and wrong, worthiness and unworthiness, good and bad, better and worse. Let there be a possibility of choice in moral and ethical spheres and conscience is present. It signifies joint knowledge. The two things known together may be two motives, for example, or two deeds.

Long before the day of the modern counselor, the concept of conscience had its recognized place. The concept arose in the Greek world, but the experience of it takes on vivid proportions in the accounts of David, Job, Isaiah and other Old Testament characters, as well as in Shakespearian characters such as Hamlet, Brutus, and Macbeth.

THE NATURE OF CONSCIENCE

The conviction that a certain course is right is accompanied by a sense of obligation. This sense of obligation or "ought" is the core of conscience. The source of this sense of ought is a matter of disagreement. The issue revolves around the question, is the sense of obligation only the result of acculturation, or is it beyond analysis? The sciences of man, especially psychology, take the first position, and some viewpoints in philosophy and religion affirm the second position. The differences in viewpoint continue. For although "ought-ness" can be exhibited, it cannot, from the latter point of view at least, be analyzed. English and English, in their definition, present two positions: (1) "that the superego, though acquired by earthly means, is conceived in psychoanalysis as functioning in substantially the same way as conscience" (a position not agreed to by religion); and (2) that conscience is "an innate or divinely implanted faculty enabling one to judge correctly on moral issues." [1]

In the scientific analysis of the nature of conscience, the first question asked is whether conscience is inborn. Allport suggests that "the best scientific answer seems to be No — in one sense, Yes — in another." [2] The "No" part of the response is based upon the recognized cultural relativity regarding what produces "guilt feelings" or is called "sin." The "Yes" part of the response is based upon the universality of conscience in the human race except in rare pathological instances. Allport warns that conscience is not the "lingering vestige of parental coercion and childhood fear" but that in the adult it is "functionally autonomous of its roots," and is an "arbiter of adult values." [3] We turn to a further discussion of these two positions, accompanied by illustrations from the life of the counselor.

THE PSYCHOLOGICAL VIEWPOINT

Conscience is the product of acculturation. It is learned by the individual through experiences in his environment, and is essentially the pressure of the community on the "ego." Moral obligation is purely a sociological phenomenon. Allport defines it as "the knife-edge all our values press upon us whenever we are acting or have acted contrary to these values," [4] and again as "the indicator of the measure of agreement between our conduct and our values, whatever they be." Jourard, in accord with this view, refers to conscience as "the values, ideals, rules, taboos, goals, and so on which an individual holds with respect to his own behavior and inner experience." [5] There are obligations that can be accepted as universal, such as refraining from murder, theft and adultery. These prohibitions have been found by societies to be necessary, and obedience to them has been taught and enforced. Anthropologists have impressed upon us that obligations are relative to time and place. Man is affirmed as the product of history and society. The youngster who is taught early

[1] Horace B. English and A. Champney English, *A Comprehensive Dictionary of Psychological and Psychoanalytical Terms* (New York: David McKay Co., Inc., 1958), p. 111.
[2] Gordon W. Allport, *The Individual and His Religion* (New York: The Macmillan Co., 1950), p. 87.
[3] *Ibid.*, p. 89.
[4] *Ibid.*, p. 90.
[5] Sidney M. Jourard, *Personal Adjustment* (New York: The Macmillan Co., 1963), p. 237.

to steal pop bottles and sell them, or to "lift" small articles in the large chain stores, or to cheat on examinations has a learned sense of obligation and resorts to what he considers reasonable means for justifying his action to himself and to society at large. In his summary on conscience, Jourard writes: "Conscience is a constraining influence upon a person's behavior and experiencing. In some forms, conscience can undermine the health of personality, whereas in healthier patterns, it can foster the fullest development of the individual and permit guilt-free gratification of needs." [6]

The conscience that Jourard refers to as undermining the health of the personality is characterized by Fromm as an immature conscience. He considers the mark of an immature conscience to be its authoritarian nature. It is ridden by a sense of obedience, self-sacrifice, duty and resignation. The mature conscience is animated by adult sentiments and self-chosen goals. [7] Allport agrees with this analysis, except that he does not share Fromm's opinion that a religious conscience is almost of necessity immature. Allport believes that the individual "in his maturing may rediscover for himself the essential truths of his religion and thus incorporate them into a wholly productive and rational conscience." [8] These are clear expositions for those who view conscience as one-dimensional. Are there not, however, decisions of conscience that foster the fulfillment of the person and are unrelated to need gratification in the psychological sense?

Is guilt experienced only when one behaves in a matter that is socially unacceptable, or does it occur also when one commits an act of perjury against his inner self? Are there not people who remain guilty even after they have completed the steps suggested by Jourard for the removal of guilt, and even after they have been forgiven by those they wronged? Are these people "unhealthy" psychologically or is their guilt due in part to a healthy awareness of one's inner self?

The socio-psychological viewpoint of conscience is contingent upon a certain definition of the sense of "ought." The sense of "ought" is one-dimensional in that it bears direct relationship only to one's experience. Rollo May defines it as "one's capacity to tap one's own deeper levels of insight, ethical sensitivity and awareness,

[6] *Ibid.*, p. 266.
[7] Erich Fromm, *Man for Himself* (New York: Holt, Rinehart & Winston, Inc., 1947), p. 89.
[8] Allport, *op. cit.*, p. 91.

in which tradition and immediate experience are not opposed to each other but interrelated." [9]

Conscience, then, must answer the question, is it acceptable not only to myself but to the wider interests of the community? The conflict lies in which will be favored, personal values and interests or community values and interests. The counselor is involved in helping the counselee to reach an appropriate compromise in which he will have a measure of freedom as an individual but will also be acceptable to, and accepted by, the community — home, school and society. The student who succeeds in making such a compromise is said to have made a good adjustment.

In such a situation and with this viewpoint the counselee does not distinguish between the desired and the desirable. Any counselor who reflects upon this will recall how consistently the students endeavor to prove that the desired is really desirable. They say it is necessary to learn to play tennis not because they enjoy the game but because they need it for their well-rounded development. Or the counselor hears the high school senior defend his need for a car on the basis that if he has a car he will save time for his studies, or he will be able to also take a part-time job, or he will not always be interfering with the plans of his parents in his need for transportation. Evidently in our effort to convince ourselves and others that what we desire is also desirable we have to defend our desires by proving that they are in accord with some wider system of values than our own interest.

Consider some illustrations of the various forms of the working of conscience in terms of the one-dimensional socio-psychological point of view.

Mary enrolls as a freshman in a large state university. Experiences in her high school have indicated to her that it is important to be popular and that to be popular one must conform. Although her friends tell her that a freshman must study and that one may be popular without pleasing everyone, Mary is unable to listen until her grades force her to reconsider.

John comes from the same high school to the same university. He was popular although he recognized that it was to the detriment of his grades. He begins to think of himself as a student; he identifies in his thinking with those on the honor roll; he takes pleasure in the idea that at some future time he will be a scholar. He applies him-

[9] Rollo May, *Man's Search for Himself* (New York: W. W. Norton & Company, Inc., 1953), p. 215.

self to his studies. Despite the many opportunities to become involved in many social activities, he engages in a minimum of carefully chosen ones.

Both of these students were highly influenced by their high school community. In college, Mary chose goals that were in accord with the former community. John ignored the former community and chose in terms of a new community, which existed at first only in his imagination and made no overt claims on him. The counselor needs to become more aware of the degree to which conscience performs in terms of one or more communities. The counselor must know these communities to understand their influences on the individual.

Four counselors at a national convention were informally exchanging notes on their experiences. They were all experienced and had shared in this kind of communication more than once. Frank described a problem about which he was concerned. "Louise is an intelligent, good looking girl, the daughter of one of our science teachers," he began. "She is seventeen and a senior. In my office she told me that she was pregnant and expected her baby in five months. She doesn't want to marry and neither does the boy. In fact, he wants her to leave town on some pretense until after the baby is born. A couple of things seem to stand out; she feels very selfish; she worries that her behavior will disgrace her family and that it will bring the whole school down on her. She says she never intended this to happen and knows that she can't expect to go against what everyone thinks is right without suffering. I talked with her parents. They were quite upset. 'After all we have done,' they told me, 'she throws away her good name and spoils her chances, to say nothing of disgracing us. She must have known this was the wrong thing to do, her common sense should have told her that.'

"At the Board of Education Meeting just before I left, it was decided that neither Louise nor the boy could continue in school. So there it stands. Her concern doesn't seem to stem from her action, as such, but from the fact that it was unacceptable to her family and the community."

Bill added, "They seem to take as a guide what is done in their homes and communities, and what they read about or see on TV. Not long ago, Freida, one of our popular girls from a so-called good home, came in. She too was pregnant, and only sixteen, with two years to complete in high school. She said that when her family moved to the community a year ago she wouldn't have considered this behavior, but that the girls were all doing it and the boys expected it. She apparently had no conscience of her own. Her own sense of values seemed to have receded into the background, and she had taken over the values of the immediate community. When I talked with her parents they were surprised and said that they had not discussed values and behavior with her but that they had noticed how much more important it had become to her to be well liked by her peers."

In both of these illustrations conscience is a one-dimensional approach to difficulties in human relationships. Both also exemplify the dilemma of the individual who lacks internalized personal values and, instead, considers the offense in terms of immediate cultural expectations.

In the case of Louise, the situation revolves around the balance between the effects of benevolence and the effects of selfishness as indicated by her conscience. Her chief concern was that she had disregarded accepted ethical codes and in so doing had broken the harmony between herself and her parents and the community. In accordance with Shaftesbury,[10] conscience in this situation would be considered as the emotional reaction to the harmony between self-relatedness and relatedness to others.

In the case of Freida, there was both an exaggerated need for acceptance and lack of development and insight concerning her own values. Apparently Freida identified strongly with others and introjected their approval or disapproval of her action as her own decision. Such action could be expected to develop to serious proportions when a teenager or adult has an unusually great need for love due, in large measure, to the lack of experiences in which one is loved for oneself and has means of expressing in acceptable ways his reactions to his feelings of worth. Concerning those who have exaggerated needs for identification, David Hume[11] and Adam Smith[12] have written that sympathy with the other person becomes the basis of conscience.

[10] Anthony A. C. Shaftesbury (Right Honorable Anthony, Earl of Shaftesbury), *Characteristics of Men, Manners, Opinions, Times* . . . (London: J. Darby), 1727.
[11] David Hume, *Essays Moral, Political and Literary*, T. H. Green and T. H. Grose (eds.) (New York: David McKay Co., Inc., 1898), p. 136.
[12] Adam Smith, *The Theory of Moral Sentiments* (London: G. Bell Sons, 1880), p. 421.

These two situations exemplify the emotional-harmonistic interpretation of conscience; the counselor may also expect to encounter those who handle problems of conscience in other one-dimensional strategies. Some may make decisions and carry out actions on the basis of duty. They consider it a duty to have a conscience, which becomes an obligation to be conscientious. The objective of their conscientiousness depends on the situation and on the cultural milieu of which they are a part.

Society expects people to "have a conscience." This in many instances is interpreted as being conscientious. Some teenagers grow up in homes where one of the chief or perhaps *the* chief duty is to be conscientious. What one is expected to be conscientious about varies with the situation, the time, and the particular duties connected with his vocation. These responsibilities are generally in accord with the psychological demands of the current pattern of society.

For teenagers who grow up under such a philosophy, the suffering of guilt comes when they fail to be conscientious in furthering the mores which they have integrated.

Conscience is, according to Fichte,[13] the certainty of the pure duty independent of anything except its own certainty. The danger is that when conscience comes to grips with a concrete situation it will become obedient to a well-calculated system of economic services. It will be then only as pure as the controlling system of values relevant to the problem. This lack of its own intrinsic direction means that the conscience may tolerate or be a party to immoral influences. The result may be that the conscientious person will eventually have a conscience that is not discriminating.

Some individuals have an immovable certainty that conscience expresses the absolute right and wrong. They believe that conscience knows within and out of itself what law and duty are, and that it is not necessary to acknowledge anything except what conscience tells us is good. The difficulty with this formal and subjective understanding of conscience arises when it is put to the test in the individual's relations with family and society. In these circumstances the subjective certainty may yield and become indistinguishable from the rational contents embodied in the approach to the situation. Then the conclusion is dominated by rationality and devoid of the certainty of the absolute right of the subjective self-consciousness.

[13] Johann Gottlieb Fichte, *Science of Knowledge,* a critical exposition by Charles Carroll Everett (Chicago: S. C. Griggs & Co., 1884), p. 263.

THE PHILOSOPHICAL AND
RELIGIOUS VIEWPOINT

Philosophy and religion are interested in what has been termed by Tillich the "transmoral conscience." Experience has demonstrated to us that the feeling of separation due to a wrong done to another is not of the same order as any physical distress; nor is it like the feeling of disappointment when our scientific hypotheses fail. The difference between the moral and unmoral emotions is one of kind and not of quantity. This leads to the concept that the knowledge of right is constitutional. Thus, according to Kant, "An erring conscience is a chimera." The sense of "ought" is considered innate, a quality not the result of the process of education. We can evoke but not create the voice of conscience. To anyone who has not energized it, it may be impossible to impart a transmoral conscience.

Those who have energized the transmoral conscience ask not the question of expediency but the question "Is it right for me to do so?" Obligation, not inclination, is the focus here. This transmoral conscience is defined in such terms as "any aspect of the self's judging its actions and attitudes in which a sense of obligation in contrast to inclination is expressed." [14] Conscience is man's capacity to receive progressively a revelation of what is right, in religious terms, the righteousness of God.

How to transmute this revelation into action has to be learned. The Apostle Paul prayed that his friends might improve in moral discrimination (Ph. 1:9; Col. 1:9). We know that the conditions of poverty are wrong; we have to learn how they can be alleviated. Man is a natural judge of himself, and the verdict that results from self-examination brings either peace or uneasiness. Sometimes we try to escape the uneasiness by tranquilizers, by some diversion, or by work.

One philosophical position in particular takes a different view of the transmoral conscience. The existentialists, in developing a philosophy, have derived a concept of the transmoral conscience following the general lines of Bruno and Nietzsche, but of vastly different significance. Heidegger, a representative of existential philosophy, considers "the call of conscience as having the character of the demand that man in his finitude actualizes his genuine potentialities,

---

[14] Reinhold Niebuhr, *The Self and the Dramas of History* (New York: Charles Scribner's Sons, 1955), p. 13.

and this means to become guilty." [15] Since it is impossible not to act, and since every action implies guilt, one must act with resoluteness to command the situation rather than be determined by it.

How may a counselee with a transmoral conscience be expected to respond? Let us examine this by returning to our four counselors. Bob continues the conversation in this manner. "The situation I faced with Jean was very different. She was the daughter of the principal of the school. The family was very religious. The girl became pregnant at the beginning of her senior year. She was very broken up about it. She felt that she had done wrong, that she wasn't fit to be a member of the family, and she wanted to run away. She said she loved the boy but that it was still wrong to do what she had done. She said she had ruined her own life and disgraced her family.

"Not only this, but it was apparent that her self-respect was greatly diminished. She said, 'I have attended church, helped with church school classes, I have prayed and tried to do right, but I guess I wasn't the person I thought I was after all. I am not worthy of all the good things I have had. I wish I could die.'

"Her parents were disturbed. They seemed unable to believe what had happened. They then felt hurt that she would do such a thing, and aggressive toward her. However, after they had talked a while they were apparently sorry for her and ready to forgive her and to even share some of the probable causes for her behavior.

"Although Jean and her parents talked several times and they tried to help her to feel that she was, as always, a member of the family, Jean could not accept forgiveness. She felt her action was unforgivable.

"She continued coming to see me. She was depressed with feelings of unworthiness. Her concern was that she 'had done wrong,' and felt unforgiven.

"She talked, at first with great difficulty, of Biblical and other situations about which she had read. She seemed to be struggling to find some basis for believing that she could be forgiven. It was a painful struggle. I wondered often if she was making progress, if I was helping her. I wanted to assure her, but I felt it wouldn't help. So I listened, accepted, clarified occasionally, and sometimes reflected the meaning of her comments.

"Gradually the depression decreased; the tone of her comments

[15] Martin Heidegger, *Essays in Metaphysics: Identity and Difference,* trans. by Kurt F. Leidecker (New York: Philosophical Library, 1960), p. 74.

changed. One day she said, 'You know, don't you, that I feel better now. I have to go on, there's a lot of good I can do. Although I don't see myself as I did, I feel acceptable and that I belong now.' From then she began to look to the future, to plan life in a normal way."

The counselor has to be able to understand the person who does not judge his actions by, or seek meaning in, only the pragmatic one-dimensional outcomes of life. Such a person cannot be unified through the re-establishment of relations with those affected by the outcomes of his action. Such a person was Jean. Her resolution was not only moral; it was above the moral demand. A conscience that has both horizontal and vertical dimensions is referred to as "transmoral."

There is another way of reacting to the vertical perception of the seriousness of the guilty act. This was what Hugh found in his experience. "I talked with a girl in the same situation who also seemed to recognize the seriousness of her behavior but whose reactions were very different from Jean's," said Hugh. "Elsie was also in her senior year. She was known as a serious and deeply happy person much in love with life, who seemed able to achieve academically with ease.

"Her parents came to my office at the school late one afternoon to explain to me what had taken place. They expressed their concern that Elsie did not seem to see the gravity of her action, and discussed their fears about the effect of the community attitude on the girl's future. They said that they would encourage her to come in to talk with me.

"Elsie made an appointment and came in a few days later. The essence of what she told me was that her parents were upset and she herself was sorry. What had happened would undoubtedly affect her own plans and would also be hard for her parents to live with. Then she began to discuss her analysis of the situation. It took this form: 'No one is perfect, we all do wrong, you know. . . . The only way you could keep from doing wrong would be to do nothing. Just to live, that is, if you really live, is to be guilty. There are lots of girls who think they are pretty good, but they are kidding themselves. All of them have done something they shouldn't have done; it's just a matter of degree. We should actualize our potentialities, and to do this you have to act. If some actions turn out badly you have to accept the bad with the good.'

"I was somewhat surprised by this approach. She was serious. I really think she had looked at the seriousness of her behavior but seemed to accept the fact that being guilty was part of existence — almost an indication that you were alive and developing."

At first thought the counselor might conclude that Elsie is an unusual girl. But he may be forced to revise this position, and should be ready to do so. Elsie is living in a world impregnated with the philosophy of existentialism. But although no one is perfect, it is not generally conceded that this is sufficient reason for acting irresponsibly. Elsie and Jean both recognized the vertical dimension of their behavior, but their reactions were markedly different. Whereas Jean acted responsibly on all levels of relationship, Elsie assumed no responsibility. Whereas Jean established morality, Elsie added to the destruction of morality through a goal below morality.

Many writers have analyzed moral conscience, but they have maintained the reader's respect for it. These empiricists, including Freud, did not attempt to cut away the foundations. Heidegger has attacked the foundations, and this position may gradually seep into thought and action.

It is accepted that the mark of the counselor is sensitivity. He is interested in helping others to become more sensitive. However, the more his capacity for sensitivity toward his own actions and for understanding others increases, the greater the discrepancy between the real and the ideal self becomes. Those who attain this level can hardly escape the question of the "transmoral" conscience. In fact, the counselor may well realize that depth psychotherapy is dependent upon the "transmoral" conscience. In order for health to be restored the counselee must look inward. He must recognize and accept his own conflicts, and he must suffer because of what they are. Recognizing what he has become as the result of them, he must not attempt to suppress them and hide them from himself. The counselor must continuously broaden his perspective with reference to the powerful value of influences which surround him and his counselees. He must have respect for his own conscience and for that of the counselee. He must recognize the central place of conscience in therapy but also realize that its influence may take many forms, not all of which lead to psychological health and moral behavior.

CONCLUSIONS

Conscience is a part of each counselee. Its functioning, however, varies widely from one person to another. Likewise, counselors vary in their recognition and interpretation of conscience and its functioning in therapy. The greatest congruence among counselees as well as among counselors is in the degree to which each persuades himself that his desires are in agreement with an overarching system of values and that although some obligations are accepted as universal many change with time and place. The greatest difference is in relation to the concept of "ought." To some the sense of "ought" is the product of reason; to others it is a separate entity, carrying with it its own sense of obligation, which may or may not be in accord with the product of reason, or may go beyond reason. Those who identify the sense of "ought" with reason judge their actions on the basis of community expectations, on the basis of the effect they may have on relations with others, or on the basis of what would be the conscientious thing to do. Those to whom the sense of "ought" is a separate entity, carrying with it certainty of pure duty, may end with a conscience that does not discriminate. Or they may claim that by listening to conscience one can be certain of the right action to take. This kind of certainty runs the risk of becoming one with the rational contents in the problem and of reaching conclusions on a purely rational basis. Still others take the position that in this world of varying shades of grey, the only requirement is to determine to act. To them the right and proper decision is to act with resolution, since only in this way can one actualize himself. A final position is one which is held by the person with a sense of "ought" who has a two-dimensional approach to behavior. He reviews his action not only in terms of its effect on his community with others but also in terms of a deep sense of obligation, the "inner choice." The counselor who understands the several avenues of conscience is in a much better position to understand the meaning of the counselee's action.

QUESTIONS

1. What difficulty may the counselor experience if he considers conscience only the product of acculturation?
2. Why do some authorities consider the possibility that conscience may be innate?
3. Why should the counselor have an understanding of the "transmoral conscience"?

FOR FURTHER READING

Gordon W. Allport. *The Individual and His Religion* (New York: The Macmillan Co., 1965).

This book examines conscience within the perspective of mental health and within the framework of psychology and religion. Chapters in the book bear such titles as "The Religion of Youth," "The Religion of Maturity," "The Nature of Doubt," and the "Nature of Faith." The author emphasizes that the individual must have the freedom to see clearly the forces of conformity that invite him to be content with merely a second-hand, immature religion. He believes that many attain a religious view of life without suffering arrested development and without self-deception.

Paul Tillich. *Morality and Beyond* (New York: Harper & Row, Publishers, Inc., 1963).

The author is concerned with pointing out the possibility of accepting the person who is unacceptable, and of healing the person who is morally sick. He asserts that being precedes action in everything that is, including man, although in man, the bearer of freedom, previous action also determines present being. Within this framework he affirms morality and points beyond it to its religious foundation. Particularly helpful are the two chapters, "The Religious Element in Moral Motivation," and "The Transmoral Conscience."

Erich Fromm. *Man for Himself* (New York: Holt, Rinehart & Winston, Inc., 1947).

The author discusses the problem of ethics in the realization of man's self and his potentialities. He criticizes the rationalism of the last two centuries as narrow in its concepts. He considers it impossible to divorce psychology from philosophy, ethics, sociology and economics. He discusses philosophical concepts within a psychological framework. In part four, "Problems of Humanistic Ethics," he devotes 30 pages to an examination of conscience. He defines conscience as "man's recall to himself." The counselor will find thought-provoking and rewarding his discussion of the "Authoritarian Conscience" as "the voice of an internalized external authority," and the "Humanistic Conscience" as "our own voice, present in every human being and independent of external sanctions and rewards."

4

THE WILL

What mother or teacher has not asked, "How do I get Johnny to do his work?" Much research has been undertaken in attempts to answer this question. The research has taken several forms, but all has assumed that there are certain conditions that, when established, will produce desirable and predicted behavior patterns. The conditions and their effects varied.

FUNCTION OF THE WILL

It is the function of reason to clarify outcomes and bring them into focus; the will then gives an affirmative or negative response, or no response. It is reason that analyzes the ends in view and compares their relative merits in relation to the self's total ends or in terms of some more inclusive system of values. The will, then, participates in the making of decisions and assumes responsibility for effecting them.

This is the case in regard to all levels of action, and in relation to both immediate and ultimate ends. John may desire to become a good tennis player in order to be eligible for membership in the club, and to excel in science in order to win a scholarship to study abroad, and to do both in order to win the respect and interest of a particular brunette. He desires all of these because they are consistent with his ultimate goal — a good life as a competent high school science teacher. In order to reach his goals John must pursue them consistently, with a minimum of erratic and unrelated activity. Reason has assisted him in formulating these goals and may help him to detect inconsistency in his activities with reference to his goal. But it is the will that enables him to persevere and be consistent in his pursuit.

The act of will determines to what degree, if any, the adolescent will endeavor to meet the anxiety that arises as he achieves freedom. The counselor hopes that the counselee will move from dependence upon parental protection to new levels of freedom and integration. But the initiation of that movement is the work of the will.

THE PSYCHOLOGICAL VIEWPOINT

The term "will" is little used in contemporary psychology. English and English define it as "the capacity for voluntary action." [1] Instead of focusing upon this capacity, psychology has directed its attention to those conditions conducive to the use of this capacity. It has assumed that if these conditions could be understood the voluntary action would follow.

Two general approaches have received the greatest attention. One focused on the conditions that would induce a person to behave in the desired manner. Reinforcement of a desired verbal expression or act by the appropriate verbal agreement, support or encouragement or the giving of a suitable reward following a desired act, and punishment if the act was not performed or inadequately performed, were found to be effective methods. By such methods persons were conditioned to respond in certain ways to the stimulus situations. Through experiments with animals, chiefly rats, conditioning methods have been greatly refined and the dependability of the outcomes increased. The principles of conditioning and reinforcement have become widely used in education as one of the chief methods for the inducement of learning.

Counseling is also experimenting with the reinforcement of appropriate responses to motivate change in the counselee. This method has now been used so widely and with such success that it is considered possible "that men may be conditioned by other men to develop any number of desired characteristics." [2] One of the most comprehensive summaries of the conditions most likely to induce desired behavioral outcomes is that provided by McClelland in his article, "Toward a Theory of Motive Acquisition." He lists in table form the "variables conceived as entering into the motive change process."

[1] Horace B. English and A. Champney English, *A Comprehensive Dictionary of Psychological and Psychoanalytical Terms* (New York: David McKay Co., Inc., 1958), p. 590.
[2] B. F. Shriver, "Freedom and the Control of Men," *American Scholar*, 1955–56, Vol. 25, pp. 47–65.

The counselor will be particularly interested in the character of the reinforcing interpersonal relations, e.g., "personal warmth and support," and "support of the reference group." [3]

The second significant approach to finding the conditions conducive to voluntary action relies on different assumptions. It assumes that each person desires to make the best of his potential, and that he can know himself better than any other person can know him. The person who is not motivated does not need reward or punishment, but assistance in understanding, accepting and working through the psychological problems that prevent him from knowing what he desires. As he understands, clarifies and accepts for himself he becomes motivated from within in a constructive direction.

It is to be expected that as a leading proponent of this theory, Carl Rogers is in strong disagreement with the conditioning theory. He writes, ". . . the human person, with his capacity for subjective choice, can and will always exist, separate and prior to any of his scientific undertakings. Unless as individuals we choose to relinquish our capacity for subjective choice, we will always remain free persons, not simply pawns of a self-created behavioral science." [4]

These approaches to understanding man's capacity to act voluntarily illustrate the lack of interest among psychologists in exploring the will per se. One outstanding exception exists in the life and work of Otto Rank. In fact, he gave the will a central place in his system, and wrote, "Whence comes the will and why psychologically must we interpret this will, not understood in its origin, now as will to power (Adler) and again as sex drive (Freud) and more than that, why must we interpret it at all, instead of being able to recognize its true psychological nature?" [5]

McClelland, among others, makes room for an intervening variable that to some degree is unpredictable. In each of his twelve propositions concerning how to increase motive acquisition, he includes the words "most likely." He recognizes that he is not explaining the full process, and that whether or not action is initiated, it is not completely predictable. That is, despite the use of all methods of conditioning and reinforcement in the most conducive

[3] David C. McClelland, "Toward a Theory of Motive Acquisition," *American Psychologist*, 1965, Vol. 20, pp. 321–333.
[4] Carl R. Rogers, *On Becoming a Person* (Boston: Houghton Mifflin Company, 1961), p. 401.
[5] Otto Rank, *Will Therapy* (New York: Alfred A. Knopf, Inc., 1936), p. 12.

psychological climate, the person may not act. This the counselor may be unable either to understand or to accept.

THE PHILOSOPHICAL VIEWPOINT

The counselor is interested in what causes the initiation of change. Whether the will is free to act or not or is in bondage to the total self has been an issue of long standing. The two philosophical points of view were illustrated in the debate between Luther and Erasmus. In the debate on the freedom and bondage of the will, Erasmus conceived of the freedom of the will as the freedom of the self over its impulses. This point of view, which originated in the Renaissance, has had great influence even to the present time. Luther, a representative of the Reformation viewpoint, considered the will to be in bondage. That is, he believed that as part of the self the will was subject to the internal change in the self in exercising its influence.

Renaissance thought, then, took the position that the will, although part of the self, is free and able to control its impulses. This means that the will can extricate itself from the demands of the self and by its own strength can commit the whole self to a pattern of action. In practice, then, the will independently initiates action. Imagination and feeling, if not in agreement, are repressed, and the will accomplishes the outcomes determined by reason.

Freud at first believed that such repression resulted in anxiety states; later he concluded that it was the anxiety that caused the repression. Discoveries such as this demonstrated that the will was integrally part of the self and that when the will exceeded its proper function as part of the self, the self no longer functioned in a healthy manner. The gyroscope man of the nineteenth century showed that the internalization of external rules, compartmentalization of will and intellect, and repression of feelings led to anxiety, rigidity, dogmatism and inability to learn and change. Captains of industry of that period are now recognized as forms without selves — "hollow men." Thus the injunction that more will power was needed came under increasing criticism.

The second viewpoint, sometimes called the Reformation position and implicit in Luther's position, considers the will an integral part of the self, so that the influence of the will is contained within the total self. The unification of the self in the pursuit of a goal makes compartmentalization and isolation unnecessary and tends to increase openness to experience and the improvement of mental health. As Kierkegaard explains, "let your heart in truth will one thing, for therein is the heart's purity." [6]

The counselor, then, who believes in the second viewpoint wishes to create for the counselee those conditions which will be conducive to the activation of the will as the spokesman of the total self, moving the self in a more desirable direction. This he hopes to do by providing a psychological climate that is permissive and supportive and also permits the individual to have and use a high degree of freedom. The assumption is that each individual does have goals, and that he can become more aware of them and is inclined by the will to try to accomplish them.

CONTRASTING METHODS AND VIEWPOINTS IN COUNSELING

What counselor has not heard a high school student say, "I made up my mind to hit the books but I didn't. I just never got around to it"? What does the counselor do in such situations? Counselors, of course, do different things depending upon their beliefs and their insights.

Some counselors proceed to help the counselee to clarify the various possible outcomes and encourage him to pursue the one that appears most useful and realistic. These counselors rely on reasoning and imagination to make the goal more distinct and more interesting and on reinforcement to ensure that the counselee takes steps to attain it. They assume that if the counselee can make a clear-cut decision he will move toward attaining the goal, that once a decision is reached, the will initiates action accordingly.

Other counselors proceed differently. If the counselee does not try to carry out his decision the reaction may be, "Well, he really didn't make a decision in the first place." Such a conclusion leads to the examination of possible reasons, frequently psychological, why a firm decision was not made or why, if made, it was not carried out.

Occasionally, however, there is a counselee who, despite his understanding of a situation, his conviction concerning the action he should take, and his decision to do so, does not act. In such situations the counselor confronts the fact that there is a step between deciding and doing. He may recognize that the person is not subject to his

---

[6] Søren Kierkegaard, *Purity of Heart Is to Will One Thing,* trans. by Douglas V. Steere (New York: Harper & Row, Publishers, Inc., 1948), p. 31.

reason, that he has a freedom to act, not to act, or to disregard reason in acting. Or he may not recognize this, and once again may attempt to help the counselee to reach a reasonable decision. In this case the counselee's true problem eludes the counselor. His problem is that he does not will the initiation of change, regardless of his conviction that it would be an improvement. If the counselor does recognize this, he does what is possible to create a situation in which the counselee assumes responsibility and is free to choose. He should, of course, realize that the counselee may *not* choose, or may choose "death" instead of "life." In accepting this fact lies the deep respect for the counselee that is honored more in the breach than in the observance.

BELIEFS IN ACTION

Whether the counselor is aware of it or not, his counseling method reflects his belief concerning the will of the counselee. This belief is, of course, embedded in his over-all theory of counseling.

Miss Smith was delighted that Bob, her counselee, had signed up for the college preparatory course. She knew that he had the ability to make it through and become a professional leader. One evening as she was tidying up her desk before leaving the office, Bob stood in the doorway. What was the trouble? Bob said hesitatingly that he didn't think he wanted to continue in the college preparatory program. Why? It was just that in order to keep up with his work he was having to give up some school activities that he enjoyed. As he left the office forty minutes later, Bob looked much better, more purposeful, Miss Smith thought. They had worked out a study schedule, and decided upon those activities to be relinquished. Throughout the session she had been able to interject mention of the satisfactions that would come his way if he persisted. In fact she wondered now, as she finished recording the interview and placed the folder bearing his code number in the file, if perhaps she had been too sure about what Bob should do.

Some time passed before Bob came in again. This time his problem was whether or not to try for a scholarship. Miss Smith reviewed with him the pros and cons, in terms of his chances of securing it and the advantages and responsibilities that would result. Bob seemed a little hesitant, she thought, but on the other hand he appeared interested and aware of the advantages to be gained. She encouraged him, not outright, but by reinforcing indications he gave of wanting to try for it and by taking a slightly positive position regarding the advantages of a scholarship. She felt that it would do him considerable good, and she was pleased when Bob decided to try for it. Later she felt a little uneasy, as she reflected that Bob really should not have needed her help to make that decision. He had all the facts and was aware of what was involved. Was he becoming dependent upon her?

Miss Smith based her counseling on the belief that if Bob really understood what was best and could see the rewards in his imagination, he would make the right decision. This is the Renaissance position. She expected him to use his will to carry out the dictates of his reason. In other words, she believed that the will was capable of acting freely on its own, and could ignore or repress the emotions connected with the problem.

Miss Smith had been counselor in this high school for four years and had chalked up, as she saw it, a number of successes. Not even she herself knew why she succeeded or why, at times, she failed. Occasionally she found herself thinking about a student, "He didn't have what it takes." It may be that some of her successes are now more dependent than they should be, or might have been. They may be doing what they don't like to do or may not know what they desire. On the other hand, maybe some of her encouragement-advice was so good and the students were so free that they came to realize what was best and what they themselves really desired. Or they may have reviewed and reflected upon their decisions and decided that what they wanted to do was different from, or similar to, or in complete agreement with, the ideas they had assimilated from the counselor.

Mr. Jones is a counselor in the same high school. He too wonders about the success of his work and finds difficulty in living with ambiguity. But his method is different. He is counseling with Frank, a sixteen-year-old in the eleventh grade. Frank is being "pressured," as he sees it, by everyone to get into school social activities. But his girl friend Jean and he "aren't for these big affairs." They like to be "with Bill and Mary," and Frank especially does not want to take part in sports, in school drives, or in clubs or fraternities. These are not for him.

Mr. Jones has realized for some time that Frank is missing opportunities to learn social skills, to communicate his ideas to groups, to learn how others of his age think, to learn to compromise and keep his respect, and to discuss without becoming defensive. He wishes that Frank would have these important experiences, but Frank insists, "I don't enjoy these clubs, they're just a waste of time. I tried them and they're not for me."

"You tried them, Frank, but they don't make much sense to you, is that it?"

"I can't see what good they are; a few make all the decisions and the activities aren't interesting anyway."

"The organizations seem to you to be poorly run and uninteresting."

"They might not be any better if more had a chance to decide things, but they're a bore right now. That's why I've dropped them."

"Whether or not the programs were any better, you think they would be more interesting if more students took part in the planning."

Mr. Jones is assuming that the will is integrally part of the total self. He believes that whatever decisions are finally reached by the total self will have the affirming and initiating support of the will. Mr. Jones realizes, no doubt, that the total self may not reach any firm decisions, but waver among alternatives. He also knows that the decisions reached by the self may not be what the counselor perceives best but may, nevertheless, be put into effect by the will. Mr. Jones works within the philosophy of the Reformation.

INERTIA OF THE WILL

Phil's graduation from high school was in doubt. This became increasingly apparent to his teachers, to his parents, and, of course, to Phil, as the year progressed. To all of them including Phil, it was bewildering, because he had never experienced any difficulty in anything. His life flowed smoothly, and he had few decisions to make.

The counselor examined some of Phil's themes and other writing along with the usual information in the cumulative folder before talking with him. The writing caught his attention. The word usage, the sentence formation and the style set it apart as brilliant, but on rereading it, he had an uneasy feeling that it lacked the spontaneity of a purposeful author.

The counselor became more and more puzzled as the number of sessions with Phil increased. Phil was not apathetic, he was not without ambition, and he was concerned that he "would let his parents down." He realized that he needed further preparation to lead a productive, economically independent life. Granted he was not sure what he wanted to do. At times he thought of becoming the manager of a hotel-restaurant business, at another time, a journalist. But the counselor concluded that such vacillation was not unusual at his stage of development.

He almost enjoyed his sessions with Phil, who was alert and rather philosophical at times, and quoted quite well from literature and philosophy. When not delving into his problem, he had a cheerful mien, although in one interview he let it be known that this was not the way he really felt.

On reflection, the counselor realized that he was hard pressed to see much change taking place in Phil. In the tenth interview Phil seemed more ready to look at himself. After some superficial talk he said, "I just can't keep still at home. I go from one thing to another but I don't hit the books. Now Bill comes over sometimes and I help him with his math, but I just can't get myself to study."

"You can't get yourself to study but when Bill comes over you help him."

"Yeah, I wonder why I help Bill and don't study for myself when I need to so badly."

"It's hard to understand why you don't get around to studying."

"I know I can't afford to fail. I just have to make it but I have to work to do it and I'm not working. [Pause.] I have never failed in school; in fact, I have always thought that I was pretty good. Could it be that I really don't think I'm that good and I'm afraid to put it to the test?"

"You mean you are not studying because you're really afraid to put yourself on the line."

"It could be that I don't study so that if I do fail I can always say, 'I could get it if I studied but I just wasn't interested.' "

"In that way you could go on believing you really have a lot on the ball."

"That may be it. I feel as if I'm in a real battle most of the time. If I could just use all this energy on the books something would happen."

"You are using energy in sort of arguing with yourself which could be used another way."

"I guess I just can't take the risk. Now I believe I can succeed well in any academic work but if I really work at it, I may find I can't. I don't like to think that I may not be so hot, after all."

The above protocol illustrates the problem and the torment suffered by the counselee, whose reason tells him what to do but whose will refuses to initiate action. In such a situation the counselor is forced to recognize the central place of the will.

Counselors find counselees like Phil among the most difficult to work with. Some resort to encouragement, advice, or emphasis on the rewarding outcomes of constructive action. Often they are surprised when the counselees are unaffected or "seek an out" through rationalizations.

When the counselee wills to change, he wills at the same time that something die. He is aware that something has to die in order that something else may be born. But this something that must die is the familiar, which he has come to accept and which he may no longer view as a hurtful alternative. It has become a way of life — his way of life. Therefore some apprehension arises, even some opposition to willing, that the old should die. What, then, is needed in order that the counselee will take the decisive step of willing the new, knowing that the old forthwith must die?

The counselee is involved in a risk, for although his reason and imagination indicate that the new is preferable, there is no guarantee that it will be better. Hence the risk. What can the counselor do to enhance the possibility that the counselee will take the risk of willing the new? He can assure the counselee that improvement can be expected if he moves in the direction suggested. That is, he can try to ignore the risk that he cannot remove. The risk remains; this the counselee knows. If he does will the change, it may be only on the advice of his counselor, a pseudo-willing, "If you say so, all right," kind of willing, for which he does not take responsibility and which lacks the vital surge of free involvement and free will.

The counselor may impress upon the counselee the less promising prospects if he allows matters to continue as they are. He may indicate that the situation will almost certainly become worse if the counselee does not do something, the something being what he has suggested or what has been hinted at by the counselee himself. At this juncture the counselee may will to change; this is a pseudo-willing, a "there isn't much else that can be done" kind of willing, an avoidance or a resignation that reduces vitality to mechanical motion and intelligent action to an afterthought.

The counselee who initiates action on the advice and encouragement of the counselor, or changes because it is the only solution to the dilemma in which he is involved, may eventually genuinely change. If this occurs it is the result of the counselee's becoming the evaluator of himself in relation to the situation. This requires the involvement of the total self in which the will, active as a part of the self, plays a decisive role. That this does take place, we know. To how many, or under what circumstances, we are uncertain.

The counselor may endeavor to become involved in the problem, attitudes and feeling of the counselee. This approach makes a different demand on the counselor. His understanding must be deepened; he must come to love the counselee; he must see him as a person and, through loving care, free him and provide him with the support that may encourage him to take the risk of willing to change. However, there are risks in this method also. The counselee may not decide to change, or the direction he decides to take may be less constructive and useful than that which could have been encouraged by the counselor. The positive factor is that whatever decision is reached by the counselee, it has the support of the will as part of the total self in carrying it through to fruition.

The tragedy that engulfs so many young people today due to improper and unwise behavior may be so personally devastating to them that even the acceptance and love of the counselor leaves them still with a heavy load of guilt and unable to affirm themselves and life. It is then that Luther's assertion may become a reality, making possible for these young people the acceptance of their condition and the movement again toward life. This, of course, has the greatest possibility of taking place in a community that surrounds them with understanding rather than condemnation.

CONCLUSIONS

The counselor depends on the will for change to take place. As the importance of the decision increases, the action of the will becomes more significant.

Regardless of the counseling method, some assumption regarding the will is always implicit. Some counselors employ methods that require for their effectiveness that the will assert itself independently, if necessary, of the emotions or reason. This is the Renaissance position. Other counselors employ methods that assume that the will is an integral part of the total self. This is the Reformation position. Each assumption regarding the will has built-in risks. If the will overrides feeling and emotion, anxiety and repression may result. Or if the will is stimulated to act through advice and encouragement, a dependent relationship with the counselor may result. On the other hand, delayed action, or no action, may result if the will remains integrally related to the self.

The counselor who recognizes the function of the will takes a more realistic, sober attitude regarding the methods he uses and the beliefs he holds.

QUESTIONS

1. How would you explain a counselee's failure to do something when he has made a strong declaration that he would?
2. What relationship, if any, do you perceive between operant conditioning and the functioning of the will?
3. How do you explain inertia of the will?

FOR FURTHER READING

D. F. Pears, *Freedom and the Will* (New York: St. Martin's Press Inc., 1963).

Most of the essays in this book were presented in a program over B.B.C.; therefore the greater part is written in dialogue form. A sample of the chapter titles reads: "Freedom and the Will," "What Is the Will?" and "Acts of Will and Legal Responsibility." The chapters contain an astute and painstaking analysis of the will and the relation of freedom and the will. A few of the questions discussed regarding the will are: Can you distinguish between an effort of will and an act of will? Is the outcome of willing always some overt action? What is meant by the statement that someone did something of his own free will?

Otto Rank, *Will Therapy* (New York: Alfred A. Knopf, Inc., 1936).

The author places the construct of the will at the center of his therapeutic work. Seizing upon a concept that psychology has ignored, he employs it in a new understanding of will as it appears in human relations and especially in the therapeutic relationship. The chapter entitled "The Basis of a Will Therapy" deserves particularly careful and thoughtful reading.

William James, *Principles of Psychology,* Volume II (New York, Holt, Rinehart & Winston, Inc., 1918).

In volume II, Chapter 26, "The Will," James has written an incisive, clear discussion of the will. The counselor will find this chapter provocative, useful and interesting. A key idea is that the "effort of attention is thus the essential phenomenon of will."

5

LOVE

In recent psychotherapeutic literature, love has been increasingly recognized as the solution to our widespread separateness, aloneness, anxiety and neurosis. Recognition has also been given to the necessity that the counselor be a person capable of loving and that he love the counselee.[1] Since loving has been accepted as a prerequisite to almost everything worthwhile, counselors, teachers, parents and others assume that any feeling of good will is love and thus avoid any searching consideration of its nature. The importance we place upon love and the great lack of understanding of its meaning are apparent.

The counselor is dismayed as he views the panorama of symbiotic attachments that masquerade as love on T.V. and movie screens and billboards, in magazine advertisements and in literature. He comes to recognize that the adolescents whom he desires to help are bombarded everywhere by a cheap emotionalism labeled "love." Not only is there misunderstanding, but many people apparently have not developed the strength of character that would make it possible for them to love rather than to indulge in the all too common dependency relationship that passes for love. One author, who insists that courage and maturity are necessary if one is to become capable of truly loving, takes a dim view of our situation. According to him we live "in a society which is always talking about love but has so little of it."[2]

The counselor talks daily with teenagers who, because they are confused and uncertain of their values, are unable to understand

[1] C. Gilbert Wrenn, "The Status and Role of the School Counselor," *Personnel and Guidance Journal,* 1957, Vol. 36, p. 182.
[2] Rollo May, *Man in Search of Himself* (New York: Harper & Row, Publishers, Inc., 1953), p. 246.

themselves or their relationships with their peers. Lacking self-awareness and self-respect, they are unable to affirm and appreciate the potentialities of others. They assume that they are in love, but their need to be loved is so great that they cannot examine the situation. In such relationships neither girl nor boy perceives the other as a person. Each is to the other an object to which to cling. There is an unspoken agreement to support and satisfy each other's needs.

It may be that only the minority is capable of loving in its true sense. *Love is the capacity, willingness, and desire to give, expecting nothing in return.* Foote considers love to be the relationship between two people that is most conducive to the optimal development of both. This development is to be measured in terms of increased competence in interpersonal relations. May writes, "We define love as a delight in the presence of the other person and an affirming of his value and development as much as one's own." [3] Fromm writes, "The essence of love is to 'labor' for something and 'to make something grow'. . . . To love a person productively implies to care and feel responsible for his life, not only for his physical existence but for the growth and development of all his powers." [4] Spinoza has stated it thus: "He who loves God truly does not expect to be loved by Him in return." [5] The artist Joseph Binder believes that art requires that the artist be able to love, which is to be able to give, without thought of being rewarded. Poets have sung of the ecstasy in love. Such ecstasy becomes possible only through the fullest interdependence in human relations. However, one can merge himself in such ecstasy only as he has gained the prior capacity to be a person in his own right, to stand alone.

The paradox is that those who need love the least are those who are capable of loving the most. This is what Robert concluded in his counseling with Sandra. After Sandra had described her home conditions, her harsh father who was unfaithful to her mother, and her own feeling that she never did anything acceptable, he understood why she needed love so desperately. He began to understand why she did not follow the dictates of her own reason and why she became involved with Tom, who used her and abused her while trying to make her believe that he loved her. He began to sense the turmoil

[3] *Ibid.*, p. 241.
[4] Erich Fromm, *The Art of Loving* (New York: Harper & Row, Publishers, Inc., 1956), p. 26.
[5] Benedictus Spinoza, "Ethics" and "De Intellectus Emendatione," trans. by A. Boyle (New York: J. M. Dent & Sons, Ltd., 1955), p. 201.

she was in, trying to be free from Tom, whom she knew did not really love her, and at the same time being drawn toward him because of her desperate need.

APPROACHES TO THE MEANING OF LOVE

Although love is the most important quality of life and living, contrasting viewpoints exist concerning its origin and nature. This is to be expected since "any theory of love must begin with a theory of man, of human existence." [6] Since there are rather dissimilar theories concerning the nature of man, dissimilarity is also to be expected concerning love.

The Psychological Approach

Each discipline has arrived at its own conclusions concerning love. Much has been learned from the scientific approach. There is evidence, for example, that love develops gradually through interpersonal relationships. In this regard a baby's first experiences with its mother are very important. The child who is loved responds to the person who loves him. In this view love is a quality added onto life. It is brought into being and developed in relation to the maturing quality of the interpersonal relationships.

In order for the child to develop his ability and desire to move toward others psychologically, he must be helped in his relationships to develop a personal center. This requires that his parents genuinely love him and also that their unconditional love be experienced by him. It is difficult for parents to love their children genuinely and unconditionally. They are affected in this as in other things by strong cultural influences. Parents tend to love children more if they keep clean, if they are obedient and well-mannered, if they are successful academically. The children come to recognize that they are loved in direct relation to their performance.

This tendency is, however, difficult for parents to perceive or accept. In fact, when the idea was tentatively suggested in a meeting of parents of third-grade children, the parents loudly disagreed with it. One parent, a lawyer, exclaimed, "That is all bosh!" Other parents voiced their dissent in this manner: "Now, we let our children know that we love them; we tell them; we get them things." When parents become interested in exploring their relationships with their children,

[6] Fromm, *op. cit.*, p. 64.

and willing to do so, they invariably defend the practice of showing more warmth when the child conforms. "But you have to socialize them, do you not?" Rogers suggests that if the child is to remain secure, through admission to awareness and accurate symbolization of all relevant evidence of his experience, the parents must genuinely accept the feelings of satisfaction experienced by the child regarding his acts. They must accept the child himself, and their own feeling toward him, even when his behavior is unacceptable. To love the child in spite of his behavior is one of love's most difficult tests and is experienced as such by parents, teachers and counselors alike.

It is often apparent to counselors that their task would be minimal if parents passed the test of unconditional love for their children. One counselor received a phone call at midnight from a mother in a city 500 miles away. She asked him to go to the college hospital to see her daughter, who had flu. When the mother insisted, the counselor agreed to go immediately, and to report back. He found the girl awake, and when he told her the reason for his visit, she looked at him and said, "My mother doesn't love me," and turned her face to the wall. The counselor left. Some days later in his office as he talked with the student, he understood her feeling. Although the girl had so many party dresses that she supplied all the other girls in her wing of the dormitory, it was clearly evident when the facts of her relationship with her mother were known, that the daughter had reason for saying that she was not loved.

In fact, counselors are so frequently faced with symbiotic forms of attachment in the home that they rightfully conclude that if progress is to be made they must understand the parents' relationships with each other and with their children and work with all to improve these.

The empirical tools of research have been applied to the separation of love into types. We have become accustomed to speaking of brotherly love, teenage love, married love and sexual love as discrete and describable entities. The most controversial of all the kinds of love is sexual love.

If love is considered only a quality added to life, a learned way of behaving, it may be correctly placed in the chain of cause and effect relationships. It operates in predetermined ways and outcomes are predictable. From this point of view love is a sign. It is something we comprehend fully and believe we discover in its entirety. It is within our accomplishment. Thus attentiveness, graciousness, gifts, beautiful clothes, the right hairdo become the means of acquiring love. Love is the result of certain actions and may decrease if these actions are not sustained. When love is believed to be a quality added to life, youngsters are encouraged to learn the art of loving in order that they may be attractive to the opposite sex and eventually successful in securing a life partner. Parents feel it is a duty to show unequivocal indications that they love their children. Counselors are told that they should love the counselees, always, of course, with the right kind of love, which is described as offering to the counselee deep acceptance and deep understanding.

In this view, love is closely linked to behavior. The implication is that the more conforming and pleasing the behavior, the more love will result, or that love will be withdrawn if one does not perform in accordance with the wishes of another.

The Philosophical Approach

There is a second approach toward the understanding of love. This approach differs from the psychological one in several important respects. One of these differences is that love is not considered an addition, or something that comes into being only through interpersonal relationships, but one of the constitutive elements of life. In this view there are no types or kinds of love. There are only qualities of love. All love has only one purpose, the reunion of the separated.

The truth of this viewpoint became apparent to one counselor in an unexpected manner. Joyce was a sophomore. She had been "going with" Bill for almost a year. "Bill," she said, "wanted to get serious," but for some reason, despite the fact that she liked him and enjoyed being with him, she did not feel that she loved him. Several interviews later she realized that Bill in certain ways resembled her brother whom she had greatly missed since his joining the navy. What she actually desired was to be with her brother again.

This approach does not presume to provide a completely satisfying explanation of love. In fact, it views love as a symbol, beyond the possibility of being fully comprehended. This idea of love is not popular. It contains too much ambiguity and uncertainty. It is too inexact, too foreign to our customary ways of perception and analysis. We find it more natural to compartmentalize everything into concepts, things, and activities. This is the world we have known; we are nominalists. However, when pressed, we are forced to admit that we are incapable of either explaining love or proving to another that we love a certain person.

Jim Smith, a counselor, felt that Mr. Jones didn't really love his son, Bob. In fact, he was convinced that this was one of the chief reasons why Bob had recently become delinquent. In talking with Mr. Jones, the counselor tactfully asked him if he loved Bob. Mr. Jones was a bit surprised and answered, "Of course I love him." When the counselor asked again, he said, "What do you mean, do I love him? Of course I love him. He's my son."

Assuming that love cannot be fully explained, the philosophical viewpoint holds some further understandings. To these we now turn. In this context love is the result of the need to overcome separateness. This feeling of separateness can exist within oneself but is more easily recognized and more generally considered to exist between individuals.

All acts of love are considered to have within them varying degrees of certain qualities. We shall begin by examining these qualities, which in actuality are inseparable but are distinguished here for purposes of description. At the present time three qualities have been distinguished. They have been given these names: *epithymia,* the desire for sensual self-fulfillment, *eros,* the striving "for union with that which is the bearer of values because of the values it embodies" [7] (this includes not only union with persons, but with the beauty in nature, and mystical union with the source of the beautiful and the true), and *philia,* love toward self, the affirmation of self and maintenance of a personal center.

The most controversial among these qualities is epithymia (sexual desire). Some prefer to consider a wide gap to exist between this quality of love and those which they consider higher and essentially different. Others would reduce all love to this quality of sensual self-fulfillment. Such extreme attitudes become a barrier to understanding those who emphasize this quality of love in their relationships. Some consider sexual compatibility as the *sine qua non* of the perfect love relationship. Others consider sexual love as a different, lower kind of love. Each position hinders the understanding of true love. According to the former position, intimacy established through sexual relationships completely encompasses love. Separateness has only one meaning, physical separateness, and the logical conclusion then is that separateness is overcome by physical union.

Further misunderstanding results when the pain-pleasure principle is used as an explanation of this quality of love. The hedonistic principle actually only explains perversion in this instance. From the philosophical viewpoint all living beings strive for union with

[7] Paul Tillich, *Love, Power and Justice* (New York: Oxford University Press, 1954), p. 30.

that to which they belong; they strive to overcome separateness. These strivings express themselves normally as desire for food, movement, sexual union, and participation in a group. With the fulfillment of each of these desires comes pleasure. However, it is not pleasure as such that is desired; it is the union that fulfills the desire.

Counselors report the increasing difficulty that sexual union among high school adolescents is presenting for them and for school boards. Many school boards consider such behavior in terms of the pain-pleasure principle and outrightly condemn it. For them there is no integral relationship between sexual desire and other qualities of love.

Such a position tends to lose sight of the person. Rather than making some plan to help the individual, those who hold this position proceed on the basis of some rule that because of its nature ignores the particular problem of the particular person. Condemnation of the person and decision on the basis of some ruling is the logical outcome of the conviction that sexual desire is a lower passion of the body unrelated to the higher feelings and qualities of love. If members of school boards, counselors, parents and others interpret the problem of sexual union among adolescents as only a striving for pleasure, they neglect the essential elements in the situation. Such misunderstanding will seriously mitigate the possibility of their understanding and helping these adolescents.

Sexual desire (epithymia) is not evil in itself as desire. It becomes evil only when desire falls under the tyranny of the pleasure principle. Then the other becomes an object, a tool, a means of pleasure. This is the hazard of love in which epithymia takes ascendance. This is the case especially when some form of symbiotic union masquerades covertly, and to a degree unconsciously, as love.

The quality of eros drives us toward union with the forms of culture and nature, and with the sources of these. Eros is joined with epithymia (sensual desire) in the normal desire for vital self-fulfillment. This we experience in our movement toward others in terms of sincere, positive feeling. Plato described it as motivating the union of the true and the good; Aristotle considered it the power moving everything to its highest form as the object of love. It is the transpersonal dimension in the love relationship.

Eros, the "reaching out" quality, is the driving force in all cultural creativity and mysticism. But to reach out and become truly involved entails a risk. This risk may be avoided by engaging in a pseudo-involvement which often takes the form of an aesthetic detachment. But whatever form of escape from the risk is sought, it influences our reaction to culture and the striving of the eros drive becomes ambiguous. As evidence of this we may note how difficult it is for us as members of an organization to assume the responsibilities of membership.

The counselor is aware of how great is the resistance of the adolescent to the responsibilities incurred because of his membership in the school. The ambiguity that results from the avoidance of genuine involvement becomes a ready avenue for escape from the realities and needs of the culture. Often there is a detachment from and disappearance of participation in community, which finally gives way to a lack of any sense of responsibility for the community. The result is that culture in every respect is irresponsibly enjoyed. The counselor should recognize that such behavior is based in the lack of love of self, i.e., of a personal center, which prevents the adolescent from becoming normally involved in accepting responsibilities. The counselor who senses this will then attempt, and will encourage others, to do what is possible to help these adolescents to build a solid self-respect based on realistic understanding of self and on achievement.

Philia represents this love of self. A person reaches out to the environment and to others to the degree that he loves himself. He must be able to affirm himself. Philia and eros, then, are interdependent. The person does not experience the eros quality of love if he lacks a personal center. If one is unable to relate himself as an "I" to a "thou," he is also unable to relate himself to the true and the good and to the ground in which they are rooted.

Philia and eros are united not only in the individual relation but also in the communion of social groups. This, in fact, is the ideal to which groups in group process tend and a prerequisite if group therapy is to take place. In community, national and family groups special philia relations may be lacking, but "the desire for participation is directed toward the power of being which is embodied in the group." [8] The philia quality of love then presupposes some degree of familiarity with the other one, the object of love. Philia is possible when psychological and other barriers are absent.

Regardless of the degree of eros and philia in the love relationship, epithymia is always present. This is easily affirmed by the fact that eros and philia are united with sexual attraction. However, we would do well to recognize that each of us has an urge to fulfill himself through union with others. This is a universal urge and it under-

[8] Paul Tillich, *Love, Power and Justice* (New York: Oxford University Press, 1954), Chapter 2.

lies the other qualities of love. There is an element of libido in all love relationships.

Self-respect, self-regard and self-affirmation, characteristic of the philia quality of love, are also jeopardized by the ambiguities in interpersonal relationships. Counselors, teachers and parents are involved with the problems that result when some young people receive preferential treatment and others are implicitly or explicitly rejected. Parents are sometimes amazed at the efforts children will make in order to be acceptable and desirable to the in-group. It is, of course, true that in both primary and secondary groups some individuals are preferred to others. It is when an attachment forms out of compulsive needs, either sadistic or masochistic, and bonds become so fixed that each person is bound in servitude to the needs of the other that a relationship loses its creative and life-giving qualities.

AGAPE, A DEPTH DIMENSION

An undestanding of love from the viewpoints of science and philosophy is not all-inclusive. There is another dimension called *agape:* "the depth of love or love in relation to the ground of life. . . . [It] enters from another dimension into the whole of life and into all qualities of love." [9] Each quality of love permeated by agape transmutes love into a constructive and creatively fulfilling act. With agape, epithymia (sexual desire), takes its proper place as a quality of love rather than *the* quality of love. The loved person is seen as having a center, a uniqueness, values, a destiny partly seen and partly hidden, an inwardness, an inner choice. Sexual desire is now diffused with other qualities of love, and the combination, permeated by agape, encourages one to see the other in his center, to relate to his being, to respect him, and to unite with him at the center of his being. In this perspective, sexual union becomes the high act of giving, an ecstasy of relatedness.

The operation of this depth quality in love is illustrated well by J. A. T. Robinson. He writes: "To the young man asking in his relations with a girl, 'Why shouldn't I?' it is relatively easy to say, 'Because it's wrong' or 'Because it's a sin' — and then to condemn him when he, or his whole generation, refuses to listen. It makes much greater demands to ask, and to answer, the question 'Do you love her?' or 'How much do you love her?' and then to help him to accept for himself the decision that if he doesn't, or doesn't very deeply, then his action is immoral. Or, if he does, then he will respect her

[9] *Ibid.*

far too much to use her or take liberties with her." [10] Such love may only be possible to those who are open to "the inner choice."

All qualities of love or, more correctly, love composed of their complete integration, are severely limited without the depth quality, which has been termed agape. Agape significantly influences behavior and outcomes in many situations. The influence of this quality is evident in a mother's risking her life so that a child might live, in a convict's volunteering for the sake of research to risk injections that may cause cancer, in a student's revealing that he cheated on an examination in order that others will not suffer condemnation, or in the forgiveness of infidelity in business or in love. It may not be too great an exaggeration to say that without this depth quality communion and communities might degenerate.

Equally significant is the fact that it is not possible to predict in whom this depth quality will exert its influence. Whether the counselor will act in a selfless, positive manner in love depends, no doubt, upon factors known and unknown. If he is one whose ideal is to be guided by loving concern, the possibilities may be increased that in a difficult situation agape will guide his decisions and actions.

This is our hope since love "has a built-in moral compass, enabling it to 'home' intuitively upon the deepest need of the other [and] can allow itself to be directed completely by the situation. It alone can afford to be utterly open to the situation, or rather to the person in the situation, uniquely and for his own sake, without losing its direction or unconditionality." [11] In Tillich's words, "Love alone can transform itself according to the concrete demands of every individual and social situation without losing its eternity and dignity and unconditional validity." [12]

QUESTIONS

1. What is the common characteristic of the authorities' definitions of love?
2. How may a dependency relationship be distinguished from love?
3. What are some of the implications if love is only the outcome of a learning process?

[10] John A. T. Robinson, *Honest to God* (Philadelphia: The Westminster Press, 1963), p. 119.
[11] *Ibid.*, p. 115.
[12] Paul Tillich, *The Protestant Era* (Chicago: The University of Chicago Press, 1948), p. 155.

4. What is unique about the view that love is one, and that there are qualities but not kinds of love?
5. Why is philia considered to be the pivotal quality of love?

FOR FURTHER READING

Erich Fromm, *The Art of Loving* (New York: Harper & Row, Publishers, Inc., 1956).

The author explains in the foreword that the purpose of the book is to show that love is not a sentiment but rather loving requires the development of one's total personality. Satisfaction in individual love, he emphasizes, can only be attained as one develops the capacity to love one's neighbor. This capacity demands humility, courage, faith and discipline. In a culture in which these capacities are rare, the attainment of the capacity to love remains a rare achievement.

Ashley Montagu (ed.), *The Meaning of Love* (New York: The Julian Press, Inc., 1953).

This book probes the meaning of love. The authors, all authorities on the subjects on which they write, examine the various meanings of love. The object of the inquiry is to obtain a clue to why man does not secure satisfaction from his loving. The articles explore the possibility that the answer lies in what man has been taught, or how he has learned, or that he has learned something else, which he has confused with love. A sample of authors and topics are: Lawrence K. Frank, "On Loving"; Leon J. Saul, "Maternal Love"; Alvin Johnson, "Love of Friends"; O. Spurgeon English, "Sexual Love," and James Luther Adams, "Love of God." Throughout the book an attempt is made to restore something of the meaning of love to the understanding of human beings and the vocabulary of human expression.

Paul Tillich, *Love, Power and Justice* (New York: Oxford University Press, 1954.)

This is an analysis of love, power and justice and their ethical implications. The author considers all concepts fundamental in the mutual relations of human beings, of social groups, and of man and God. His concern is to save the concepts from sentimentality, vague talk and cynicism. This he proceeds to do by penetrating to the essential or ontological meaning of the words, love, power and justice. The book is brief, clear, stimulating and provocative.

THE
HUMAN
SITUATION

❧

II

6

MODERN VALUES

Constantly and continuously, the counselor confronts values that come from many sources, operate at many levels, and are frequently permeated with ambiguity. The task of value analysis and understanding is exceedingly difficult. It is not surprising that many counselors seldom engage in serious consideration of the value systems to which they and others, often unwittingly, subscribe.

A BRIEF SURVEY OF VALUES

Our present culture has characteristics unique in history. This is a time of mass production and distribution of goods. This has a profound effect on economic and political structures, and also on the innermost center of personal life. This is seen more clearly in the different approaches to the use of reason related to the panoramas of societal change. The panorama of modern times reveals three eras of change: the period of middle class revolutions, the victorious period of the middle class, and our present crisis. Each era had its guiding principle.

Reason as the Principle of Harmony

In the first era, that of the middle class in revolt, the guiding principle was the belief in reason. It was assumed that reason would control nature in and beyond man, since reason and nature were regarded as being in harmony. The ends to be pursued were beyond the existing order and somewhat "utopian," although the means of achieving them were conservative.

The revolutionary reason, symbolized in the adoration of "reason" as goddess in the French Revolution, was the basis of the struggle against feudalism and other forms of tyranny. The goal was the liberation of reason, which, it was believed, would in turn initiate a system of harmony between individuals and society. It was assumed that in the various spheres of activity — economic, political, religious and educational — a harmonious community would result because of the theory of integral unity and development that was given philosophical expression in Leibnitz's theory of the monad.

Reason was interpreted as "the power of truth and justice embodied in man as man." [1] Each man, regardless of his rank, felt a part of the spiritual reality that bore him into the future. In the later part of this period, the common ground of universal authority was replaced by a common ground of devotion, defense of religious doctrine, struggle against forms of authoritarianism, and a virtual crusade to establish the Kingdom of God.

Reason as the Tool for Progress

The principle of reason as the basis of harmony was transformed as the bourgeois revolution succeeded. In the compromising of political groups, reason became a tool in the service of the industrial revolution and the fast developing technical society. Concern shifted from goals beyond the existing order to the stabilization of the existing order. Man now applied his technical reason to the making of machines, and ushered in a world-wide mechanism and with it a mechanized way of looking at man. This approach to man was objective and evaluational in terms of the quality and quantity of his production. Although man surpassed his dreams in the control and manipulation of physical nature, he became a slave to his own creations. His world became less and less predictable. The movements of production and consumption were in part incalculable. The middle class especially felt that they had lost control of their destiny. Human reason no longer had the ability to control man's historical existence. The evidence of this condition is plainly visible in the two world wars, with their psychological and sociological consequences.

In the later stages of this era individuals emerged with developed minds and strong wills. These men were the bearers of technical reason. Willpower and technical rationality were united to build great monopolies and the mechanism of the capitalistic society. The

[1] Paul Tillich, "The World Situation," *The Christian Answer*, ed. Henry P. Van Dusen (New York: Charles Scribner's Sons, 1945), p. 2.

price was high. The classical and humanistic ideals of personality faded. At all levels of society the individual became part and parcel of the purposes of the age. But these purposes lacked ultimate meaning, and the sensations and adjustments entailed were without a center. Although the individual enjoyed music, literature and art, he was not shaped by them. Instead, he was shaped by the demands of the economy. The naturalistic laws of the machine world became increasingly plausible as the means of explaining human existence.

The common ground and common spiritual purpose disappeared. The family unit no longer existed, and the family became a number of individuals, each living for himself in the service of the mechanism about him. Men's sense of responsibility for one another's welfare gave way to impersonal mass cooperation. Neighborhoods, whether rural or urban, lost their meaning as communities. Competition held universal sway in all areas of life.

Reason for Control

So man moved into the third period, the present crisis. Now he asks how he can gain control again, and make proper use of the results of his continuing scientific advancements. No doubt in this predicament we would like to turn back, either to some form of unrecognized laissez-faire in which responsibility is shuffled off, or to some form of absolutism that does not have to recognize the fact that persons are treated as objects. A creative solution must be found. This is the problem of all and especially that of counselors, who confront the elements of life and must take action.

The Atomization of Life • The counselor faces on all sides the atomization of life and its accompanying feeling of solitude, loneliness and meaninglessness. The counselee rebels against control by merely utilitarian reason whether by parents, teachers or counselors. This revolt in its various forms — "urge to mature," "competitive thrusts," "sadistic drives," "will to power," or *"élan vital"* — reveals the dynamic center. Man senses that he is not fully explained on the foundation of, and in interdependence with, rational factors. It is a vitalistic protest against the mechanization of man. The problem is most difficult for the counselor. This is not surprising, of course, since the mechanism of mass production does not provide a spiritual center for community. Instead individuals feel like atoms, lonely and competitive. They have been driven apart by the demands of the mechanized society.

Loss of Meaningful Communication · The sustenance of life through meaningful communication and the growing into community with others through education has gradually disappeared. It was supplanted by an educational and counseling method focused on means rather than on the development of persons as persons.

With the ascendance of technical reason the humanistic ideal of education lost its influence and became a decoration for social prestige. Education bowed to the demands of a technical society. Counseling in a formal sense appeared as vocational education for an ideal humanity, and "adjustment" became the key word. The successful person was one who could adjust, and the successful counselor was the one who could assist him in doing so.

An increasing number "took" education. Everyone attended public school, and technical education was extended and improved to meet the demands of large scale industry. Since the mechanism of production was foremost, everyone was to some degree subject to the ideals and norms of the system. Education took its key from the emphasis on production, and counselors tried to help students to understand and take advantage of it. "Educate everyone to his fullest potential," became the slogan, and the process was considered developmental. The traditions of humanism and religion were considered useful but seldom relevant. They became peripheral since they were no longer recognized as significant expressions of human possibilities and ultimate realities.

The Marketplace Orientation

A competitive society that is geared to mass production and that idealizes technical and planning reason cannot expect its citizens to be sincerely interested in or feel responsible for one another, even including members of their own families.

Today, throughout his life, each individual to some degree is reminded, through personal experiences or as he watches the experiences of others, that he is valued according to what he produces. Mary learns early in childhood that her mother loves her more when she conforms to her mother's wishes. Mary has no basis for self-respect; her significance is unrelated to her beliefs, her values, or the fact that she is a person. She must demonstrate her worth by what she can and does accomplish. She never knows real security, since she is always threatened by the dismaying possibility that she may fail. She is incapable of loving because she is not aware of her true feeling; if on occasion she has a glimmer of it she becomes confused about how to show it. She cannot accept true love because she is uncertain about the sincerity of her lover. In fact, to be truly loved would be threatening, since it would necessitate an evaluation of her own feelings. Mary has been conditioned by innumerable experiences to accept the fact that her worth depends upon what she produces and how she is accepted by others. She has become just another commodity on the market. She is a means of satisfying, and is satisfied by, others, but she is not a person in her own right. This is the "market-place orientation" so well described by Erich Fromm. Referring to the different skills and qualities of man, he writes, "As with any other commodity it is the market which decides the value of these human qualities, yes, even their very existence. If there is no use for the qualities a person offers, he has none, just as an unsalable commodity is valueless though it might have its use value." [2]

As all forms of society became saturated with the philosophy of technical and planning reason permeated with pragmatism, persons lose their individuality. They become depersonalized, products on the market like the machines they have helped to produce. It is not wisdom or understanding of persons that is considered significant knowledge, but the impersonal knowledge of mechanistic naturalism. "The concrete relationship of one individual to another has lost its direct and human character and has assumed a spirit of manipulation and instrumentality." [3]

Counselor Reactions

In the schools, some counselors became expert in techniques and safeguards against erupting irrational powers that were inclined to be destructive both for the individual and for the accepted educational aims. For such irrational outbursts have been more and more common, as education, permeated with the mechanistic and pragmatic goals of modern society, has gradually put aside its understanding of, and respect for, truth and justice, and thus its ultimate meaning. Symptomatic of this eruption in the search for meaning is the increasing incidence of school dropouts and student demonstrations and riots. Both counselor and counselee are embedded in this complex culture. All are inhabitants; unfortunately some are inmates.

Other counselors, perceiving the counselee as a person, motivate him to commit himself to understanding himself and his problem.

[2] Erich Fromm, *Escape From Freedom* (New York: Holt, Rinehart & Winston, Inc., 1941), p. 19.
[3] *Ibid.,* p. 118.

This Rollo May considers a fundamental principle in counseling. "The patient must find or discover some point in his existence where he can commit himself before he can permit himself even to see the truth of what he is doing." [4]

It may be that the line of separation between those counselors who release the curative forces of healing and growth within their counselees and those whose relationship with their counselees only initiates and strengthens the superficial mechanisms of adjustment becomes apparent in their approach to persons. Tournier explains that we may see the world "in nothing but things, mechanisms, from those of physics to those of biology and even of psychology. Art, philosophy, religion can also become things, collections of concepts, formulae, definitions." [5] This method of trained observation that asks the questions of utility is useful in studying objects, but is superficial, one-sided, and partial in its usefulness for understanding persons. Yet for many it encompasses the only basis of value or orientation.

In fact, the surprise is not so much that we tend to see persons as objects, but rather that we ever see them as anything else. Throughout our education we are taught to know things, to isolate them, identify them, count them, measure them and classify them. Small wonder that we become less capable of perceiving that which is not measurable or objective and cease to believe in its existence.

We assume that a field of common experience waits for us to impose our value upon it. That is, it is there for our use or our pleasure; it is a means of our self-actualization. But we ourselves are part of the common experience in the human situation. Thus we need to ask not only, "How shall we value the world," but also, "What value have we in the world?" It is not only, "What are we to make of the world?" but in addition, "What is the world to make of us?" Only when he does this is the counselor able to grasp the field of common experience as a whole.

The counselor, then, discovers that he is not moulding experience but is in a cooperative relationship. Like the experienced swimmer, who expects, accepts and works cooperatively with the buoyancy of the water, the counselor needs to recognize that he is, partial, temporary and dependent. The realization that he is a

[4] Rollo May, Ernest Angel, and Henri F. Ellenberger (eds.), *Existence: A New Dimension in Psychiatry and Psychology* (New York: Basic Books, Inc., 1958), p. 28.
[5] Paul Tournier, *The Meaning of Persons* (New York: Harper & Row, Publishers, Inc., 1957), p. 179.

dependent creature of the world instills a different approach to reality and to persons than either the utilitarian or aesthetic. The counselor, like the swimmer, relies upon and works with the eternal purposes of the universe, the buoyancy of life.

INFLUENCES OF RELIGION AND HUMANISM

Any religion taken seriously involves the whole person in his total destiny. This is so regardless of the nature of the religion. The interpretations that the individual places upon the teachings of his religion reflect his needs and mental health. These interpretations have also varied with the interests and goals of each generation. Formal religion is not currently the accepted bearer of values that it has been in other times. Its symbols, which conveyed meaning in the past, lack meaning in an age of technical reason and planning. This is a scientific age concerned with the productive use of knowledge from many disciplines in solving the problems of the present. The thought patterns and symbolic language are apparently irrelevant. The message of religion clothed in mythical or metaphysical robes does not make itself understood by or interesting to the very great majority. This fact is recognized by perceptive students of this age, who analyze the situation, make assumptions and offer suggestions. Some assume that religion as always is the bearer of values, and that its stock in trade are the ultimate concerns of man, but also that "the old order changeth, yielding place to the new."

One of these critics, Harvey Cox, examines and analyzes two approaches to recapturing the relevancy of religious values for our time. He dismisses the premetaphysical hypothesis of Martin Heidegger and Heinrich Ott as a step backward, a return to the tribal stage of religion in which literalism and anthropomorphism hid the possibility of further understanding. He is also critical of the existentialists, especially Rudolf Bultmann, because he considers their thinking "antitechnical, individualistic, romantic, and deeply suspicious of cities and science." [6] He believes the world has already moved beyond the metaphysical interest that is the focus of existentialism. Cox concurs with Van Peursen, who calls for the reading of the Bible without metaphysical presuppositions. Cox believes that politics does today what metaphysics once did.

In this day of technical reason and technical planning, truth is unified not only by the scholar in his study, but more often by the

[6] Harvey Cox, *The Secular City* (New York: The Macmillan Co., 1965), p. 252.

intellectual teamwork of many from disparate specialities who come together to do something about a pressing problem that affects them and people in general. This certainly does not mean that the past is ruled out — only that it is used in a different way. The emphasis is on reflection on the issues at hand, but these issues are studied in light of the great religious events of the past, hopefully to gain understanding of "the hints God has dropped in the past in order to make out what He is doing today." [7] This approach to religious values, requiring maturity, insight and knowledge, is a challenge to all engaged in the betterment of mankind. It rightly assumes that not religion, but its formal expression, is outdated. There is need for the counselor and others to advance in knowledge and understanding in this area as they have done in the areas of science and politics.

He who is able and willing to put aside premetaphysical and metaphysical concepts of religion, and, out of an honest desire to help, speaks to another in his concrete need, brings religious and humanistic values to fruition. But he must interact; he must be committed; he must be willing to drink of the same cup. When we restore men to each other in mutual concern and responsibility, we are engaged in the work of religion. In this effort something is present which the participators in the drama are sure of, but which they have always found it difficult to describe in scientific terms.

The religion of many, counselors and others, is childish and immature, and their lack of knowledge further emphasizes its unimportance in their thinking. Even the counselor who is sufficiently secure and open to search for religious understanding takes with him habits of thought and methods of validation that are not useful. The tools of measurement and the patterns of thought that have served him so well in his scientific quest are of little help. He must develop respect for other methods of gaining truth. It is difficult for the counselor to recognize and accept the fact that the values most crucial in the counseling relationship do not yield to scientific measurement.

The quality and helpfulness of the value interpretations of religion are a function of the ability and health of the interpreter. It has been long understood that a healthy religion encourages health in persons and that insecure, threatened, closed-minded persons place interpretations on theological constructs in accordance with their psychological needs. Sick persons have a sick religion. This is the

[7] *Ibid.*

message of Carroll Wise in his book, *Religion in Illness and Health.*[8] Recently Clinebell, with counseling and clinical training in psychology and also in theology, wrote, "The popularity of authority-centered religious groups in our society is one indication of the prevalence of emotional cripples. . . . Healthy religion encourages a person to accept himself as he is . . . imperfect, finite, sinful . . . and then to move ahead. Self-acceptance based on God's acceptance is the starting point of spiritual growth."[9]

INFLUENCES OF PRAGMATISM
AND EXISTENTIALISM

Significant and pervasive in its effects has been the influence of pragmatism. Peirce first enunciated the pragmatic principle in America in 1878.[10] He made the claim that to develop the meaning of a thought it is necessary only to determine what conduct it is fitted to produce; the result is its sole significance. The value of an idea or action, then, is revealed by how satisfactorily it works out for the person using it. Through its explication by Charles Sanders Peirce, and by William James, John Dewey and others, it has become the most accepted and most widely influential pattern of value thinking in the country. Among its appraisers are scientists, psychologists, philosophers and theologians in the United States and other countries.

The idea or practice "counts as true" only to the extent that it gratifies the individual's desire to assimilate the novel in his experience. The new truth "makes itself true, gets itself classed as true by the way it works; grafting itself then upon the ancient body of truth which grows much as a tree grows by the activity of a new layer of cambium."[11]

Pragmatism, then, is first a method and second a generic theory. As a method it has given impetus to great scientific advancement. As a value system it has come under criticism. One psychologist, Louis P. Thorpe, comments thus: "Pragmatism has provided a powerful stimulus to scientific study and practice. Indeed, it is the

[8] Carroll A. Wise, *Religion in Illness and Health* (New York: Harper & Row, Publishers, Inc., 1942).
[9] Howard J. Clinebell, Jr., *Mental Health Through Christian Community* (Nashville: Abingdon Press, 1965), pp. 36, 43.
[10] Charles Sanders Peirce, "How to Make Our Ideas Clear," *Popular Science Monthly*, January 1878.
[11] William James, "What Pragmatism Means," *Pragmatism and American Culture* (Boston: D. C. Heath & Company, 1950), pp. 1–23.

handmaiden of nearly all scientific endeavour. . . . Where pragmatism as a philosophy of life has its greatest drawbacks, however, is in the field of character and conduct. One can quickly sense the weakness of reducing the standard of right and wrong in this realm to mere expediency. . . .[12]

Pragmatism became predominant in the early years of this century; its effect in the area of social welfare did not become apparent for some time. Religious and humanistic principles were still considered to have some influence upon and relevance to the developments of the society of technical reason; the real nature of pragmatism, although criticized outside, was not recognized in America. Bertrand Russell wrote: "The two qualities which I consider superlatively important are love of truth and love of our neighbor. I find love of truth in America obscured by commercialism of which pragmatism is the philosophical expression; and love of our neighbor kept in fetters by Puritan morality." [13] What was not clear was that, although Puritan morality left much to be desired, it was based on eternal values and offered a life based on faith and hope. Under these conditions pragmatism was still under the influence of religion. As such, it was a refined pragmatism and, grafting itself on the current religious and moral values, it penetrated the vital tissues of the individual and society.

Wherever humanistic values and religious principles were compartmentalized and dismissed as irrelevant, and discussion of them was considered entertainment for the impractical or naive, the true nature of pragmatism in its crude form became evident. Thorpe defines it as the "relatively uncontrolled philosophy of life in which expediency based upon ego-centric purposes guides the shifting destinies of the individual. Persons with this code cannot comprehend fair play, and are scarcely on speaking terms with duty, honor, courtesy and other qualities which characterize the socialized individual. To them the man who does what is right because it is expected of him and because there are other people to be considered besides himself is an object of wonder." [14]

Many counselors, unaware of the impact of pragmatically value-laden systems on the adolescents they try to help, are not equipped to understand the underlying motives of their counselees. They as-

[12] Louis P. Thorpe, *Personality and Life* (New York: David McKay Co., Inc., 1949), p. 214.
[13] Bertrand Russell, "Obstacles to Free Thought," *The Freeman*, 1922, Vol. 5, pp. 272–275.
[14] Thorpe, *op. cit.*, p. 217.

sume that truth, honesty, fair play, responsibility, dependability and trustworthiness are the basic virtues of the majority of their clients. Such a conclusion is too far removed from the actual facts to be a useful operational assumption. Even when Thorpe's description fits their colleagues they will not let themselves accept what their eyes have seen. The counselor must not ignore or distort such value systems when they present themselves. On the other hand, he should not conclude that all adolescents and all adults can be characterized by any one value system. Value systems of the counselees span the whole range of those discussed under the three periods of modern values. For the counselor to be open to and to live with value systems that differ from his own is difficult.

One disillusioned and troubled teacher went to a counselor. For three consecutive years she had had occasion to discuss cheating with her third grade group. Each year she discovered the same attitude: "Copy from someone who knows it, and be sure you don't get caught." The counselor took the position that either she misunderstood or the children were not serious. Observation of the children's performance demonstrated without a doubt that the counselor was wrong.

Such conditions emphasize the need for knowledge concerned with life. This is the counselor's predicament. What does he know for certain? How can he have some certainty about his conclusions? "Existential truth" has come to his aid. This is a new kind of truth, a personal truth, truth for him who perceives it. It is not general truth to be accepted on its rational basis. Detached analysis and verifiable hypothesis are irrelevant in dealing with this truth. Its validity is based on its adequacy for dealing with the concrete situation. "Existential truth in its many forms has one common trait, it has no criterion beyond fruitfulness for life." [15] Nevertheless, it opens up a new avenue for interpersonal understanding. It challenges the counselor to recognize and to become involved with truth in a situation as the counselee perceives it. This requires a new approach. It also requires commitment. The counselor must be willing and become able to commit himself to understanding the world as the counselee views it. But for the counselor there is grievous danger, first that he may come to think that this is the only truth, and second that he may consider this truth to have universality. The counselor needs to retain his respect for the truth that has demonstrated its ultimacy over the centuries and continues to do so. This he may find

[15] Tillich, *op. cit.*, p. 6.

difficulty in doing, since he may perceive modern interpretations of this truth as the elimination of the truth itself.

Existential truth has strong appeal. It presents itself as a legitimate means of casting off all that resembles what formerly was known as eternal truth. It is a truth that to counselee and counselor alike appears to be living, concerned with life now and with those who are making decisions in the present. However, it is relativistic and individualistic. Although existentialism is concerned with "being," it is being as each philosopher viewed life. Each philosophy of existence bears the trademark of the individual philosopher — Kierkegaard as the lonely individual concerned about eternity, Marx as the disinherited proletariat concerned about the future, Nietzsche as the dominating aristocrat concerned about power over life, Bergson as the vital intuitionist concerned about the fullness of experience. This new form of truth is here to stay. Its influence is difficult to discern. It is in the bloodstream of the counselor's values. The counselor needs to be aware of its weakness in that it surrenders reason and uses technical rationality to support its non-rational purposes.

IN THE MIDST OF CHANGE

The counselor must keep his awareness of the limitations of existential truth in the midst of change unprecedented in his lifetime. For example, what form should counseling take as we face the fact of an economy of abundance in which the traditional link between jobs and incomes is broken? Wealth produced by machines is still wealth. In the distribution of this wealth, may it not be that every family will receive an adequate income as a matter of right? What change in values is inherent in the fact that the amount of leisure will far exceed the number of working hours for everyone except those in certain services and professions? What would it mean if national policy were aimed less and less at the welfare of the productive process and more and more at the welfare of the people? If we decrease the research emphasis on processes, and increase the emphasis on creative interests and activities that are non-profit-making, what will this mean for the counselor? The demand on the counselor and educator because of the increased number of activities relating persons to persons will inject a new challenge to become, to know, and to do.

With the era of abundance comes a much enlarged possibility for a democratic society in which all those affected by the outcomes have a significant voice in determining the means and the ends. To whom shall we turn that we might learn to understand democracy in action, to believe in democratic procedures, and to become skilled in their use? Surely the counselor will be expected to be one of those in a position to give leadership.

The rate of change is, of course, unpredictable, but the change itself is imminent. Cybernation assures it and, coupled with the "Human Rights Revolution," it gains momentum. Many millions are beginning to understand and to demand a life that is decent and free of want and that is now deemed possible.

CONCLUSIONS

We are living in a time in which technical thinking and planning has a pervasive influence. The sense of community has in large measure succumbed to depersonalization in all forms of relationships in home, school, office and factory. Persons have lost their sense of identity and well-being. Their values are second-hand introjections from many, often conflicting, sources. People are treated as objects, and their worth is reckoned in terms of what they can sell or produce. Such treatment minimizes opportunities for full expression. The emotional life of persons finds no legitimate outlet in the planning and ordering of their lives.

Humanistic reason and regency of eternal verities are relegated to the periphery of life and become increasingly irrelevant, bowing to technical reason and planning. Pragmatic modes of thought and value gain ascendancy. Value becomes more and more a function of how well an idea or action "works." This trend further diminishes the relationship between religious values and daily life. Religion and religious values become compartmentalized and related only to certain functions and times. Disrespect and confusion result from lack of knowledge and the attempts to measure value by using the tools of science.

The pragmatic and scientific tests applied to values leave a gap, since only a part of the person is active in the valuational process, and since the principles and demands of technical reason are not fully satisfactory in every situation. Since technical reason is not sufficiently comprehensive or fully relevant as a guide to action, existential truth becomes more and more acceptable.

Existential truth provides the counselor with a further and different means of understanding the counselee, but this "truth" is relativistic. It also surrenders reason and uses only technical rationality for the evaluation of its non-rational purposes. Since it does not include the criterion of truth that could be supplied by humanism and religion, it lacks a safeguard against irrational forces.

In working with individuals or groups, the counselor discovers that the combination of pragmatism and existentialism has removed the anchors of value and judgment that are inherent in humanism and religion, and on which depends reasonable and responsible behavior.

IMPLICATIONS FOR THE COUNSELOR

Many counselors are like voyagers in a small craft on a broad, fast-moving river, without any map of the topography to indicate where the gorges and falls exist. The counselor must become well acquainted with the topography of modern values. He should be a student of social change, and should be sufficiently expert at least to sense the relationship between social change and the changes in values and motivation incurred thereby in his colleagues and counselees.

The counselor must be able to recognize the basic value structure underlying the behavior of those with whom he works, the materials he studies, and the counselees he seeks to help. It is necessary for him to become more aware of his own value structure, to recognize the degree to which the values of the culture flow in his bloodstream. It is important that he remain aware of, and learn to understand and evaluate, not only his personal values but also those within the culture that are based on religious or humanistic reason and those which are experimental, relativistic and expedient — whose criterion is technical rationality. Understanding of what happens to persons when they are treated as objects and ability to recognize the times when and the possible reasons why he treats them in such a manner are essential. He needs to differentiate between ultimate and existential truth and to recognize that "only by a proper union of the two can the intellectual needs of our present world be met." [16]

QUESTIONS

1. Why should the counselor be a student of modern values?
2. What change in the image of the person has accompanied the age of technical reason?

[16] Tillich, *op. cit.*, p. 12.

3. What is meant by the pragmatic viewpoint and what are its implications for counseling?
4. What are the limitations of existential truth?

FOR FURTHER READING

Richard Farson (ed.), *Science and Human Affairs* (Palo Alto, California: Science and Behavior Books, Inc., 1965).

This book is a compilation of the lectures of outstanding authors in a variety of fields. Each lecturer in his own scientific discipline dares to combine with his learning his intuition and subjective knowledge. Such an approach has provided fresh insights and new ways of looking at human behavior. The editor considers these leaders in the behavioral sciences to be "addressing themselves to such vital human concerns as conflict, resolution, prejudice, creativity, esthetics and personal growth." They return us to the study of human beings in a naturalistic manner and in relation to meaningful human concerns.

Richard Thruelsen and John Kobler (eds.), *Adventures of the Mind* (New York: Vintage Books, 1960).

The writers in this book of essays have a common concern that man make the best use of his mind and the knowledge he has inherited. Mark Van Doren, in his introduction, interprets their quest to be a response to the question, "Do we know what we are doing?" The authors are authorities in their respective fields. Among them are a scientist, a theologian, a moralist, an historian and an artist. The contents include: Jacques Barzun, "The Misbehavioral Sciences"; Paul Tillich, "The Lost Dimension in Religion"; J. Robert Oppenheimer, "The Mystery of Matter"; Walter Gropius, "The Curse of Conformity"; and Bertrand Russell, "The Expanding Mental Universe."

John W. Gardner, *Excellence* (New York: Harper & Row, Publishers Inc., 1961).

The author states in his introduction that he is concerned with the social context in which excellence may survive or be smothered. He examines the characteristics of several aspects of American society. He clarifies its strengths, exposes its weaknesses, asks penetrating questions, and hints at possible changes that he believes would lift the whole tone of the nation's thinking. The book is divided into four parts: "Equal and Unequal"; "Talent"; "Individual Differences";

and "The Ingredients of a Solution." The author deals frankly and in a straightforward manner with today's problems, especially those which are concerned with the development of the abilities of the young.

7

ANXIETY

Everyone is aware that anxiety is a pervasive and profound phenomenon. Frequently, however, counselors consider the anxiety of adolescents normal and attribute it to physiological change and new demands for adjustment. Although, as Erikson emphasizes, this time of personal growth is a period of unusual stress and intrapsychic conflict,[1] the amount and intensity of anxiety common today is different in both kind and degree from what could be considered normal. The now trite expression, "age of anxiety," points directly to the fact that the anxiety felt by most adolescents today far exceeds what might be expected as a normal function of development.

Expressions of anxiety take many forms. Each form is perceived as a plausible, or perhaps the only, means of coping with life. For example, several high school students from a community in which almost all go to college face failure in courses required for college entrance. A college education has been the goal of these students and their parents for years. This ideal has been discussed frequently, financial plans have been worked out for it, and life has almost come to revolve around it. Each of the students now confronts the fact that he is disappointing his parents, that he will be seen as a "failure," that his future is uncertain, and he is unsure about himself. He wonders if he might have been successful if . . . Each confronts these anxious thoughts and feelings in addition to those which accompany his developmental state of growth.

Often adolescents are anxious, guilty, dissatisfied, uneasy with nagging inferiority feelings. Some isolate themselves, feel defeated,

[1] Eric H. Erikson, "The Problem of Ego Identity," *Journal of the American Psychoanalytic Association,* 1956, Vol. 4, pp. 74–79.

and are unable to tell anyone. They wonder whom to tell, what to say, what good it would do! They may cease confronting the fear of failure directly, and try to forget it or by-pass it. Or they may settle for just accepting the feeling of misery, frustration and despair. And so defeat sets in.

When it is not confronted directly, anxiety takes many forms. The teacher notices that George is becoming quiet, passive, not only in science classes but even in student government, where his voice was usually heard. Is he losing interest, she asks herself? When she hints at this on the way to the study hall, George replies, "Oh I'm all right," in an off-hand, assumed manner of assurance.

Miss Wilson reports that Hugh, who was always so co-operative and helpful, has been interrupting and bothering the girls, that his work is untidy, and that he was almost sullen when she spoke to him about being noisy in the study hall.

"Jean," reports Mr. Dodge, mathematics teacher, "can hardly be separated from her work lately. She is doing more than her assignments and has asked me for extra help, and she also notes carefully the success or failure of the others. If working can do it, she may surprise us. Too bad she finds math so difficult."

"It's strange," began Miss Ross. "Jacqueline, who has always been in the center of things, asked me if she might wait till the rush is over in the halls because all the kids filling up the hall and rushing ahead bothers her. She feels she can hardly keep from screaming."

"At PTA the other night," Mr. Smith remarked, "John's mother talked to me and she seemed in trouble. She wanted to know if I saw any difference in John. She said that he washes his hands after everything he does around the house, and that he makes trouble if anyone moves any of his hangers in the clothes closet. At first I couldn't think of anything, and then I recalled that he was last finishing the history quiz and he continued to check his answers long after he had finished writing."

Each of these teen-agers has found his own way of handling the anxiety that resulted from the fear of impending failure. Many such attempts remain inconsequential unless they are very extreme in form and disruptive to the school routine.

THE PROBLEM

Many teachers and counselors lack the training to recognize and help students who are unsuccessful in coping with anxiety. The lack of interest and emphasis in this area may be our "widespread tendency . . . to avoid and look askance at 'irrational' phenomena and to refuse to admit them in our own experience." [2] Generally we accept without further investigation those aspects of experience which can be made to appear rational. Thus we have given more attention to "fears," and have tended to suppress anxiety or to rationalize it in terms of "fears." For "fears" are experienced as specific and definite, and can be studied by measurement techniques, but anxiety is generally experienced as a pervasive, irrational phenomenon.

As counselors we do not distinguish between anxiety and fear because we have been trained to depend on the counselee's reason, and fear lends itself to this rational attack. Counselors have been influenced by the age of mathematical rationalism and technical reason.

HISTORICAL DEVELOPMENT

The emotional, or irrational, has long been suppressed by the belief that only what can be calculated and measured has practical utility. Following Descartes the general position was that physical nature, including the human body, could be understood and controlled by means of mechanical mathematical laws.[3] Thus fear could be overcome by courageous dedication to reason, and so the problem of anxiety could be ignored. This appears to be the position of many school counselors today.

There were, however, historical exceptions to this rational position. Although Pascal had a high respect for reason ("To think well . . . is the principle of morality"),[4] he considered it undependable in the practical issues of life ("pliable to every sense"), and considered the prevalent confidence in reason faulty since it did not recognize the power of the emotions. He viewed the emotions as positive as well as negative: "The heart has reasons which the reason knows not of." [5]

The revolutionary belief in autonomous reason (reason as divorced from feeling and will) in the seventeenth century gave way to

[2] Rollo May, *The Meaning of Anxiety* (New York: The Ronald Press, 1950), p. 18.
[3] Will Durant, *The Story of Philosophy* (New York: Simon and Schuster, Inc., 1926), p. 167.
[4] Blaise Pascal, *Pensées*, ed. and trans. by G. B. Rawlings (New York: Peter Pauper Press, 1946), p. 35.
[5] *Ibid.*, p. 38.

technical reason. Technical reason was a faith in mechanical principles and their use, which developed until each science, understood on the basis of mechanism, was considered distinct from the others. By the nineteenth century this trend had brought about an era of "autonomous sciences." [6] The compartmentalization vividly opposed by Ibsen in *The Doll's House* became the pattern of life. Reason and emotions were separated, and the will was the arbitrator. Repression of the emotions became the pattern. As an outcome of these forces, the concept of anxiety emerged and set the stage for the work of Sigmund Freud.

In the middle of this period and preceding Freud, Kierkegaard, in searching for a new basis for the unity of personality, developed a profound study of anxiety. Kierkegaard was regarded on the continent as "one of the most remarkable psychologists of all time, in depth, if not in breadth, superior to Nietzsche, and in penetration comparable only to Dostoievski.[7] Following are a few of the important insights presented in his book on anxiety: [8] (1) reality can be approached and experienced only by the whole individual, as a feeling and acting as well as a thinking organism; (2) anxiety is to be understood as oriented toward freedom, and the capacity for freedom brings with it anxiety; (3) there must be differentiation between normal and neurotic anxiety; (4) in the developmental stages anxiety enters the picture when a conscious choice becomes possible between "knowledge of good and evil," as the myth states it; (5) self-awareness is important — "the more consciousness, the more self"; (6) anxiety involves inner conflict, it "is a desire for what one dreads, a sympathetic antipathy." (7) guilt feeling is a concomitant of anxiety; (8) the creative person does not avoid but tries to move through anxiety and guilt.

Thus two theoretical approaches moved across the centuries — the wholistic approach of Kierkegaard and the trait approach of Freud, in which segments of persons are related to outer coordinates and traits may operate independently or jointly in relation to the requirements of the outer environment. Traits may be described in terms of here-and-now attributes or by explanations pointing to un-

[6] Werner Brock, *Contemporary German Philosophy* (Cambridge: 1935), p. 70.
[7] *Ibid.*, p. 75.
[8] Søren Kierkegaard, *The Concept of Dread*, trans. by Walter Lowrie (Princeton, N. J.: Princeton University Press, 1944), p. 75.

derlying motives. They may also be pseudo. For example, the giver, in spite of all appearances, may not be a truly generous person.[9]

Freud's approach poses several difficulties for the counselor. One is that traits are not wholly independent of one another; another is that their self-consistency is only relative, and contradiction and conflict among traits is to be expected. A different problem for the counselor is explaining the integration of traits. This forces him to accept the possibility of some consciousness that makes integration possible. Anxiety and freedom are experienced by the person in totality.

According to Allport, the trait approach has received much greater acceptance in America, almost to the exclusion of the wholistic approach. Both approaches must be understood by the counselor unless he is content with treating symptoms while the counselee frequently suffers on the deeper levels of his being.

DISTINGUISHING BETWEEN
ANXIETY AND FEAR

The better the counselor's recognition and understanding of the difference between anxiety and fear, the better his judgment should be in deciding how best to help the counselee. The following distinctions are useful.

As stated earlier, all anxiety is a diffused apprehension, whereas fear is reaction to a specific danger. The counselee experiences fears on the basis of a security pattern. They are troublesome, but they can be recognized and understood and an adjustment can be reached. This is not the case with anxiety. Anxiety is not specific; it is "vague." When anxiety is intense the counselee feels uncertain and helpless in the face of an unidentifiable danger. This condition is very harmful because, unlike fear, anxiety has no known or soluble cause, but is a threat to the counselee's security pattern itself.

A certain degree of anxiety is normal to the process of "becoming." Such anxiety, however troublesome, does not reach abnormal proportions or hinder to a significant degree the carrying out of one's responsibilities. As May states, "anxiety is the apprehension cued off by a threat to some value which the individual holds essential to his existence as a personality." [10] The causes of anxiety vary in the same

[9] Gordon W. Allport, *Personality, A Psychological Interpretation* (New York: Holt, Rinehart & Winston, Inc., 1937), based on pp. 319–341.
[10] May, *op. cit.*, p. 191.

way as the values at the center of the personality vary from one counselee to another. The threat or apprehension may have to do with success, physical health, acceptance or rejection by others, or meaninglessness. The individual suffers in many ways because feelings of anger, hostility and guilt permeate his total self.

Since the threat is to the totality rather than to an aspect of the self, the counselee in anxiety is not able to "stand outside" the threat and objectify it. This is an insight sometimes missed by school counselors. When the basis of one's perception of what makes him different from the world of objects is threatened, it should not be assumed that he can objectify the source of the threat.

In proportion to the increase of his anxiety, the counselee feels diffused as if his life were pouring out like grains of sand on the desert. His awareness of himself as an object related to objects in the outside world becomes confused and vague. It is hopeless to attempt now to discuss with him what is troubling him, for he doesn't know.

Jersild,[11] in his experimental study of children's fears, found that the fears described did not even resemble those misfortunes which the children had actually experienced. For example, fears of gorillas, wolves and lions accounted for 19 percent of their fears. In explaining this, May concludes that these are not actual fears, but rather appearances in objective form underlying anxiety. The objects described are not specific stimuli.[12] As Symonds[13] has indicated, the anxiety of children and adults as well is often displaced upon ghosts, witches, and other objects that have no relation to the actual experience but fulfill significant functions for their subjective needs. There are, of course, reasons for this displacement. The child feels that he cannot say to his mother, or perhaps even to himself, "I am afraid that you do not love me," or the employee to the employer, "I know you are trying to find ways to get rid of me." In such situations the anxiety is displaced. Children displace it upon "imaginary" objects and adolescents and adults, now skilled in rationalization, make their displacements logical or reasonable. Schmideberg[14] views children's

[11] A. T. Jersild, F. V. Markey, and S. L. Jersild, "Children's Fears, Dreams, Wishes, Daydreams, Pleasant and Unpleasant Memories" (Child Development Monograph No. 12) (New York: Teachers College, Columbia University, 1933), pp. 265ff.
[12] May, op. cit., pp. 92–94.
[13] Percival Symonds, The Dynamics of Human Adjustment (New York: D. Appleton-Century-Crofts, Inc., 1946).
[14] Melitta Schmideberg, "Anxiety States," Psychoanalytic Review, 1940, Vol. 27, pp. 439–449.

fear of animals as projections of hostile feelings toward adults, especially members of the family. These projections are made necessary because the children feel that they would suffer if the direct feelings were expressed or demonstrated.

Such an interpretation, May points out, explains the unpredictability and shifting quality that Jersild found in his study of children's fears. If these fears are appearances in an objective form of underlying anxiety, the anxiety could focus on different objects at different times.

A strong indication that this form is anxiety rather than fear is the fact that verbal reassurance is ineffective in helping children to overcome these so-called fears. Such a situation is often experienced by counselors. How disappointing and puzzling it is that their reassurance and support are so ineffectual in helping some of their counselees.

PSYCHOLOGICAL THEORIES OF ANXIETY

Each theorist referred to in this section is interested not only in the personal genesis and meaning of anxiety but also in the interrelationship of these to the cultural and historical context.

Viewpoints of Theorists

Sigmund Freud • Freud considered anxiety the "fundamental phenomenon and the central problem of neurosis." [15] His thinking on this topic was in the process of continuous evolution. Even at the close of his career he considered his conceptions only hypotheses. The trends in his thinking can be summarized as follows: (1) His thinking concerning libido in relation to anxiety underwent change. From viewing anxiety as an automatic conversion of libido he came to see it as a description of the individual perceiving a danger and using libido (energy) in coping with this danger. (2) He moved from his earlier belief that anxiety is only an intrapsychic process to the conclusion that it arises out of danger situations in interpersonal relationships. He states, "We have become convinced also that instinctual demands often become an (internal) danger only because of the fact that their gratification would bring about an external danger — because, therefore, this internal danger represents an external

[15] Sigmund Freud, *The Problem of Anxiety*, trans. by H. A. Bunker (New York: W. W. Norton & Company, Inc., 1936), p. 111.

one." [16] This is a significant evolution in Freud's thinking. It encompasses the whole difference between seeing anxiety as a more or less exclusively intrapsychic process and seeing it as arising out of the individual's endeavor to relate himself to his environment. (3) A final trend was Freud's emphasis on the topology of the psyche. In applying his topology he held that in neurotic anxiety the ego is made helpless by its conflict with the id and superego. Perhaps it was expecting too much to think that Freud would move beyond the mechanistic viewpoints of his age. Even in his last writing he describes the ego as "developed out of the cortical layer of the id." [17]

Karen Horney • The central thesis of this theorist and those who follow in this chapter is that anxiety arises out of disturbed interpersonal relationships. According to Horney, sexual and other desires do not become drives unless and until motivated by anxiety. Even then it is only when the frustration of the desire threatens some value or relationship that is vital to the security of the individual that drives result.

Horney distinguishes among normal, existential and neurotic anxiety. She refers to neurotic anxiety as basic anxiety in two ways: (1) as the basis for neurosis, and (2) as developing in the early life of the child out of disturbed relationships between the child and the significant persons in his environment, especially the parents. She views anxiety as the reaction to the threat to any pattern upon which the person feels his safety depends. Thus anxiety is cued in different persons by different threats. What may be a security symbol for one individual may be unimportant to another. Thus she writes, "Anything may provoke anxiety which is likely to jeopardize the individual's specific protective pursuits, his specific neurotic trends." [18]

Anxiety involves contradictory trends within the personality. For example, the adolescent is dependent upon adults but on the other hand he has a great need to be independent. The two needs are contradictory, and his inability to be free of his parents generates feelings of hostility. This feeling of hostility provokes anxiety. Horney writes, "Hostile impulses of various kinds form the main source from which neurotic anxiety springs." [19] But these hostile feelings cannot be ex-

[16] *Ibid.*, p. 152.
[17] Sigmund Freud, *Outline of Psychoanalysis* (New York: W. W. Norton & Company, Inc., 1949), p. 110.
[18] Karen Horney, *The Neurotic Personality of Our Time* (New York: W. W. Norton & Company, Inc., 1937), p. 199.
[19] *Ibid.*, p. 62.

pressed without impunity, and the intrapsychic impulses to express them only increase the anxiety.

Harry Stack Sullivan • The human organism is viewed by Sullivan as engaged in two kinds of activities: (1) the gaining of satisfactions such as eating, drinking, sleeping and (2) the gaining of security, which is related "more closely to man's cultural equipment than to his bodily organization." [20] This second activity is the more important and is interpreted as his need to expand in ability and achievement or to actualize himself. It is the "power motive" that is to some extent inherent in the human organism as such.[21]

Sullivan places importance on the infant-mother relationship, and considers anxiety an outcome of the disapproval of significant persons in the infant's interpersonal world. It is in the infant's necessity to cope with anxiety-creating experiences that the self is formed. The self endeavors to preserve the feeling of security, and does so, by conforming to the limitations enforced by reward or punishment. Anxiety is experienced whenever "we tend to overstep the margin." [22]

This restricting of activities to what significant others approve is seen as an anxiety-creating experience not only because of the prohibition of action but also because of the limitations of awareness. Sullivan summarizes this view as follows: "The self comes to control awareness, to restrict one's consciousness of what is going on in one's situation very largely by the instrumentality of anxiety with, as a result, a dissociation from personal awareness of those tendencies of the personality which are not included or incorporated in the approved structure of the self." [23]

O. H. Mowrer • From his early animal studies Mowrer concluded that man was distinctive in his ability to engage in integrative behavior — that is, the capacity to bring the past and future into the psychological present. He distinguished between adjustive behavior (drive reduction) and integrative behavior (need fulfillment).[24]

From his viewpoint of man as a "time-binding" being, Mowrer

---

[20] Harry Stack Sullivan, *Conceptions of Modern Psychiatry* (Washington, D.C.: The William Alanson White Psychiatric Foundation, 1947), p. 4.

[21] *Ibid.*, p. 6.

[22] *Ibid.*, p. 10.

[23] *Ibid.*, pp. 21–22.

[24] O. H. Mowrer and A. D. Ullman, "Time as a Determinant in Integrative Learning," *Psychoanalytic Review*, 1945, Vol. 52, pp. 61–90.

recognized that man views his behavior in terms of symbols developed over the centuries and that he can be fully understood only in the broad context of history. He related the problem of neurotic anxiety to the problems of social responsibility and saw the involvement of the person in the social dilemma as a precondition to anxiety. He sees this "social dilemma" commencing with the anxiety of the child in relation with his parents, which is heightened because he is dependent on his parents at the same time that he fears them. Thus, in agreement with Freud, he sees anxiety as resulting from the repression of real fears. He accepts Freud's description of the genesis of anxiety: real fear → repression of this fear → neurotic anxiety → symptom formation as a solution to the anxiety. But in disagreement with Freud, who endeavored to explain anxiety in terms of instincts, Mowrer saw the conflicts that are most likely to cause anxiety to be of an ethical nature. The individual most fears social punishment and withdrawal of love. The repression of these fears and the associative guilt become neurotic anxiety.

Rollo May · May agrees with Mowrer that anxiety develops in childhood as an outcome of the child's dependency on his parents, whom he also fears to some degree. May, too, believes that the child most fears social punishment and withdrawal of love. He adds the following insight from his experience. He noted that when "aggressive, sexual, or other behavior in egocentric form" emerged in the analysis, his patients "showed no anxiety." But when the opposite needs and desires emerged — i.e., to have responsible and constructive social relations — "there appeared much anxiety . . . [especially] with defiant, aggressive types of patients." [25] He also describes what may happen when the counselee has a heavy load of guilt and anxiety. The counselor may endeavor to reduce the guilt feeling, and succeed, only to find that "the genuine, if confused, insights of the patient into himself have been violated and obscured; and that the most valuable and objectively accurate motivation for change is lost." [26] The counselor is unwilling to share in the desperate feeling of the counselee and, perhaps threatened by the force of the counselee's anxiety, may cause more damage than good. When this occurs the problems underlying the anxiety go unsolved and become buried in a complicated system of repression.

[25] May, *op. cit.*, p. 110.
[26] *Ibid.*

Types of anxiety may be grouped under those of most interest to psychology (normal and neurotic) and those of most interest to philosophy (existential anxiety or the anxiety of being).

Normal Anxiety • Everyone experiences normal anxiety to some degree. Normal and neurotic anxiety are each experienced as "diffuse, painful, persistent feelings of uncertainty and helplessness," [27] but with one important difference: normal anxiety is proportionate to the actual threat to values that the individual holds as essential to his existence. May gives the following characteristics of normal anxiety as distinguished from neurotic: "(1) It is proportionate to the objective threat; (2) it does not involve repression or other mechanisms of intrapsychic conflict . . . ; (3) [it] does not require neurotic defense mechanisms for its management but can be confronted constructively on the level of conscious awareness or can be relieved if the objective situation is altered." [28]

Each time the individual moves toward creative freedom he faces some anxiety threat. Actually, significant change rarely if ever takes place without anxiety. This is the "objective anxiety," as termed by Freud, or the experience of "separation" throughout the individual's life, as described by Otto Rank. Kierkegaard interpreted this anxiety as "the possibility of freedom." He considers anxiety the concomitant of self-awareness. From the time the child acquires self-awareness and exercises conscious choice, anxiety accompanies the portentous nature of possibility and of the responsibility associated with it. As the person moves toward individuation (becoming a self), anxiety is part of the experience of taking a stand *against* or at other times *with* one's environment. Creative decisiveness (willing to be one's self) is the decisive criterion of the self but is not attained without working through anxiety. "Self-strength" develops out of the person's successfully working through anxiety-creating experiences; this is the road to maturity of the self." [29]

Neurotic Anxiety • May lists three characteristics that differentiate neurotic anxiety from normal anxiety: (1) neurotic anxiety is disproportionate to the objective danger; (2) it involves repression (dissociation) and other forms of intrapsychic conflict; (3) as a corollary, it is managed by means of various forms of retrenchment of activity

[27] May, *op. cit.*, p. 194.
[28] *Ibid.*
[29] Kierkegaard, *op. cit.*, pp. 104ff.

and awareness, such as inhibitions, the development of symptoms, and the various neurotic defense mechanisms.[30]

The individual who lacks security and confidence and is uncertain about his values may perceive as threatening situations that do not appear threatening to others. He succumbs more easily to anxiety since he is less able to deal with psychological patterns and conflicts. Unable to assert his inner resources, he represses the object of anxiety. This pattern of dealing with threat commences in the child's relations with parents and generally continues through life. Repression sets up contradictions within the personality and consequently the child is more easily shaken by everyday problems. Also, he has less ability to distinguish and cope with real dangers. The child who represses a good deal of aggression and hostility assumes a compliant and passive attitude and is exploitable by his peers.

The child matures in a community. He must progressively relate to his parents on different levels, each level within a broader social nexus. Inability or blockage in his development either with his parents or in his broadening community relationships engenders anxiety. Such anxiety, if not understood, influences negatively the healthy development of the "self."

SOCIOLOGICAL THEORIES OF ANXIETY

Fromm, Horney, Kardiner and May all agree that much of our anxiety has its roots in the culture. Kardiner views the rising concern with success and prestige as a major cause of our increasing anxiety. From his study of Plainville, he concludes that the various means of self expression are channelled in the direction of achieving social prestige, or wealth as a sign of social prestige. The struggle for success becomes such a powerful force because it is the equivalent of self-preservation and self-esteem.[31]

Fromm commences his analysis of the roots of present day society with the emergence of individuality in the Renaissance. He considers that the freedom from ecclesiastical, economic, social and political restraints created deep feelings of insecurity, powerlessness, doubt, aloneness and anxiety.[32] This he believes was true especially for the middle class. They became threatened too by lack of control

[30] May, op. cit., p. 197.
[31] Abram Kardiner, The Psychological Frontiers of Society (New York: Columbia University Press, 1945), p. 376.
[32] Erich Fromm, Escape from Freedom (New York: Holt, Rinehart & Winston, Inc., 1941).

over the rising capitalism and the recognition that they were becoming more and more the pawns of the market-place. Fromm emphasizes that, unlike the Europeans, Americans were concerned with preserving law and order, and therefore repressed anxiety, which according to Horney serves to increase hostility.

The values of the market-place became the highest criteria. A person's worth was his salable market value. Fromm summarizes the point in part: "If he is 'successful,' he is valuable; if he is not, he is worthless." [33] May also writes, "feeling of isolation and anxiety consequently occur not only because the individual is set in competition with his fellows, but also because he is thrown into conflict about his inner valuation of himself." [34]

Both May and Horney consider competitiveness one of the chief causes of anxiety in our day. May concludes that "goals are dominant in our culture." Each one is striving for success, and not success in relation to one's potentialities but success as measured against the status of others. One is successful when he excels and triumphs over others. Success validates the self in one's own eyes and in the eyes of others. Lack of success or failure produces anxiety since it threatens the values held essential to one's existence as a person. Horney provides an excellent description of the inroads of competition in our culture in the following statement: "It must be emphasized that competitiveness and the potential hostility that accompanies it, pervades all human relationships. . . . It pervades the relationships between men and women, . . . it greatly impairs the possibilities of reliable friendship . . . it pervades school life. And perhaps most important of all, it pervades the family situation, so that as a rule the child is inoculated with this germ from the very beginning." [35]

Some counselors are aware that our society is faced not with brief unrest but with a radical change of structure. Threats felt today by both counselor and counselee are significantly different from any they have ever before experienced. The threats now are those related to "ends" rather than "means," and cannot be removed on the basis of cultural assumptions. Because of this situation of ambiguous threat, the counselor can expect many to be thrown into anxiety at the prospect of even some minor change. This is not because the change is a threat to subsistence or prestige. Rather it is seen as a

[33] Erich Fromm, *Man for Himself* (New York: Holt, Rinehart & Winston, Inc., 1947), p. 72.
[34] May, *op. cit.*, p. 174.
[35] Karen Horney, *The Neurotic Personality of Our Time* (New York: W. W. Norton & Company, Inc., 1937), p. 284.

threat to basic assumptions that have been identified with the existence of the culture. The individual, as a participant in the culture, identifies the threat with his own existence.

The counselor needs to recognize that many are anxious because nothing new compels or "grips" them. Even the symbols of "competitive success" and "love" have lost their power, and anxiety deepens when "blowing on the coals of the heart" has no effect.

It isn't that we lack the capacity to symbolize; we lack available contents for symbols because we do not believe in anything beyond our understanding sufficiently to make a full commitment of ourselves possible. Counselors face an almost impossible task in trying to help those who, having no moorings, drift to and fro.

PHILOSOPHICAL THEORIES OF ANXIETY

Existential Anxiety

Fromm, May, Mowrer, Horney, Tillich and others recognize another form of anxiety, *Urangst,* or the existential anxiety of knowing that we are finite, that someday we die. Horney is careful to differentiate between this existential anxiety and neurotic anxiety. *Urangst* does not connote hostility or provoke inner conflict leading to neurotic defense measures. Fromm views contingency in the face of death as a possible motivation for increasing the common bonds among persons. May emphasizes that existential anxiety cannot be intelligibly identified with fear or termed neurotic.[36]

Tillich believes that existential anxiety is basic to all anxiety. He wrote, "A more exact analysis shows that in the anxiety about any special situation anxiety about the human situation as such is implied. It is the anxiety of not being able to preserve one's own being which underlies every fear and is the frightening element in it." [37] He distinguishes three types of existential anxiety "according to the three directions in which nonbeing threatens being": (1) "Nonbeing threatens man's ontic self-affirmation (his affirmation of his own being), relatively in terms of fate, absolutely in terms of death. (2) It threatens man's spiritual self-affirmation, relatively in terms of emptiness, absolutely in terms of meaninglessness. (3) It threatens man's

[36] May, *op. cit.,* p. 112.
[37] Paul Tillich, *The Courage To Be* (New Haven: Yale University Press, 1952), p. 38.

moral self-affirmation, relatively in terms of guilt, absolutely in terms of condemnation."

Existential anxiety has always been present in human existence. But in times of great sociological upheaval anxiety becomes much more general and more intense. At such times, the overwhelming anxiety of great numbers of persons expresses itself in certain ways relative to the particular traumatic change. Tillich perceives our age as the third main period of anxiety in man's history. The precursors of this state he considers to be "the breakdown of absolutism, the development of liberalism and democracy, the rise of a technical civilization with its victory over all enemies and its own beginning disintegration." [38] This situation emphasizes the anxiety of emptiness and meaninglessness. This is the age of the threat of spiritual non-being. Our anxiety flows from attempts to be creative and courageous by the expression of detachment. Conformity helps us to elude the threat of meaninglessness, which is ever present. Conformity may provide some degree of creativity from our viewpoint, but the courage to replace the old with the new is lacking.

The force of this existential anxiety drives man toward the creation of certitude in systems of meaning, which are supported by tradition and authority. At times when his anxiety increases, he makes his castle more secure and surrounds it with a moat to ensure that he will not be troubled by questions from without.

Guilt

The adolescent is not merely uneasy, confused, inhibited, and uncontrolled; he also feels guilty. The genesis of this feeling of guilt is complex. Odier[39] suggests that guilt has two sources. He describes one kind of guilt as "functional guilt." It is that which accompanies anxiety resulting from social suggestion, the must-nots of society, and the loss of love of others. The other he calls "value guilt," and it is the genuine consciousness of having betrayed an authentic standard, a free judgment of the self by the self.

Tournier believes that the "distinct phenomena are less in question than different aspects of one complex mechanism in which each viewer sees what supports his own psychological theory, his own

[38] *Ibid.,* p. 61.
[39] Charles Odier, *Les Deux sources, consciente et inconsciente de la vie morale* (Neuchatel: La Baconniere, 1943).

conception of mankind." [40] He refers to the fact that for Adler, the sense of guilt stems from a refusal to accept one's inferiority, for Jung, from a refusal to accept oneself wholly, for Buber, from some violation of human relationships resulting in a breakdown in the I-Thou relationship. In agreement with the Rank school and psychotherapists akin to Jung (e.g., Plattner), Tournier would add "a new depth to this vision — that of guilt towards God." [41] He emphasizes that these attempts to define guilt are really the same assertion expressed in three linguistic forms: "guilt towards oneself in the psychological language of C. G. Jung; guilt towards others in the existentialist language of Martin Buber; guilt towards God in the religious language of the Bible." [42]

Tournier does not leave the matter here. He is concerned first that a distinction must be made between the "functional" guilt described by Freud and "value" or "true" guilt. True guilt results from estrangement from God as recognized in the innermost heart of each individual. Then he proceeds to show that the refusal to accept oneself and the separation from others are both forms of true guilt. If one is to continue toward maturity, he must, according to Tournier, distinguish between these two kinds of guilt and become increasingly able to govern his life according to the autonomous sense of true guilt rather than by the functional or false guilts suggested by society or parental reproof.

One of the causes of the high degree of anxiety and guilt among adolescents is that our society has become pluralistic, dynamic, secular and scientific. The permeating influence of pragmatism has made it exceedingly difficult to advance beyond the functional stage of false guilt. The adolescent is weighed down by the fear of social judgment and the disapproval of peers and adults. May reports that in the analytic sessions, great anxiety accompanies the recognition that one is unable to form constructive social relationships, but no apparent anxiety accompanies the expression of sexual, aggressive and antisocial urges. [43]

Somehow we have failed to encourage the necessary climate, or to encourage the adolescent to face himself. Too many adolescents feel that they are not loved for themselves and are therefore not free enough to look at themselves in a genuine manner. They have, in a

[40] Paul Tournier, *Guilt and Grace* (New York: Harper & Row, Publishers, Inc., 1962), p. 66.
[41] *Ibid.*
[42] *Ibid.*, p. 67.
[43] May, *op. cit.*, p. 110.

neurosis of opposition, created their own gods or, in a neurosis of submission, made gods out of their parents or significant others. The adolescent who feels that he is accepted only when he is successful is unable to love himself or others. Since it is his nature to love, he has an anxious "longing" as doubt concerning his social acceptability.[44] To him it is a problem of adjustment, and it is too frequently viewed as such by counselors. As long as school counselors see their responsibility as merely the improvement of adjustment, there is little likelihood that many adolescents will develop real selves.

IMPLICATIONS FOR THE COUNSELOR

Since childhood is one of the crucial times in the development of a normal approach to situations, the counselor should devote more time to assisting parents in helping the child to correctly symbolize his experiences. He might work with parents and teachers to help the child attain and keep a proper respect for his decision-making abilities.

The counselor needs to become more understanding of the meaning of children's projections of their fears. Much study will be required of the counselor to become versed in the genesis of anxiety and guilt feeling. He must become more capable of recognizing symptoms as such. He must be able to relate well to the normally anxious and those who are becoming defeated.

It is not easy for the counselor to respond helpfully to those who express guilt feelings. But unless he can become comfortable with expressions of guilt, he will not avoid the restriction of the adolescent's progress by the dilution and depreciation of his intimations of feelings of guilt.

Parents, teachers and administrators are in key positions in helping children and adolescents in the matter of guilt feelings. Can they and the counselors work as a team to create a climate in which students can express real feeling? It is hoped that they can and will provide more opportunity for students to be taken seriously and to express themselves honestly without fear of results.

All those who are helping to shape the lives of children and adolescents need to become more knowledgeable concerning the difficulties and threats faced by the young. There should be much more discussion of the particular dynamics of the present culture among

[44] Fred Berthold, Jr., "Anxious Longing," *Constructive Aspects of Anxiety,* ed. Seward Hiltner and Karl Menninger (Nashville: Abingdon Press, 1963), pp. 69–86.

adults — parents, teachers, administrators and counselors. Each in turn should encourage the children and adolescents in discussion and try to develop the setting in which children and adults can learn from each other.

The counselor should provide leadership in the development of interest in, and knowledge of, the forms taken by anxiety, This is a matter that too often has been glossed over. It requires concentrated attention and study if counselors, teachers and others are going to be equipped for progress in this area.

If anxiety is going to be correctly and fully understood, those concerned must recognize and accept the fact that each child, adolescent and adult has a depth dimension. This dimension must be honored and respected, for each finally depends upon it for normal and optimum development.

The counselor is not engaged in trying to free the adolescent from anxiety. He values anxiety as an opportunity for growth. Therefore he is interested in helping the counselee to accept anxiety as a constituent of life. He hopes to be successful in helping the counselee to discover and to take issue with his anxiety, accepting what cannot be changed and changing what can and needs to be changed, both within himself and in the external world.

Anxiety-creating influences are increasing. It is urgent that we become more intelligent concerning anxiety and work to develop the environment and the qualities of character that will enable us to encounter anxiety constructively.

QUESTIONS

1. What is the common point of view held by various theorists regarding the present increase in anxiety?
2. Why should the counselor understand existential anxiety?
3. What is the distinction between true and false guilt?
4. How would you distinguish between fear and anxiety?

FOR FURTHER READING

Søren Kierkegaard, *The Concept of Dread,* trans. by Walter Lowrie (Princeton, N.J.: Princeton University Press, 1944) (originally published in Danish, 1844).

This is an inquiry into the philosophical background of the problem of anxiety. It illuminates one phase of the historical background of the problem of anxiety in our society. The author objected to the traditional dichotomy between mind and body and the tendency to suppress the "irrational" aspects of experience. He felt that "truth" and "self" could be defined only dynamically, i.e., dialectically. His key idea is the relationship between anxiety and freedom. Anxiety, he insisted, is always to be understood as oriented toward freedom.

Rollo May, *The Meaning of Anxiety* (New York: The Ronald Press Co., 1950).

This study organizes in one volume the theories of anxiety offered by explorers in the disciplines of philosophy, psychology and psychotherapy. The common elements in the theories are formulated and presented in such a manner as to encourage further study. The author tested his theoretical synthesis by investigation of actual anxiety situations, using the case study method. The study serves to bring the problem of anxiety into sharp focus, especially as it exists in the Western World.

Seward Hiltner and Karl Menninger (ed.), *Constructive Aspects of Anxiety* (Nashville: Abingdon Press, 1963).

This book is the outcome of dialogue situations between theologians and psychiatrists. The editors consider the results incomplete, but hope it will encourage further discussion. Anxiety is viewed not only as part of the world's misery but also as a reliable instigator of self-help and, therefore, to some degree a blessing in disguise. Anxiety is also treated as part of the larger concrete process of becoming aware of danger or challenge and taking whatever action is necessary to deal with it. The signal system of anxiety is considered the same regardless of what the signal may be. It is the action taken in relation to it that determines the outcome.

_8_

FREEDOM AND
RESPONSIBILITY

No one is completely bound or completely free. Many are unable to use constructively the freedom that is theirs. This is because of the integral relationship between freedom and responsibility. We may expect to relinquish our freedom when we are irresponsible, for when we do not manage ourselves, others direct us. Teachers and counselors should help children to understand this at an early age.

Each of us exists within a framework that is established partially by himself and partially by others. The boundaries of the inner framework are directly related to our developmental age, our mental health, our physical well-being and our self perception. The boundaries of the outer framework are defined by family, school or business relationships, and by city, state, national and world situations.

Need satisfaction and self-actualization depend not only upon the existing amount of freedom, but also upon the responsible and best use of the freedom that each person has. Christopher Burney records in his book, _Solitary Confinement,_ that during a period of eighteen months in his six-by-six cell he survived without book, paper or pencil by the use of "freedom of the mind." Each day he reviewed lesson after lesson that he had been taught in various subjects.

THE NATURE OF MAN'S FREEDOM

Man is, in some way, and to a certain degree, free. This does not ignore the rigorous determinism of modern philosophers, including Spinoza. Each of these philosophers has left man with vestiges of freedom to know, learn, strive, grow and create.

_100_

Psychology places a low estimate on man's freedom. "It knows so many limitations upon freedom that it inclines to assume that in the last analysis all conduct is determined and no act is free. It knows that personality is dependent on many "givens," on the inherent capacities and limitations of the human species, on native constitution (physique, temperament, intelligence), on the social environment in which personality is fashioned and from which it draws nutrient; it is dependent also upon the immediate situation which calls forth one or another of the potential modes of conduct available in the nervous apparatus. Such dependencies weave a net of determinism whose strength is greater than the person knows." [1]

Some freedom remains. Although Freud was an avowed determinist, he acknowledged freedom of choice. In *The Ego and the Id,* he writes that ". . . after all, analysis does not set out to abolish the possibility of morbid reactions [in patients], but to give the patient's ego freedom to choose one way or the other." [2]

Existential psychology sees man as living in a human world, and in its definition of human existence as "fundamentally free, fundamentally refers to the fact that by free choice man exposes his behavior to become conditioned by freely selected cues and signs." [3]

The Religious and Philosophical Viewpoint

Religion has always maintained the existence of man's freedom for significant choice. Niebuhr writes, "The self which stands outside itself and the world cannot find the meaning of life in itself or the world. It cannot identify meaning with causality in nature; for its freedom is obviously something different from the necessary causal links of nature . . . man contradicts himself within the terms of his essence. His essence is free self-determination. His sin is the wrong use of his freedom and its consequent destruction." [4]

[1] Gordon W. Allport, *Pattern and Growth in Personality* (New York: Holt, Rinehart & Winston, Inc., 1961), p. 561.
[2] Sigmund Freud, *The Ego and the Id* (London: Hogarth Press, 1927), p. 72.
[3] Adrian Van Kaam, "Commentary," in Esther Lloyd-Jones and Esther M. Westervelt (eds.), *Behavioral Science and Guidance, Proposals and Perspectives* (New York: Bureau of Publications, Teachers College, Columbia University, 1963), p. 113.
[4] Reinhold Niebuhr, *The Nature and Destiny of Man,* Volume I (New York: Charles Scribner's Sons, 1946), p. 16.

A similar point of view is slightly differently expressed by Victor Frankl. He writes ". . . an adequate view of man can only be properly formulated when it goes beyond homeostasis, beyond self-actualization — even beyond man himself! . . . to that transcendent sphere of human existence in which man chooses what he will do and what he will be in the midst of an objective world of meanings and values." [5]

Man can be singularly free because of his consciousness of self. The more consciousness of self the greater his freedom potential. When the counselor helps the adolescent to stand outside the chain of stimulus and response, to pause and consider, he helps him to experience freedom. When one is uninhibited by influences from within and without, his freedom potential increases. He is thus able to examine alternatives in relation to evidence and his inner values.

It is not easy to become free. The truly free man, Kierkegaard informs us, is he who "extols reality." He perceives freedom as the goal of personality development. "The good is freedom." [6] The astute insight of Meister Eckhart counsels us thus, "When you are thwarted, it is your own attitude that is out of order."

The adolescent may view freedom superficially as the right to say "yes" or "no." He should be helped to understand that his freedom depends upon the way he faces the realities of life and upon whether he perceives the undetermined possibilities. The counselor can help him to see that his freedom is determined by the way in which he relates to such facts as high ability, low grades and disturbed parents, or to low potential, low grades and lack of opportunity or recognition. Will he be bound by resentment or discouragement, or will he use his freedom to develop psychological and spiritual integration?

Pseudo-freedom

We lack an understanding of true freedom and the sense of responsibility that makes its constructive use possible. We allow ourselves to drift into pseudo-freedom rather than critically examining it. One of the forms of pseudo-freedom is living without a plan. We fail to recognize that we become the victims of circumstances. We delay, and may repress, difficult but challenging opportunities to express our freedom. In reaching a decision we consider only part of the available

[5] Victor Frankl, "Beyond Self-Actualization and Self-Expression," *Journal of Existential Psychiatry*, 1960, Vol. I, p. 17.
[6] Søren Kierkegaard, *The Concept of Dread*, trans. by Walter Lowrie (Princeton: Princeton University Press, 1944), p. 99.

evidence. We allow ourselves to succumb to mass patterns of social conventions and gradually surrender our inward psychological and spiritual freedom. How frequently it becomes apparent that we are not really interested in the activities in which we participate, but conform rather than become intelligent about the cause.

As we become increasingly uneasy because something important is slipping away, we grasp at the best possibility of regaining our freedom. For the adolescent this may be competition in grades, athletic prowess, or social distinction. For adults it may be economic aggrandizement. Gradually this effort becomes the last remnant of individuality and symbolizes the complete meaning of freedom.

In a society that encourages competition and in which even members of the same family treat one another as objects, everyone is forced to relinquish some of his freedom. The greater his relinquishment the more he is praised, and the greater the alienation from his ideal self-image. Gradually resentment and hostility replace freedom. Latent hate and resentment become a means of preserving a degree of dignity and with it a false sense of freedom. Teachers, counselors and parents find it difficult to accept expressions of resentment, especially when directed toward them. There is no place in our relationships for expressions of hate, even when genuinely and honestly offered. Yet this is the way of return; resentment and hatred must be worked through if genuine freedom is to be accomplished.

Another form of pseudo-freedom is rebellion. Rebellion easily becomes confused with freedom because it is a normal interim move toward freedom. "Rebellion acts as a substitute for the more difficult process of struggling through to one's own autonomy, to new beliefs, to the state where one can lay new foundations on which to build." [7]

It is especially difficult to relate to a counselee who gains a sense of direction and vitality from attacking existing standards. The counselor frequently receives rebuttals rather than receptiveness and readiness to "reason together." Nonetheless, rebellion is a hopeful sign, and should be recognized by the counselor as a means that if understood may be an opportunity for helping the individual develop his own standards and mores.

CONDITIONS OF FREEDOM

It is agreed that influences within and without the person make it difficult to use freedom wisely. Of these two areas of influence

[7] Rollo May, *Man's Search for Himself* (New York: W. W. Norton & Co., Inc., 1953), p. 154.

it is assumed that those within the person are more determinative, since perception is the guide to action.

Within each of us there is a basic propensity to move forward, to use our freedom toward becoming. One psychologist writes, "[the] urge to grow, pursue meaning, seek unity is also a 'given'. . . . Growth toward this end is a law to which most personalities seem to conform. The promise I see for myself is the essence of my freedom. When a critical situation challenges me I call forth this promise — it becomes a major factor in the solution of the problem in hand." [8]

It is possible, however, to use our freedom to decrease our self-awareness, to withdraw from life. We may use our freedom unwisely and wrongly, and it is a reasonable assumption that wise use of freedom is a greater potential of the emotionally mature. Knight describes the choice of the healthy person as follows: "The healthy person has a combined feeling of freedom and of inner compulsion. He feels that his course is determined by standards, beliefs, knowledge, aspirations that are an integral part of himself and he can do no other; yet at the same time he feels free . . . it [sense of freedom] connotes feelings of well being, of self-esteem, of confidence, of inner satisfaction based on successful use of one's energies for achievement that promotes the best interests of one's fellowman as well as one's own . . . this kind of freedom is experienced only by emotionally mature well-integrated persons." [9]

HOW WE RELINQUISH OUR FREEDOM

Retaining and increasing our freedom is a never-ending struggle. Goethe forcefully expresses the ultimate lesson learned by Faust:

> Yes! to this thought I hold with firm persistence;
> The last result of wisdom stamps it true:
> He only earns his freedom and existence
> Who daily conquers them anew.

Rather than take the risk of venturing into the unknown, or of standing in isolation or rejection, many frequently seek to escape the realities of life. Both counselees and counselors in handling problems may resort to methods that limit their freedom.

There are various ways of relinquishing one's freedom. A very

[8] Allport, *op. cit.*, p. 563.
[9] Robert P. Knight, "Determinism, Freedom and Psychotherapy," *Psychiatry,* 1946, Vol. 9, p. 256.

common and almost unconscious method is the submergence of the individual in a group, society or cult. He becomes very adaptable, meeting each situation without effort. He fulfills the expectations of others. The risk is that he relinquishes contact with himself; gradually genuine individuality and spontaneity disappear.

A person may lose his freedom by rejecting the poignant feelings of doubt concerning the meaning of existence. The adolescent discontinues the question, "Why"? The counselor assumes routine duties, working on a "horizontal" level that makes any real confrontation with life unnecessary. Thus we escape from our freedom by asking only the questions that can be answered and by accepting answers imposed upon us authoritatively. Such retrenchment unfortunately provides a false sense of being in command of life, a feeling of belonging. Doubt is rarely present. "Meaning is saved but the self is sacrificed. And since the conquest of doubt was a matter of sacrifice, the sacrifice of freedom of the self, it leaves a mark on the regained certitude; a fanatical self-assertiveness." [10]

Modern civilization has loosened the ties that bound the individual to his tradition and to his family. The result has been greater freedom, more freedom than some could use wisely. The use of such freedom necessitates the establishment of a meaningful relationship between the self and values that lie beyond. An important function of the counselor may well be to help the adolescent attain this relationship.

Many counselees do not wish to accept the moral responsibility that accompanies the acceptance of freedom. To be responsible for one's self and one's actions is a challenge and a burden that many prefer to avoid. Learned Hand emphasized this in his statement that freedom was a burden to all but the rare individual.[11] Albert Camus stated dramatically that "at the end of all freedom is a court sentence; that's why freedom is too heavy to bear, especially when you're down with a fever, or are distressed or love nobody." [12]

If each adolescent and adult is to develop the ability to use freedom, he must nourish the qualities that make him a free and responsible person, and assist others to do the same. But this is not enough, he must also honor and cherish values beyond the self.

[10] Paul Tillich, *The Courage To Be* (New Haven: Yale University Press, 1952), p. 49.
[11] Learned Hand, *The Spirit of Liberty* (New York: Alfred A. Knopf, Inc., 1952).
[12] Albert Camus, *The Fall* (New York: Alfred A. Knopf, Inc., 1960), pp. 130–133.

THE NATURE OF RESPONSIBILITY

Responsibility has two meanings. In one sense it means "responding" or to "respond to." [13] It also has a second and different meaning. Webster's New Collegiate Dictionary defines responsibility as a "state or quality of being responsible, specifically; accountability, also moral accountability; as the responsibilities of parenthood."

Responsibility as "Respond To"

In accordance with this concept the person responds according to the degree that he is free. This is not to assume that an individual ever becomes completely free but that he becomes more conscious of the deterministic experiences in his life. The possibilities of responding are increased with the increase of self-awareness. Increased awareness of self and the world develop concurrently. The goal of the counselor who accepts this meaning of responsibility is to help the counselee to respond in normal fashion to the exigencies and demands of life.

The counselee becomes a decision-making person who has a centered self. Also, he both confronts and responds to the world. He responds after deliberation and decision. However, his response does not necessarily conform to the moral demand. Although the psychologically healthy person is likely to act morally, according to "the inner law of his true being," he may do otherwise. "This [freedom] is his greatness but also his danger; it enables him to act against the moral demand. He can surrender to the disintegrating forces that tend to control the personal center and to destroy its unity." [14] Lack of responsibility contradicts the self-realization of the person as a person and leads to disintegration.

Although the counselor may greatly increase the counselee's freedom to respond, the moral character of his responses depends upon his personal center. The counselor hopes that he will use his freedom responsibly. Moral responsibility is not the outcome of therapy alone, since it is grounded in the cultural and religious functions of the counselee's personal center.

[13] May, *op. cit.*, p. 157.
[14] Tillich, *op. cit.*, p. 62.

Assisted by insights from Gestalt psychology, ethical relativism is now in eclipse. The contrast in moral demands in separated cultures is now recognized as a different expression of a common, fundamental principle. "Man by nature (in Christianity by creation) has an awareness of the universally valid moral norms. This awareness is potentially given to every man." [15] This given potential of awareness is present in all men, although it receives varying cultural expressions.

The religious dimension of moral responsibility is its unconditional character. This is the "ought to be" dimension of each moral decision. A conditional decision becomes unconditional when the result, in some irreversible way, affects at least the participants. For instance, "You ought to leave now, if you wish to catch your plane." This is a conditional decision, and you may decide to remain a few hours and take the next plane. But if you are a surgeon and you must catch the plane to perform an operation upon your arrival, then the conditional decision becomes unconditional. To miss the plane would be an anti-moral act, affecting you in a disintegrating manner.

Freedom and Responsibility

Autonomy without responsibility is one of the main sources of anxiety in this half-century. We have failed to accept the truth that freedom and responsibility are integrally related. We have not encouraged a balanced relationship between them.

At one time, undue emphasis was placed on freedom, with little attention or concern regarding responsibility. "A decade or two ago our task in counseling and therapy was simply to set the person 'free,' and, therefore, the values held by the therapist and the society had no part in the process. The therapists most under the influence of this assumption made a dogma out of never making a 'moral judgment,' and saw guilt as always neurotic and therefore a 'feeling' that ought always to be relieved and gotten rid of in counseling and therapy." [16] This emphasis on freedom, without corresponding emphasis on re-

---

[15] Paul Tillich, *Morality and Beyond* (New York: Harper & Row, Publishers, Inc., 1963), p. 19.

[16] Rollo May, "Freedom and Responsibility Re-Examined," in Esther Lloyd-Jones and Esther M. Westervelt (eds.), *Behavioral Science and Guidance, Proposals and Perspectives* (New York: Bureau of Publications, Teachers College, Columbia University, 1963), p. 103

sponsibility, merely increases the counselee's anxiety and deceptively removes the structure required to give meaning to life.

The encouragement from many quarters and through various media to conform to the moral and social controls of society is not an effective solution. Such a process may weaken and destroy the ability to cope with life's problems through intelligent decision making. It causes repression of the desire for freedom, and removes the necessity of accepting responsibility. Such a destructive outcome is superbly described by William H. Whyte in *The Organization Man,*[17] in which he writes of "mild looking groups of therapists who . . . would be doing what they did to help you."

A third solution is that proposed by operant conditioning. This is not new, but is receiving widespread emphasis as a new benefit. Teachers, parents, counselors, employers and others tend to engage in this conditioning process. Each decides the characteristics he wishes the students, children, counselees, employees and others to emulate, and then proceeds by methods as subtle and as painless as possible to condition these individuals (objects) to act in the desired fashion. Thus while the manipulators triumph with ego satisfaction, the manipulated relinquish their freedom, or secretly rebel and devise means to keep their identity.

The counselee is an object and the counselor, who is now a manipulator, finds satisfaction in the expression of the counselee's conforming behavior. He is apparently unaware, or lacks the courage to encounter the fact, that the counselee is giving up his right to weigh alternatives, make decisions, and put them into action. The counselee has sacrificed the "pearl of great price" for a "mess of pottage." The pragmatic principle that the end justifies the means must be recognized not only as inadequate but also as the destroyer of personal freedom and responsibility.

The increasing complexity of interpersonal relationships places a growing premium on the quality of responsibility. In desperation, we attempt to ensure this quality by means that increasingly rob the individual of his personhood. Apparently we do not see that responsibility without freedom is nonexistent.

RESPONSIBILITY IN OUR TIME

Conditions of modern living place a premium on the necessity of moral responsibility. Urbanization, automation, population in-

[17] William H. Whyte, Jr., *The Organization Man* (New York: Simon and Schuster, Inc., 1956).

crease and family mobility make a high level of responsibility increasingly necessary. One irresponsible flagman, typist, accountant, teacher, counselor, lawyer or surgeon can, to an extent unparalleled in history, cause disaster, suffering and death. Any employed citizen can testify to the increasing need for morally responsible employees. It is difficult to recall a newscast that did not describe at least one fatality or serious injury or damage due to irresponsibility.

What motorist would not like to be certain that other drivers are responsible? What pilot would not like to be certain that the mechanics who maintain his plane are responsible? What teacher would not like to be certain that students in elementary school, high school and college are responsible? Lack of moral responsibility is one of the critical problems of our time. It is deeply rooted in the core and fibers of our society.

A close examination reveals that our interpersonal relationships are not conducive to the development of moral responsibility. They are inadequate in the following ways:

(1) *Cultural patterns minimize the possibility of developing responsibility.* To the degree that parents, teachers, employers and counselors enact the principle that the end justifies the means, responsibility becomes irrelevant. Emphasis on the materialistic, status-giving and other "horizontal" values minimizes the necessity for evaluation in terms of the effect of one's actions on others. As the practice of meditation, reflection and introspection recedes, the climate and soil that nurture the sense of responsibility diminish. A culture that supports the dictum, "every one for himself," and insists that individual competition is necessary, healthy and constructive tends to eclipse the fact that responsibility is so basic as to be necessary even to its own survival.

(2) *Religion and humanism often fail to relate their principles to current decision making.* Although the philosopher, clergyman, medical doctor, teacher, counselor and others endeavor to assist others to understand and relate moral and religious principles to their daily living, they recognize that their efforts are inadequate. There are at least the following explanations of this. Those who most need this kind of assistance are unable to actually hear and assimilate it. This is so partly because their own psychological needs for dependence, security and identity greatly inhibit them, and partly because the risk they anticipate in trying to integrate these teachings into their daily experiences is too great and too threatening to their established way of life. The second explanation is that the presenters themselves experience great difficulty in (1) giving visibility to these principles,

(2) envisaging the relationship of these principles to current life, and (3) supplying illustrations that would kindle the imagination of those who do long for a better way. Perhaps our interpersonal relationships handicap our endeavor most of all. Until we ourselves can point the way to a moral, responsible community we resemble an authoritarian teacher trying to teach democracy as a way of life. The whole situation is a disastrous façade.

However, because of, or in spite of, all the influences of culture and significant persons, there are those for whom confrontation with moral and religious principles is a maturing experience. They differentiate courageously among hypotheses, beliefs and doubts — between what is reasonably certain and what is highly uncertain. They continuously and continually relate their religious concepts and beliefs to daily life and accept the difficulty of doing so. They maintain a level of thought and behavior that has a moral consistency directly related to their beliefs; the pervasiveness of their religious understanding lends a comprehensive and integrative outlook in their approach to life. They have a heuristic commitment; they are able to hold their beliefs tentatively until they either become more certain or help them to discover a more valid belief. They do not expect certainty, and do not need it to be optimistic and constructive.[18]

(3) *The methods used to attain responsible freedom are inadequate.* Responsibility as a virtue in and of itself receives little attention. It is an adjunct of what is required of the successful person. The successful person is assumed to be responsible. Since success is pragmatic in character and individualistic in nature, whatever works to the advantage of the individual concerned is termed success. What happens to colleagues, business partners or even members of one's own family in the process is a matter of circumstances, rarely of moral responsibility. An authoritarian, competitive, pragmatic society that reserves the right to treat its citizens as objects cannot expect them to be morally responsible. The individual is not aided in becoming responsible since he is not helped to respect and develop a personal center or to find meaningful experiences in groups.

Many influences hinder one's development of a personal center. Beginning at an early age, it is impressed upon the child that adults know him better than he knows himself. He learns that his parents and teachers display more affection toward him when he behaves in accordance with their wishes than when he acts according to his own.

[18] Gordon W. Allport, *The Individual and His Religion* (New York: The MacMillan Co., (1965), p. 57.

He does not develop his own intrinsic motivation since in most of his school and home activities he devotes his psychic energy to understanding what authority figures demand, and in meeting those demands. He has little opportunity to make decisions and put them into effect, and he loses the desire to do so. He receives little if any help in experiencing the direct relationship between freedom and responsibility. He has few experiences in groups, which could be expected to help him develop freedom and responsibility. His relationships with others are frequently competitive. He seldom has the experience of sharing with others for its intrinsic joy. Many teachers and parents listen for the purpose of evaluating what he says rather than for the purpose of understanding the speaker. Many group experiences offer little help in self-understanding and little encouragement in becoming responsible for other members and for the outcomes of group activity. College graduates find the concepts of learning that develop from trying to help other members in the group or of being responsible for the development of the group foreign to their patterns of thought and experience.

Many approach group experience convinced that they must defend themselves, that they must make an impression upon the other members, especially the leader. These people find group experiences of little value in their maturing process. Each is an object among objects. They expect little freedom to think, feel or act. They place all responsibility for progress and outcomes on the status leader. Many do not want responsibility, and the few who do have little opportunity to experience it and less ability to assume it.

CONCLUSIONS

Although man is not completely free, he is never completely determined. In the most limited situations he has the freedom to evaluate events and himself in relation to them. It is possible for him to make "the inner choice" and assert his way of life against great odds.

Unless man uses his freedom responsibly, he loses it. Others with more power in the situation remove his freedom from him. Freedom as license is not tolerated.

Each of us finds it difficult to use his freedom responsibly. It requires moral values, critical thought, courage and persistence. It is easier to drift into pseudo-freedoms, to live aimlessly, to compartmentalize life and assume that a small degree of freedom encompasses the whole realm of freedom. We rebel, believing that this is evidence of our freedom. We cease to doubt and to ask questions that can-not be answered by science. This provides a false sense of being in command of life.

The winning of freedom is a daily challenge. We receive little help in recognizing that the amount of freedom we possess must be balanced by the amount for which we have demonstrated responsibil-ity. Any large degree of imbalance between the two is a source of keen anxiety.

When the use of freedom affects human relations in an important and meaningful way, moral responsibility is required on the part of all as an integral part of the relationship.

Moral responsibility develops slowly. It is not a product of mat-uration. Experience and success in education and work do not assure it. Certain conditions are conducive to its development, but little attention is given to providing these conditions. Learning to be re-sponsible is generally considered incidental to learning itself.

The act of responsibility is a "centered" act, and therefore it is most possible for those who have a personal center. Since the indi-vidual inherits only the *potential* for the development of a personal center, the character of his environment and learning experiences must be conducive to its development. Certain cultural influences must be recognized as adverse forces. Our competitive and pragmatic soci-ety, with its "market place" orientation, places little importance upon, and finds less value in, moral responsibility.

The formative years are the best time to develop a personal cen-ter. Also, the responsible use of freedom should begin during the formative years. The necessary knowledge is within grasp. Will par-ents, teachers and counselors cooperatively prepare, plan and work to increase moral responsibility in our youth? It is possible for this to take place despite the adverse influences of a "market place," competitive and pragmatic society.

IMPLICATIONS FOR THE COUNSELOR

The counselor who believes in the centrality of responsible be-havior in human relations must be a responsible person. He can work with teachers and other personnel to encourage ego satisfaction for the individual for being responsible to the same extent that it is provided for academic success. He can, in his group guidance and counseling, discuss the basic relevance of responsible, cooperative and dependable behavior to satisfying, mature human relations. He can develop with school personnel informal means of emphasizing the significance of responsibility in daily living.

As a member of a team the counselor can work with individuals and groups to help students to understand possible reasons for responsible and irresponsible behavior. Students can be helped to appreciate the person who has developed a sense of responsibility. They can be helped to realize the greatness of the accomplishment by experiencing the difficulty involved.

The counselor can work with teachers at all levels to plan materials and methods to aid students in perceiving the integral relationship between freedom and responsibility. A demonstrated sense of responsibility should be a criterion in electing students to various kinds of leadership positions.

QUESTIONS

1. Describe the position that psychology takes with reference to individual freedom.
2. Why should the counselor relate freedom and responsibility in his thinking and counseling?
3. What is the relationship between responsible action and the development of a personal center?

FOR FURTHER READING

Reinhold Niebuhr. *The Children of Light and the Children of Darkness.* (New York: Charles Scribner's Sons, 1944).

The motivation for this book grew out of a recognized peril to democratic society. The author bases his conclusions on the optimistic estimates of human nature with which the democratic credo has been historically associated. He is concerned with the necessary confidence in the ability of men to arrive at tolerable adjustments between their competing interests and their responsibility to carry through justice, which transcends all partial interests. It is emphasized that a free society requires a more realistic philosophical and religious basis. This it must have in order to anticipate and understand the perils of confusion and tyranny to which it is exposed, and also to give it more persuasive justification. The author furnishes important insights regarding the relationship of freedom and responsibility, especially in the larger community.

Rollo May, *Man's Search for Himself* (New York: W. W. Norton & Company, Inc., 1953).

The author is concerned with how man may meet his insecurity and personal crises and turn them to constructive uses. He explores insights concerning the self from psychology, literature, philosophy and ethics. His synthesis includes ways in which we can nurture the capacity to love, to achieve values and goals and to assume responsibility within a realistic framework of freedom.

Erich Fromm, *Man for Himself* (New York: Holt, Rinehart & Winston, Inc., 1947).

This book is concerned with freedom and responsibility by implication. It is based upon the great humanistic ethical thinkers of the past. These were philosophers and psychologists; they believed that the understanding of man's nature and the understanding of values were interdependent. The author takes the position that neurosis is, in the last analysis, a symptom of moral failure and that "adjustment" may not mean a moral achievement. The understanding and solution of a person's moral problem necessitates the correct interpretation and use of freedom and responsibility.

9

IN SEARCH OF MEANING

Man has always searched for a framework within which to interpret the events of his life. The results of his search provide ideas in religion and philosophy, as well as legends and art. Theories are developed when his search turns to the utilitarian. These theories are dependent upon his conceptualizing powers, but separated from his feeling and inner choice. Modern science is directly related to this impersonal search.

The products of science have become increasingly dissatisfying and seemingly inadequate because they do not give substance to the core of meaning in man's life. They do not help him to know what "significance may be found in 'his' own existence, the succeeding generations of his kind and the vivid events of his inner life." [1] It is essential that counselors be open to the existential quest of their students. Many counselors assume that the high school student is interested only in those goals that provide security and status. Perhaps he dares not recognize a deeper hunger in the counselee for fear of acknowledging emptiness within himself.

"For many young Americans this search [for positive values] leads to an intense immersion in immediate experience — in a kind of cult of the present. . . . But at the same time, the search for experience is an effort, in the intensification of the present, some 'rock bottom' upon which to stand and from which to build a solid life." [2]

Educators and counselors hopefully assume that formal educa-

[1] John W. Gardner, *Self-Renewal: The Individual and the Innovative Society* (New York: Harper & Row, Publishers, Inc., 1964), p. 102.
[2] Kenneth Keniston, "The Decline of Positive Values," *The Intercollegian*, 1966, Vol. 83, p. 8.

tion, geared as it is to our technical pattern of life, will instill depth of meaning and give direction to life, and also unite thought, feeling and will in the attainment of a wise and meaningful goal. In large part, this is unlikely since education is directed chiefly and almost solely to the development of critical thought.

Joe, a young man whom I had counseled, phoned and said he was on the way to the funeral of his youngest son. He had something to talk over with me; he wanted to drop in at my home on the way. Seated in the living room, he began. "You know, for the last two years, one day has been the same as the next. Things didn't matter much. I thought if I got a Ph.D., or if I bought a nice home, life might have meaning. But all the time I knew it wouldn't. Now that my little boy just two days old is gone, something has happened to me. Life has meaning now. It is different. Do you think it will stay different? My courses in college didn't give it to me. They must have done something, of course, but now life is different. I have a new understanding."

This experience for Joe synthesized and crystallized his searching. His reason alone couldn't do this; his whole person — reason, feeling and will were apparently necessary for this insight and realization to take place. Maybe it came to Joe because he took the risk; he searched "with the whole heart."

But why did his courses in college fail to provide meaning? Not only was he apparently not fully involved, but evidently the college experience did not stimulate him to ask questions about "being" or existence. Could it have been that Joe received "training" but not "education"? In the words of Edgar Dale, "Training favors one-way communication — from teacher to taught. The textbook and lecture are usually memorized, rarely criticized. There is limited sharing of ideas and feelings in a mood of mutuality. Education, however, thrives on criticism, judgment, evaluation. It favors and requires feedback, the unlimited sharing of ideas and feelings." [3] The adolescent or college student may not find meaning because he is only a passive listener to ideas that he perceives as having little relationship to the meaning of his life.

LACK OF MEANING

Meaning cannot be transferred. It must be developed from within. Like wisdom, it requires the integrated action of the whole person.

[3] Edgar Dale, in "The News Letter," The School of Education, Ohio State University, 1965, Vol. 31.

This integration is difficult and frequently impossible. Although the counselee may talk fluently about what he *should* want — to finish college, to get a good job, to marry and have two children, two cars and a double garage — it becomes evident to the counselor and often to the counselee that these are only introjections. He doesn't actually know what he wants, or how to learn. Rollo May writes: "Many people do not know what they want. They have no definite experience of their own desires or wants." [4] What counselor has not had the disturbing experience of the young man who says, "I like Mary but I don't know whether or not I really love her."

There was a time before World War I when, as Riesman reports, the individual made his own decisions based on what he and others considered to be the eternal truths of right and wrong. He was "inner directed," relying, of course, on the standards he had been taught. From today's perspective he was inclined to be dogmatic and inflexible, but he was decisive. Although he was becoming more and more mechanistic and impersonal in his outlook, he had not yet succumbed to relativism or become submerged in loneliness. Recently a graduate class of 30 was asked to name something that could not be appraised by scientific measurements. The first and almost immediate response was loneliness.

The inner-directed man is now in the minority. Living in an environmment permeated with scientific thought and technical reason that is skeptical concerning eternal truths and impersonal in its human relationships, he strives to find guiding principles, and lacks confidence in his ability to use them. He may be less dogmatic and inflexible, but he lacks a personal center. He doesn't know who he is, what he truly desires, if anything, or how to proceed.

THE SEARCH FOR MEANING

Counselees and counselors in varying degrees recognize an inadequacy. They feel uneasy. Each day is like the last, without purpose and permeated with momentary or more lasting consciousness of emptiness. They sense that this pervasive feeling of emptiness is only a short step from meaninglessness. This engenders near-panic sensations, "must do something" compulsions, a turning to this and that to evade the vacuous feeling and the growing sense of isolation and loneliness. Not recognizing the seriousness of their condition, they try to minimize this feeling of emptiness and meaninglessness.

[4] Rollo May, *Man's Search for Himself* (New York: W. W. Norton & Company, Inc., 1953), p. 15.

By many devices they avoid being alone and the risk of having to confront themselves. They are always in the thick of things, part of the madding crowd.

How many people can be characterized in this manner we do not know. Sociologists believe that the number is substantial. In fact it is considered a well-developed trend. David Riesman, in *The Lonely Crowd,* describes them as "outer-directed." Such people, he claims, live not to achieve their potential but to "fit in." It is as if each had a radar set fastened to his head perpetually telling him what other people expected of him. In such a manner he gets his motives, objectives and values from others. He is not creatively active, merely conformingly reactive. He responds, but without choice, since he lacks his own effective center of motivation.

In the Culture

Some people sincerely search for meaning and understanding. They turn to what have always been sources of meaning and value — culture, education and religion. What they find when they turn to society is of little help. The fact is that since the advancements of science increase problems, we lag far behind in human relations. We have become much more interdependent in our schools, communities, the nation and the world, but we continue to retain individual competition as a way of life.

Bertrand Russell emphasizes that in the "world created by modern technique . . . two nations which co-operate are more likely to achieve economic prosperity than either can achieve if they compete. Competition continues because our feelings are not yet adapted to our technique. It continues in ways quite obviously capable of producing ruin to all the competitors, but it continues none the less because we cannot make our emotions grow at the same rate as our skills. Increase of skill without a corresponding enlargement in feeling produces a technical integration which fails of success for lack of an integration of purpose." [5]

There is no force for progress when each one is striving for his own gain and giving only lip service to the improvement of the community, the school or the church. The high school adolescent's psychological problems are increased when he realizes that the failure of someone else in his class helps him to succeed, especially when he

[5] Bertrand Russell," The Expanding Mental Universe," in *Adventures of the Mind* (New York: Vintage Books, 1960), p. 302.

recognizes his own desires for another's failure. Such a condition generates interpersonal fear, anxiety and resentment. He does not dare to be sincere concerning his real feelings and tries to compensate and substitute by being a hail-fellow-well-met. He joins numerous service organizations, gives generously to charities and is usually poised and affable, striving to give the impression that he is in love with life.

In Education

When the individual turns to education, his search for meaning is stifled by the idealized faith in individual reason. The common thinking of this generation is in scientific terms. The battle between such thinkers and those who insist that all cannot be explained or measured on a cause and effect basis, although still in progress, has been for the most part settled in our educational systems in favor of scientific knowledge.

When Spinoza used the word "reason" in the seventeenth century, the term indicated the whole person, that is, an attitude toward life in which the mind, united with the emotions and will, unified the person and gave him a valuing center. But such a unified approach to knowledge is exceedingly rare in our schools. Many seem to operate on the psychological insights of a half-century ago. Reason is supposed to give the answer and willpower to put it into effect; the emotions, if they get in the way, are repressed.

As early as 1949, Lawrence Kubie warned of the need to involve the whole person in the educational process. He wrote, "I think that what we need to add to the goal of education is something that can be called emotional maturation, but as far as I have been able to observe, this cannot be imparted by the same methods as those that are used for intellectual maturation.

"By emotional maturation, I mean essentially self-knowledge in depth, and the harmonious co-ordination and integration of conscious and unconscious levels of the personality. It is thus self-knowledge, a self-knowledge which penetrates below the level of conscious awareness which integrates all levels in the make-up of the human being who is the forgotten man of our educational system." [6]

Education, to be meaningful, must involve the whole person. Its efforts should be directed more intelligently and consistently to the

[6] Lawrence Kubie, "The Psychiatrist Considers Curriculum Development," *Teachers College Record,* January 1949, Vol. 50, p. 242.

expansion of the ego in the direction long recommended by the seers and poets. The student should be confronted regularly with experiences requiring him not merely to use knowledge or will or feeling, but to synthesize all three in an intimate union. The basis for meaning is accordingly provided.

In Religion

Many have turned to religion as a source of meaning, especially in the last decade. An upsurge of interest became clearly evident in the early fifties. The Departments of Commerce and Labor reported that the month of July, 1954, was the greatest church building period in American history. The New York *Times,* in a review of the books published the same year, reported that according to the sales charts the average American desired religion more than anything else.

On the other hand, traditional and institutionalized religion was ill-prepared to nourish the lives of this generation or to minister to the search for meaning. Its rituals and symbols were found to lack both aesthetic and spiritual meaning. The illustrations, symbolic language and manner of presentation made it difficult for many to become involved.

People came desiring specific answers to their everyday problems, but found that they were expected to make the applications of the truths they heard. The church took for granted that each person had a sense of self, that each was practiced in the exercise of introspection and self-transcendence, that each had a language that he could and would use in dialogue about spiritual meanings. Some of the language of the church made explicit or implicit reference to nature that had only marginal meaning, since man's relatedness to nature has been almost totally lost. Also, the language dealt with tremendous joy and deep tragedy whereas many no longer sensed the significance of these in human life. They had lost respect for the human being and his rights. For some, perhaps a great many, the meaning sought was not forthcoming.

However, none of these is the complete reason why the popular return to religion was disappointing. The reason was partly the inability of people to know their predicament. They did not realize that they were possessed by and had given their lives to the product of their time, a naturalistic materialism.

Man continues to question, and the churches are beginning to recognize the challenge of experimenting with methods and situations that may encourage each person to question and talk about his fears, concerns and hopes. In the meantime, many search for meaning through media that are posing religious questions. Their quest explains the popularity of the plays of Arthur Miller, John Osborne, Edward Albee and Bertolt Brecht, to mention a few. All of these are asking about our life in the culture and, for those who are seeking, they point to questions of meaning in depth. In this recession the youth, in the process of trying to find meaning and a place in their world, are the greatest sufferers. This has become evident to all interested adults, especially the counselor.

HORIZONTAL LIVING

We desire meaning but we are not certain what we seek. Only dimly aware of what it is we lack, we look in the wrong places and ask the wrong questions. The answers we receive point to travel, sight-seeing, promotion, position and possessions. The character of our goals reveals our horizontal living, our immersion in our world of technical reason. If the results are not fully satisfying we assure ourselves that with more knowledge and "research" better solutions will be found.

This attitude and manner of life Tillich called the "horizontal dimension." He finds on every hand examples that illustrate its character. He writes: "Indeed our daily life, in office and home, in cars and airplanes, at parties and conferences, while reading magazines and watching television, while looking at advertisements and hearing radio, are in themselves continuous examples of a life which has lost the dimension of depth. It runs ahead, every moment is filled with something which must be done or seen or said or planned." [7] Such behavior, then, prevents us from asking the meaningful questions, those which would help us to understand ourselves and relate to others with honesty and sincerity. But these questions we seldom if ever ask or discuss with our friends.

Tillich insists that "No one can experience depth without stopping and becoming aware of himself. Only if he has moments in which he does not care about what comes next can he experience the meaning of this moment here and now, and ask himself about the meaning of life." [8] How difficult this is no doubt many have discovered. But

[7] Paul Tillich, "The Last Dimension in Religion," in *Adventures of the Mind* (New York: Vintage Books, 1960), p. 56.
[8] *Ibid.*

"as long as the preliminary, transitory concerns are not silenced, no matter how interesting and valuable and important they may be, the voice of the ultimate concern cannot be heard. This is the deepest root of the loss of the dimension of depth in our period." [9]

The meaning for which we search cannot be provided by the culture. It is concealed in symbols. But many of the symbols that could speak to us do not, since they have been reduced to signs and as such point to something which is within the possibility of our understanding. A symbol points to something beyond us, beyond our comprehension. The symbol emerges in relation to the times. When a people participate only or chiefly in horizontal values, the signs suffice, and symbols disappear or degenerate into signs. We live in a time when symbols no longer beckon us to meditate on their meaning and thereby to discover the essence of life.

As early as the forties, Susanne Langer concluded that "in modern civilization there are two great threats to mental security, the new mode of living which has made the old nature symbols alien to our minds, and the new mode of working which makes activity meaningless, unacceptable to the hungry imagination . . . all symbols are gone and thousands of average lives offer no new materials to a creative imagination." [10]

"To live or interpret life in terms of signs is to remove from experience the meaning and significance of freedom, peace, justice and love. If signs and processes rule our lives, it is conceivable that freedom would mean the license to do what we can get away with: peace, the absence of conflict; justice, penalty in proportion to the infraction; truth, what works to the individual's advantage; and love, physical attractiveness and dependency." [11]

Many counselors, educators and others are aware that these concepts have ceased to stir the imagination and stimulate the search to discover their implications for life. Francis Horn concludes that the task of educators in our time is "to help young people establish a life solidly constructed upon these enduring values: truth, beauty, integrity and love." [12] Wrenn considers that "he [the counselor] must be sensitive to truth, to beauty, to the vast order of nature. Perhaps

[9] *Ibid.*
[10] Susanne Langer, *Philosophy in a New Key* (Cambridge: Harvard University Press, 1942), Chapter 1.
[11] C. Gratton Kemp, *Perspectives on the Group Process* (Boston: Houghton Mifflin Company, 1964), p. 17.
[12] Francis Horn, "Education for What?" *Teachers College Record,* 1961, Vol. 42, p. 481.

this must go even deeper than sensitivity, must involve a relationship with a God of truth — and of Love, of mercy, of justice." [13]

The emphasis on the necessity and importance of facilitating adaptation to the changing environment, however, indicates the lack of understanding of how to find meaning in depth. It is not recognized that such a method will only facilitate "horizontal" living by strengthening the process meanings already attained.

Getzels and Jackson found a deep inconsistency on the part of teachers and parents regarding the qualities of giftedness and the qualities needed for success in life. Both groups agreed that I.Q., creativity, good marks (teachers), and goal directedness (parents) were the qualities required for giftedness; for success in life, both groups agreed that the needed qualities were ability to get along with others, goal directedness and emotional stability (adjustment).[14]

In an evaluation of teachers, students rated them "below average" on "happiness, open-mindedness, originality and magnetism," and "above average" on "breadth of interest, refinement, sportsmanship, personal appearance and community participation." [15]

It is tragically significant that the teachers rated higher on the horizontal or process characteristics than on those that require symbolic content and meaning.

Adjustment may allow people more comfort, and perhaps they become more productive in working on process meanings, but it does not deepen their understanding of the meaning of existence. Doubtless it assists many to meet the demands of a competitive and conformist society. They adjust, but they do not understand. On the level of adaptation this kind of assistance is valid, but if the purpose is to assist people to truly find the meaning and purpose of their lives it must come under criticism. Adjustment should not be the primary goal of those engaged in helping others.

DEPTH, THE MISSING DIMENSION

Many are unaware of the disquieting sense of emptiness; or they accept it as the price of living in these times. Others no doubt have

[13] C. Gilbert Wrenn, "The Status and Role of the School Counselor," *Personnel and Guidance Journal*, 1957, Vol. 36, p. 182.
[14] Jacob W. Getzels and Philip W. Jackson, *Creativity and Intelligence* (New York: John Wiley, 1962), p. 119.
[15] Robert W. Richey and William H. Fox, "How Do Teachers Compare with Other Community Members?" *Education Research Bulletin*, 1948, Vol. 27, p. 239.

so "hardened their hearts" that their aspirations are finally contained completely within the satisfaction of the senses.

Even those within one of the most favorable environments for the development of awareness, responsibility, and aliveness to the meaning of life are not interested in depth. Investigators from Harvard University systematically collected from their students for over a decade descriptions of their future plans. Murray, one of the investigators, reports that the "returns show that the three most prevalent positive fantasies today are those of perfect marriage, children, and sexual conquests in that order . . . in striking contrast to students in a dozen other countries Americans at different colleges do not imagine themselves participating in great enterprises or devoting their energies to some superpersonal goal, either political or cultural. They dream of economic security, a house and a plot of land in the country, a happy family and peace for a lifetime." [16] Such a predicament is clear evidence of the success of counselors, teachers and others in their program of adjustment, and may indirectly be a reflection on their own personal values and goals.

Apparently, from their conversation and behavior, some adults responsible for educating the young have not recognized the inroads made by superficial thinking and living and have assumed that depth of understanding and dedication to deeper meanings develop as part of the maturational process. Evidence is conclusive that this is not the case. Interest in the meaning of life and in one's action in relation to this meaning must be nourished and developed by the consistent help of those who have this interest themselves and who see the need to develop the courage to ask for meaning and to live serenely with the results of the search. Mutual exploration would encourage recognition in their experiences of the validity of the teaching that "those who lose their lives will save them." In the words of a modern thinker, "Individuality is something to be built for the sake of something else. It is a structure of potential energies for expenditure in the service of an idea, a cultural endeavor, the betterment of man, an emergent value . . . an individual self is made only to be lost — that is, only to pledge to some enterprise that is in league with a good future; and thereby find itself once more." [17]

Lack of the dimension of depth, most serious in this age, has been

[16] Henry A. Murray, "Individuality: The Meaning and Content of Individuality in Contemporary America," *Daedalus,* 1958, Vol. 87, p. 43.
[17] *Ibid.,* p. 47.

the concern of many generations. Great thinkers at various times have tried to explain it or have offered suggestions for deepening the meaning of life. To note two, there is the famous dictum of Socrates, "Know thyself," and Pascal wrote, "The heart has its reasons which the mind knoweth not." Among others in our own day, Rogers hypothesizes that "there is an organismic base for an organized valuing process within the human individual," and that its effectiveness bears a direction relation "to the degree that the individual is open to the experiencing which is going on within himself." [18]

These examples, ranging over a long period of history, reveal the common assumption that meaning is not transferable. It is a personal search, a search freely initiated by the person who courageously plumbs the depths of life in order to discover its meaning for himself. He passes beyond the realms of conventionality and conformism and the rewards of horizontal living and dares to confront reality, the reality of his personal life. The tremendous difficulties involved have always been recognized. Because these are so great, we avoid them by blaming circumstances — the turmoil, confusion and pace of modern life. The individual has the capacity to act as the valuing center of his life. Nietzsche, in *Thus Spake Zarathustra,* gives the warning: "No people could live without first valuing; if a people will maintain itself, however, it must not value as its neighbor valueth. . . . Valuing is creating; hear it ye creating ones! . . . Through evaluation only is there value; and without valuation the nut of existence would be hollow. Hear it, ye creating ones!" Rogers places this fact at the heart of the difficulty in the development of mature values. For others the difficulty lies in securing the time and entering into the experience of reflection. The demand of our horizontal patterns of life are so urgent that an individual experiences feelings of guilt if he takes time out for reflection. One professor's request of a recognized university for Sabbatical leave "in order to think" was considered ridiculous.

Many of our relationships are far removed from the intention of assisting one another to understand problems and issues. We are more interested in using the ideas of others to further some objective we have in mind; or by carefully practiced subtleties we hope to win them over to our point of view, or to impress them with our friendship, or to diminish any suspicions that they may have that in the

[18] Carl R. Rogers, "Toward a Modern Approach to Values: The Valuing Process in the Mature Person," *Journal of Abnormal and Social Psychology,* 1964, Vol. 68, p. 165.

race for horizontal recognitions and rewards we have a planned scheme for using or ignoring them to our advantage. We play with another's life as we would play with a "man" on the chessboard. French, Kornhauser and Morrow maintain that "sometimes management is deliberately using the attractive symbols of democracy, participation, man-to-man discussion, group discussion etc., to create the desired atmosphere within which it can smoothly manipulate the attitudes of its employees, retain their loyalty and still run the business 'as it should be run,' without irritating interferences from below." [19]

IMPLICATIONS FOR THE COUNSELOR

Counseling reflects the functional meanings of the counselor. If he lives according to horizontal meanings it is unlikely that he will recognize statements, questions and attitudes that suggest the counselee's concern about problems deeper than those of adjustment. He will proceed as if the counselee needed help in understanding the situations that surround him. The counselor may assume that, since the counselee's problem consists only in choosing and behaving in acceptable ways, he has an obligation to motivate him to recognize the best choice and to act upon it. This he may proceed to do by a variety of techniques, such as mild suggestions and selecting and supporting the counselee's statements that he, the counselor, believes are appropriate.

Many counselors become skilled in such techniques, and their counselees often attain a high degree of adjustment. But what about the deeper uneasiness that remains and must either be repressed or find an outlet in nonconforming behavior?

Dick suffered from this deeper uneasiness. He explained to the counselor that he did not see any sense in going on to college and working at a profession. "What is the use of all of this?" he asked. The counselor could not really hear what Dick was saying. He proceeded on a horizontal adjustive level, which led to such insights as, "One has to work at something," and "Isn't your dad better off than if he hadn't gone to college?" The counselee, apparently recognizing that the counselor didn't understand, used up most of this and succeeding interviews talking about trips he had taken, hobbies he enjoyed, and problems with his brother. So the interviews ended after

[19] J. R. P. French, A. Kornhauser, and A. Morrow (eds.), "Conflict and Cooperation in Industry," *Journal of Social Issues,* 1946, pp. 44–45.

Dick had made three futile attempts to let the counselor know about his feeling of emptiness.

If counselors assume that their task is to prepare students to fit more comfortably into the scheme of mass production, to be successful in making the grade in this competitive world, they are helping them to be more adequate in superficial living. Is this all the counselee has a right to expect? Where is he going to learn the deeper meanings of life? How does he learn about fidelity, responsibility, integrity? Who is going to help him with his questions concerning the meaning of life, his life? Should not the counselor be a reliable resource in this realm also? Should counselors accept this wider, more demanding responsibility, or should they continue to give a stone when asked for bread?

Let us not be unreasonable with this counselor. He may have experienced only horizontal values. It may be that all his life his attention has been focused on them. Seldom if ever has he had occasion to be interested in anything but horizontal rewards. The ideal for him is attained through professional status, and through money and what it purchases. To expect him to recognize or be interested in any other kind of values may be close to expecting the impossible.

Fortunately, this is not true of all counselors. There are many who sense more meaning in life than merely a vegetative existence of getting and spending. They are interested in the good life for themselves and the counselee. This good life includes constructive work, socially useful leisure and recreational activities, but also a desire for something more. This "something more" is described in various terms — personal respect, integrity, relations with others characterized by openness, understanding, honesty, and brotherly affection. They long for the evidence that their lives have meaning not merely in the production of something but in bringing purpose, joy and courage to others. Some, no doubt, are aware that it is because this "something more" is so lacking that their lives have become boring and impoverished.

Only the counselor who is in touch with the inwardness of his being is free to participate fully in the problem of the counselee. This is not an easy achievement. Much of our experience is what McGregor calls "reactive" rather than "active behavior." [20] Many of the situa-

[20] Douglas McGregor, "Conditions of Effective Leadership in the Industrial Organization," in T. H. Newcomb and E. L. Hartley, *Readings in Social Psychology* (New York: Holt, Rinehart & Winston, Inc., 1947), pp. 427–435.

tions of life we have interpreted as demanding that we react for or against, for if uninterested or unable to do this, we may appear neutral or engage in mild withdrawal. When we use such "reactive behavior" in dealings with our innermost selves we reject the possibility of experiencing depth. According to Rogers we may be less sensitive and less accurate, using only the partial man. "He [the counselor] realizes that if he can trust all of himself, his feelings and his intuitions may be wiser than his mind, that as a total person he can be more sensitive and more accurate than with only his thoughts alone." [21]

Almost without realizing it, the counselor is reactive in another way. He becomes conformed to this world. He becomes so concerned about the opinion others have of him and his work that he can no longer give himself to what the counselee is saying. As the German poet Storm has written, "One man asks: 'What will result from my action?' The other man asks: 'Is it right what I am doing?' This difference reveals who is free and who is slave. The 'free' man does not depend upon the world; the fettered man does." In this sense counselors must strive to become free, to ask the question of conscience rather than the question of culture.

Counselors in relating their experiences discuss the ideas, the abilities, the plans of their counselees, and the video tape reveals why this was the focus of their interest. The counselee was an object to be diagnosed, persuaded, manipulated, informed, reassured. He was not a person, and yet counselors talk about seeing the problem from the counselee's point of view, entering into his feeling, even loving him. Through keen introspection some realize that they fall far short of this goal. They reaffirm to themselves the need to see the counselee as a person, and determine to make a greater effort.

In so doing, they set themselves a most difficult task. As counselors we have been trained to analyze and determine the possible sources of difficulty and to test our hypotheses in the course of the interview. Such training and the knowledge that psychology provides are indeed necessary, but if the "personage" [22] of the counselor takes precedence over the person, our training and knowledge becomes a distorting mirror. An eager readiness to distinguish in people's behavior the psychological mechanisms that are at work has resulted in the fact that we no longer recognize the person but see puppets. The counselee in turn has been reduced to an object; he

[21] Rogers, op. cit., p. 164.
[22] C. G. Jung used the Latin word persona not to express the idea of person, but to express the idea of a role, as in a play.

does not feel himself to be a person and is not energizing the dynamic forces of health.

As counselors we shall each remain an object among objects unless we can open ourselves to ourselves, unless we can ask ourselves questions of depth. We need to tune in on what "the inner man" is ready to tell us, to be concerned not only with questions of expediency, but with questions of right. Integration must be not solely on the horizontal levels of existence but must also be sought in the "vertical dimension." This involves a struggle of conscience in which the individual aspect of the ego confronts the universal aspect. Integration results from the unification of these two aspects — that is, of the self with itself. Integration is difficult but possible because, as Kant concluded, each is conscious of a law that is neither identical with any conventional or habitual attitude nor motivated by any consideration of expediency or benefit, but that commands unconditionally.[23] This is progress toward becoming a person. As one theologian has said, "It is by becoming persons ourselves that we discover the persons of our fellow-men." [24]

The counselor who is a person helps the counselee to feel that he is a person. Through a complete revolution, changing the climate of his life, the counselor discovers the world of persons, acquires the sense of the person, is more interested in people as persons than in their ideas, or their status, or their personage. He no longer evaluates them; he is outside the market-place orientation.

CONCLUSIONS

We are living at a time when young and old are immersed in horizontal living. The counselor himself has been conditioned to evaluate in terms of the results of his action. A random sample of 25 counselors agreed that when they had to evaluate a proposed action, they would ask only whether or not it would be acceptable to those it might affect. We tend to ask of behavior and products the same questions: are they practical and useful? We assume that the methods of technology work equally well for people.

Today's successful counselor is generally considered to be one whose counselees develop their potentialities to near maximum in

[23] Richard Kroner, *Culture and Faith* (Chicago: The University of Chicago Press, 1951), p. 163.
[24] Charles Hauter, "Les deux natures en Christ," in *Revue d'histoire et de philosophie religieuses* (Paris: Presses Universitaires de France, 1952).

becoming adjusted and flexible in meeting the demands of middle class society. They ask and find answers to the questions of horizontal living. But such answers are growing unsatisfactory to many counselors, counselees, parents and teachers. They are unsatisfactory because all those involved at deeper levels of awareness remain as uneasy as they were in the beginning.

Counseling in the horizontal dimension does not help the counselee to understand the meaning of his life or to strengthen his capacity for using his total self in confronting its issues. The counselor may consider that he has fulfilled his obligations when he has helped the counselee to make a better adjustment to his world. If so, he will often ignore, or be unaware of, the deeper concern of his counselee. He will also have to repress his own questioning, uneasiness and anxiety. It is reasonable to assume and expect that a considerable number of counselors will continue to live and counsel in terms of horizontal meanings. To consider that counselees are interested in or concerned about the meaning of life is foreign to their conceptions.

On the other hand, counselors who have found and live in touch with a vertical depth of meaning can be expected to be more aware and more at ease with the counselee who has doubts about why he should put forth effort to become, who sees no challenging purpose in life. Such a counselor would be less likely to interpret the counselee's comments and questions from only a one-dimensional, horizontal viewpoint.

Recognizing that there are many levels of meaning hidden in any situation, counselors might endeavor to be open to those which they do not generally recognize. Then a counselor who has not found it necessary to think deeply about life might respect and try to enter into the doubts and agony as well as the joy and certitude of those who have found some depth of meaning.

On the other hand, a counselor who finds reflection and introspection a meaningful experience leading into understandings of great worth should not assume that every or even most counselees are ready for assistance to enter into this experience.

Any counselor, unless he is to be content with moving around in the shoals and shallows of life, should occasionally set his sail and push out to sea. With expectancy he should drop a line into the depths, perchance to find that far down under the surface there is a foundation that is dependable and that gives meaning and perspective to each voyage into the unknown.

QUESTIONS

1. Why is it important that the counselor have a depth dimension in his life?
2. What would be indications to the counselor that he is living on a horizontal level?
3. What are the limitations of the counselor who counsels only or chiefly for adjustment?
4. What emphasis in education is conducive to a disrespect for, and loss of, the dimension of depth?

FOR FURTHER READING

Earl A. Loomis, Jr., *The Self in Pilgrimage* (New York: Harper & Row, Publishers, Inc., 1960).

The author brings together psychological and psychoanalytic concepts and a basic concern for religious searchings and truths. The book is a penetrating study of the means for the healing of sickness and the maintenance of health. He shows that free men are not nearly so free as they believe, but are often controlled by their own demons unconsciously projected onto alien societies, classes and forces. In the chapter, "The Self in Hell" he depicts hell as the torment, isolation, lack of communication, loss of identity and absence of relationship that characterize so many lives today. The central themes are the recognition of evil in ourselves as well as in others, the capacity for receiving and giving help, and the quest for new bridges of communication, assistance and forgiveness.

Roger L. Shinn, *Tangled World* (New York: Charles Scribner's Sons, 1965).

This book is based on a series of television programs that appeared under the same title. The author states in the foreword that "the purpose of the book is to help people understand what they are doing so that they can decide more responsibly." Insights are provided concerning many aspects of our society at home and abroad. But the author emphasizes that knowledge is not enough. He insists that only when it is joined to a sensitivity to human needs and to the basic loyalties of our lives can we make responsible decisions. A wide variety of problems are dealt with in a clear, straightforward, informative and convincing manner.

John Baillie, *The Belief in Progress* (New York: Charles Scribner's Sons, 1951).

Commencing with an examination of the current belief in progress as empirically observed, the author examines the writings from ancient times to the present in search of what validity, if any, exists in this belief. Following to some degree a chronological historical approach, he illuminates and evaluates the ideas of the students of progress. He provides a critique of the various presuppositions of the rationalist position and the evolutionist and developmental positions. He finally relates these interpretations to the religious understandings of progress, especially those based in Christianity. He concludes that modern progressivism may be unable to provide the spiritual satisfaction that man has sought in it.

THE
HUMAN
PROCESS

III

10

MOTIVATION

Drivers know that cars "do not run" without gasoline. Some drivers, however, are unintelligent regarding the precise function of the gasoline in the locomotion of the vehicle. Many counselors are in a similar position with regard to motivation in their clients. They recognize that the so-called "unmotivated" student does not respond in the desired manner. They try certain methods on which they depend to "motivate" the counselee. Why these methods do or do not "work" is rarely understood.

Nevertheless, the counselor knows that motivation is basic to his efforts in helping the counselee, although he is so involved in counseling that the complex problem of motivation is shoved aside. Or perhaps he has permitted himself to be satisfied with superficial indications of what is and is not effective, like the driver who is too absorbed in driving to do anything but turn on the ignition and "step on the gas."

In fairness to the counselor, however, we must admit that motivation is a complex subject on which there is much research in progress. Even those who devote a major portion of their time to the study of motivation find it a many-sided problem requiring great perseverance. One such psychologist describes it as "more confusing, more disorderly, more vexing than are the fields of sensation, learning and perception." [1] Nevertheless, if the counselor expects to understand the process of counseling he must be a continuing student of motivation.

[1] Howard H. Kendler, "Motivation and Behavior," in David Levine (ed.), *Nebraska Symposium on Motivation, 1965* (Lincoln: University of Nebraska Press, 1965), p. 2.

DEFINITION

The understanding of the term "motivation" has changed with research and study. English and English define it as "a specific hypothesized personal or organismic determiner of the direction and/or strength of action or a line of action." [2] Perrin views it as "an antecedent state of emotion which initiates directed behavior, "and contends that a "motive for an action is the reason that it is actually operative," [3] Atkinson concludes that "a motive is a relatively stable and general disposition of personality which, together with cognitive expectation concerning the consequence of action and the incentive value of the consequence, determines the strength of a goal-directed action tendency in a particular situation." [4] Leeper considers motives to be "processes that tend to produce some relatively more complex means of dealing with situations to supplement the simpler means that the reflex mechanisms provide." [5] These will adequately indicate the nature and complexity of the subject. This chapter will be devoted to a more comprehensive understanding of motivation and its implications for the counselor.

PSYCHOLOGICAL ISSUES

Basically, the issues in motivation stem from assumptions concerning the nature of man. Machiavelli believed that man was irresponsible, selfish and aggressive to the extent that he concluded that he could be socialized by trickery and coercion. On the other hand, Rousseau assumed that man was by nature "good." The belief that man must be controlled and directed required an authoritarian, reward-and-punishment society. The other belief, that man was rational, responsible and interested in self-improvement found support in a democratic society. Thus two broad cultural streams, fed by other

[2] Horace B. English and A. Champney English, *A Comprehensive Dictionary of Psychological and Psychoanalytical Terms* (New York: David McKay Co., Inc., 1958), p. 330.

[3] C. T. Perrin, "Behavior potentiality as a joint function of the amount of training and the degree of hunger at the time of extinction," *Journal of Experimental Psychology*, 1942, Vol. 30, pp. 93–103.

[4] J. W. Atkinson, An Introduction to Motivation (Princeton, N.J.: D. Van Nostrand Co., Inc., 1964), p. 65.

[5] R. W. Leeper, "The Role of Motivation in Learning: A Study of the Phenomena of Differential Motivational Control of the Utilization of Habits," *Journal of Genetic Psychology*, 1935, Vol. 46, pp. 3–40.

tributaries, have come down to the present. In politics, education and industry the trend has been toward a democratic decentralization relying increasingly upon the conceptualizing and decision-making abilities of the individual. The authoritarian theory of man depends upon the support of the theory of extrinsic motivation; the democratic theory relies generally on the theory of intrinsic motivation.

Since the concern of behavioral science is only "what is what" about motivation and about human nature in general, it considers irrelevant the general attitudes of social practice. The counselor cannot be neutral since he has no choice but to operate upon some intelligent view of motivation. He may place his trust in the traditional and dominant theory of extrinsic motivation or in the newer theory of intrinsic motivation, or he may trust one under certain specific circumstances and the other under other circumstances.

Any theory of motivation must find satisfactory answers to certain questions. Those which are most commonly asked by all theorists are the instigation question, the energization question, and the direction-hedonic question. Let us consider these and other questions and note the responses in the framework of the dominant theory of extrinsic motivation.

Theory of Extrinsic Motivation

The Instigation Question • What originates the activities of organisms and what causes cessation? Certain instigators are presumed to produce a generalized state of arousal or excitement. There are four kinds of instigators: (1) acquired drives based upon experiences in which stimuli have originally been associated with, and have become conditional stimuli for, emotional responses evoked by the various primary drive stimuli, (2) homeostatic needs such as hunger and thirst, (3) sex, and (4) strong and painful external stimuli.

The aroused behavior stops when the primary or acquired drive-stimuli cease to impinge upon the organism.

The Energization Question • What energizes activity and controls its vigor? This is explained in terms of the intensity of the primary and/or secondary or learned drives.

The Direction-Hedonic Question • How is the drive reduced? This question is answered via drive-reduction. It is assumed with animals that withdrawal indicates a negative hedonic value. In human beings the equivalence of direction to hedonic value remains an issue. A person may avoid or withdraw from a situation for one or a number of different reasons.

How is a choice made? The choice of the response is related directly to the kind of drive-stimulus that is operative and the past experience of the organism with it. From the presumed hierarchy of responses one is chosen that in the past served to reduce the drive.

What controls the choice of goals? The response to the instigation question is suitable if the short run or immediacy only is considered. If, however, the remote objectives characteristic of human conduct are to be considered, the answer has to rely on extrapolations. The evidence has come from patients in psychotherapy.[6]

What is the explanation of emotional attachment or love? The attachment to an object, person or place is directly associated with drive-reduction. The infant is presumed to become attached to the mother who reduces his hunger, his various discomforts and his anxieties based on past experience with them. Also, the "secondary reinforcements" of behavior theory are innocuous stimuli that, having been associated with drive-reduction, are presumed to signal relief from either primary drive or anxiety.[7]

What is the basis for behavioral change or learning? Learning results from drive-reduction. The new situation calls forth a response. Among the learned responses the most probable is used first. If it is unsatisfactory, further responses are tried until one serves to reduce the drive or the emotional distress originally based on the drive.

Why do the same given responses persist? Even after conditions have changed a person persists in seeking the same goal and in using the same given response. A method that has met with success a number of times becomes established — that is, counter-conditioning has taken place. The inhibitive power of the frustrations is so reduced because of their tendency to signal relief or "hope."

This dominant theory of extrinsic motivation is supported by a bulwark of empirical research. The answers it provides to the penetrating questions on motivation are simple and straightforward and lend the theory considerable weight. However, some authorities consider that, although it is true within limits, it lacks comprehensiveness in its results.[8]

[6] Sigmund Freud, "Three Contributions to the Theory of Sex," in A. A. Brill (trans. and ed.), *The Basic Writings of Sigmund Freud* (New York: Modern Library, 1938).

[7] O. H. Mowrer, *Learning Theory and Behavior* (New York: John Wiley & Sons, Inc., 1960).

[8] J. McV. Hunt, "Intrinsic Motivation and Its Role in Psychological Development," in *Nebraska Symposium on Motivation, 1965* (Lincoln: University of Nebraska Press, 1965).

Hunt concludes from his studies that activity takes place without any primary or acquired drive to motivate it. Both animals and people play, manipulate things, explore, and look for new perceptual inputs in form, color and movement. Such behavior generally occurs when painful stimulation, homeostatic needs and sex are absent, and when acquired drives based upon them are minimal. He refers to the work of Nissen, in which it was found that rats would leave their nests and cross an electrified grid to get at a Dashiell maze filled with objects that were fresh and novel to them. Also, in the work at McGill, human beings could hardly tolerate homogeneity of input for more than three or four days. On the basis of this and other evidence, Hunt concludes that the assumption that all behavior is motivated by forces extrinsic to information processing is untenable.

Although not entrely discarding extrinsic motivational theory, several authorities including Hunt recognize "an intrinsic motivation inherent in the organism's informational interacting with circumstances through the distance receptors and in its intentional goal-anticipating actions." [9] The newer evidence supports the claim that man has some freedom to make rational decisions based on available information and the openness of his belief systems (see Chapter 12). How do the proponents of the theory of intrinsic motivation answer the three main questions?

Theory of Intrinsic Motivation

The Instigation Question • Traditionally this question has been answered by reference to the transcortical, reflex-analogous association of receptor input with motor output. Sherrington's *Integrative Action of the Nervous System,* developed between 1893 and 1906, established the concept of the reflex so well that Dewey's severe criticism of it had little effect.[10]

Previous to the work of Sherrington the concept that behavior was completely instigated by the onset of primary or acquired drives had been challenged. One of the challengers was William James, who recognized that the ticking of a clock did not evoke response or awareness until it stopped and that a mother awakened to the faint cry of her child when other sounds had no effect.[11]

[9] *Ibid.,* p. 197.
[10] Charles Scott Sherrington, *Integrative Action of the Nervous System* (New Haven: Yale University Press, 1906).
[11] William James, *Principles of Psychology* (New York: Holt, Rinehart & Winston, Inc., 1890).

Hermandez-Péon, Scherrer and Jouven inferred from their research using cats and implanted electrodes that through a feedback loop the central processes can regulate receptor inputs.[12] Hunt considers this conclusion a better explanation of instigation than the reflex-analogous notion of connection between sensory input and motor output.[13]

Hunt suggests as a prototype the room thermostat. He explains that the setting of the thermostat is the *standard,* the room temperature the *input,* and the difference in the reading between the setting (standard) and the room temperature (input) the *incongruity* that instigates the operation. So conceived, incongruity becomes a kind of generic instigator and congruity between input and standard stops the operation.

There is a variety of standards. The standards differ at separate levels of human development. These standards can be conceptualized in various ways. The basic standards are considered to be those of comfort and homeostatic need and those developing out of informational interaction. Intentions and plans are also standards.

The advent of the electric computer prompted Wiener and others to recognize the analogy between computer processes and human thought. The close comparison of the components required in solving logical problems in the computer process and human process prompted certain neuropsychologists to look for their counterparts within mammalian brains.[14] Rose and Woolsey divided the cerebrum into extrinsic and intrinsic portions. The extrinsic sectors are directly connected to receptors and to effectors. The intrinsic sectors, frontal and posterior, are the centers for intrinsic motivation. The most significant function of the frontal sector is the moderation of intentions and plans; that of the posterior sector is the "storage" for hierarchically arranged coded representations of the "various invariant properties of receptor inputs from various objects, persons and places viewed from various angles." [15] Having examined the nature of con-

[12] Hermandez-Péon, R., H. Scherrer and M. Jouven, "Modification of Electric Activity in Cochlear Nucleus, During Attention in Unanesthetized Cats," *Science,* 1956, Vol. 123, pp. 331–332.
[13] Hunt, *op. cit.,* 1965.
[14] N. Wiener, *Cybernetics* (New York: John Wiley & Sons, Inc., 1948).
[15] J. E. Rose and C. N. Woolsey, "The Relations of Thalamic Connections, Cellular Structure and Evocable Activity in the Auditory Region of the Cat," *Journal of Comparative Psychology,* 1949, Vol. 91, pp. 441–466.

gruity and incongruity as an instigator of action, we now turn to the problem of what keeps it going.

The Energization Problem • We have observed that the incongruity between one's actual performance and the standard he sets for himself instigates action. This difference between our plans and our present situation is also the condition that energizes us, keeps us going. Plans may differ widely and derive from various levels. At one level the plan may derive from the incongruity between the conditions of the internal environment and the biases of the "homeostats of the brain-stem core." For example, a person feels cold and puts on a coat. On another level plans may arise from a "learning set" such as "things should be perceptually recognizable." A student re-reads the page to clarify the idea for himself, or the counselee examines the profile on the Kuder to recognize his highest interests.

In this conception of energization, when a plan is not satisfactorily completed the incongruity between it and the plan results in *unfulfilled intentions* or *frustration*. Experience has demonstrated that such a condition is a source of both emotional arousal and motivation. The motivational power of incongruity involved in an unfinished task was demonstrated in the research of Zeigarnik, which demonstrated the tendency to resume and to recall uncompleted tasks.

The research efforts of many confirm the conclusion that incongruity in information processing provides a source of arousal that can both energize and stimulate responses. Counselors will recognize the resemblance between this conception of motivation and that of the self theory of Rogers.[16] In Roger's thinking, the "standard" is the self-concept of the counselee. This self-concept is based upon information about the self in the "storage." The variance between this standard and the ideal of the counselee (what he desires to become) provides the incongruity, the motivation to attain and to actualize himself.

In Kelly's formulations the standards are called "personal" constructs."[17] Kelly views these constructs as active efforts of the individual to make sense out of what he is taught and observes. When what he observes differs from what he has been led to believe, he suffers emotional distress or anxiety. Festinger found his subjects using various means to protect themselves against information that

[16] Carl R. Rogers, *Client-Centered Therapy* (Boston: Houghton Mifflin Company, 1951), Chapter 11.
[17] G. A. Kelly, *The Psychology of Personal Constructs* (New York: W. W. Norton & Company, Inc., 1955).

was dissonant with what they believed.[18] Rokeach and others found their subjects resorting to distortion, rejection and other methods in order to avoid changing their beliefs.[19]

The Direction-Hedonic Question • The direction-hedonic question is especially interesting to the counselor since it promises further light on the familiar concept of "self-actualization." The problem it presents is the relation of the generic idea of incongruity to the hedonic direction of "self-actualization" or other concept with similar meaning. At a low level, incongruity takes place when a person reaches for the knob to open a door and finds a ring which he lifts up and turns instead of the familiar knob. Or, on another level, it is the problem a student faces when he prepares an essay in the best form and with the best possible thought and care. He turns it in, expecting an "A" and receives it back marked "C."

Such situations arouse an emotional disturbance that is like fear. Piaget observed that when his children confronted radically changed versions of things they had come to recognize, they showed emotional distress.[20]

But incongruous situations do not always evoke unpleasurable or distressing emotions. Bexton, Heron and Scott,[21] Heron, Doane, and Scott,[22] and Lilly[23] found that human beings faced for a considered length of time with homogeneous, unchanging circumstances actively seek relatively new, incongruous situations of any kind.

For a time the fact that some situations giving rise to incongruous inputs were sometimes distressing and repelling and at others pleasing and attractive was puzzling. It was concluded that there was an optimum level of incongruity. Too much incongruity repelled, while small degrees encouraged effective arousal, which made it attractive and pleasurable. The degree of incongruity that is acceptable and

---

[18] L. Festinger, *A Theory of Cognitive Dissonance* (New York: Harper & Row, Publishers, Inc., 1957).

[19] Milton Rokeach, *The Open and Closed Mind* (New York: Basic Books, Inc., 1960).

[20] Jean Piaget, *Play, Dreams and Initiation in Childhood* (New York: W. W. Norton & Company, Inc., 1951).

[21] W. H. Bexton, W. Heron and T. H. Scott, "Effects of Increased Variation in the Sensory Environment," *Canadian Journal of Psychology*, 1954, Vol. 8, pp. 70–76.

[22] W. Heron, B. K. Doane and T. H. Scott, "Visual Disturbances after Prolonged Perceptual Isolation," *Canadian Journal of Psychology*, 1956, Vol. 10, pp. 13–18.

[23] J. C. Lilly, "Mental Effects of Reduction of Ordinary Levels of Physical Stimuli on Intact Healthy Persons," *Psychiatry Research Report*, 1956, Vol. 5, pp. 1–9.

positively energizing differs with individuals. The general conclusion may be drawn that incongruity in the right amounts arouses the emotions and energizes the person toward activity in the direction of actualizing his powers in relation to intentions and plans. This provides the counselor with some understanding of the reason why the counselee seeks and uses help.

It should also be noted that this theory provides a rationale why some counselees in a relationship using intrinsic motivation may not progress as hoped. There may be too little incongruity between their present condition and their symbolic level of aspiration; on the other hand, there may be too much incongruity. Whether the incongruity is too little or too much to motivate the individual depends on his perception of it. If it is perceived as too much, the individual may distort or reject his perception of it and thus reduce the threat of the accompanying emotional arousal.

MOTIVATIONAL ISSUES

Function of Perception

A man on his knees might appear to one person to be praying, to another, begging. This is so because each of us has a different perception of what we observe. Our perceptions of the world determine the world in which we live.

Traditionally, perceptions were interpreted as relatively simple utilizations of direct sensory material. The present trend is to recognize that there are different degrees of complexity in perception and that to associate "perception" with lower levels and "cognition" with higher levels in a hierarchial system does not truly account for all situations.

Leeper favors a broad use of the term perception that would suggest emphatically that a series of propositions that have been established with reference to the phenomena of sensory perception also hold true for much more complex processes. A college student perceived his academic success to be based on the fact that he studied the right content and his success in golf on the fact that the wind was in the right direction. For some time he was unwilling to take an intelligence test and perceive himself as a superior student. When he did he legally changed his name. In this situation, perceptual abilities operated on both simple sensory and more complex cognitive levels. Leeper hypothesizes that motives are perceptual processes.

He links emotion to perception in the following manner: When emotion arouses or energizes by the diffuse discharges of the reticular system to the cortex, its influence is only through the changes induced and maintained in the perceptual processes by the diffuse discharges.

Not all perceptions are motivating. There is a continuum within the total perceptual domain. The continuum extends from motivationally neutral perceptions to motivationally strong perceptions. Neither are all perceptions correct or true. Adults have experienced the problem of changing irrational perceptions after recognizing them as such. In some situations perceptual changes are gradual and cumulative. This is the kind of change that the counselor hopes for. But the counselor also encounters the fact that the counselee is capable of making sudden reorganizations, sometimes equally powerful, such as, "I used to love him; now he disgusts me."

Many theorists in the current research have been moving in the direction of the theory of perceptual motivation. During the years 1949–1951, David Krech was urging that psychological phenomena, rather conceived in terms of separate processes of perception, motivation and learning, should be looked at as organic unities or "dynamic systems." [24] William Prentice explored the idea that "what we call motives are really a particular kind of perceptual or cognitive event." [25]

The Function of Emotion

It is now thought that emotional and physiologically based motives are on a continuum. The research on the sex motive and on the pain experienced from burns and wounds lead to this conclusion.[26] In contrast to earlier views of emotion there is now much agreement that the emotional habits should be recognized as constructively significant in the individual's development.

The thinking on motives and emotions is undergoing important revision. It has been customary to think of the former playing an organizing and directive role, while emotions played a disruptive role. Leeper suggests that a more valid conclusion is that it is necessary to see emotions as a part of a larger continuum of motivational processes that range from the most clearly physiologically based to an opposite pole of the most clearly emotional motives.

[24] David Krech, "Notes Toward a Psychological Theory," *Journal of Personality*, 1949, Vol. 18, pp. 66–87.
[25] William C. Prentice, "Some Cognitive Aspects of Motivation," *American Psychologist*, 1961, Vol. 16, pp. 503–511.
[26] D. S. Lehrman, "The Reproductive Behavior of Ringdoves," *Scientific American*, 1964, Vol. 211, pp. 48–54.

The pattern has been to consider emotions low on the scale of evolutionary development. They were considered "subcortical," or basically visceral, while the perceptual or cognitive processes were considered "cortical" processes. This view led to the placement of emotionally and physiologically based motives in one group, and all perceptual, cognitive, intellectual, representational or information-processing processes in a second group. This view is now giving way to the elimination of such a dichotomy and the establishment of a functional relationship among all of these motives. Recent research on the reticular activating systems and on the motivational subsystems within the limbic system have added to the understanding of this functional relationship. Recent books on motivation based on this research present the concept that the emotions and bodily drives produce a more intense arousal level of cortical activity through the diffused neural discharges from these subcortical systems up into the cerebral cortex.

A further issue has revolved around the functioning of the emotions. Do emotions merely arouse and energize, or do they have directional qualities as well? Cofer and Appley summarize research that gives credence to the concept that emotions are directional. The rats in their experiment learned to take one route when hungry and another route when thirsty.[27] If emotional drives operate to provide direction, is this directive quality generalized or does it have some specificity? One position is that taken by Brown, who argues that unless we consider drives to have a specific directive function we can no longer have different drives as behavior determinants but only different sources of drives.[28]

Leeper takes issue with Brown in that he considers it incorrect to talk of drive as singular. He refers to fear, explaining that this drive is not a generalized single drive of "fear," but different fears in different cases. "The process which produces the various 'motivational effects of fear' is in one case a fear of losing one's job. In another case it is fear of embarrassment and ridicule . . . and the directional qualities of behavior that come from such fears are specific to the particular kind of fear and not simply to fear in general." [29] It is reported that in the coal mines of Kentucky if the rats run up

[27] C. N. Cofer and M. H. Appley, *Motivation: Theory and Research* (New York: John Wiley & Sons, Inc., 1964).
[28] J. S. Brown, *The Motivation of Behavior* (New York: McGraw-Hill Book Co., Inc., 1961).
[29] R. W. Leeper, "A Motivational Theory of Emotion to Replace Emotion as Disorganized Response," *Psychological Review*, 1948, Vol. 55, pp. 5–21.

the wooden supports, put their heads on one side and listen, and then hurry down and scamper away, the miners immediately drop their tools and dash out of the mine, for this has become a signal that the roof of the mine is about to fall in. For both rats and men the emotional drive is directional and specific.

Emotions are now becoming accepted as functionally influential in all levels of motivation. Motives in the form of emotional drives are considered to operate on all levels up and down the scale of sensory-cognitive processes. Motives are also seen as perceptual processes, and all representational processes are seen as perceptions. What this does, in effect, is to establish a perceptual motivational theory of emotion.

These conclusions indicate a new approach to the significance of emotions. If emotional processes are motives both in the sense of arousing and of directing processes, and not merely in the former sense, attention would shift from the physiological mechanisms to behavioral or psychological relationships of emotional processes.

If emotional processes are considered to be perceptual, what is said about perceptual processes may also apply to emotional ones. For instance, it is known that perceptions tend to be dominated by past experience and personal commitments and are therefore quite difficult to modify. The same would be true of emotions. On the other hand perceptual habits can be modified by learning, and if emotional habits are perceptual habits the same possibilities would exist for them. It is accepted that perceptual processes are selective with reference even to many possibilities. Emotional processes would also have this character.

PHILOSOPHICAL ISSUES

Each of us sets standards for himself. These standards influence both the direction and effort of our motivation. Standards vary from one individual to the next. They vary even among members of the same family or between twins, despite the fact that the environmental and conditioning influences could be expected to be quite similar. Can we really claim that the differences in standards are fully accounted for by any psychological theory of motivation?

From research we have learned that one part of the brain, the frontal lobe, referred to as the intrinsic motivational area of the brain, will inhibit, deny or accept the result of the perceptual-cognitive-emotional input. The action taken by this area of the brain is said to be directly related to the existing incongruity between the individual's behavior and his "standard." Are there not situations in which the incongruity is so great that a logical approach would be to make no attempt or to take no action? Yet the person or persons involved do take action as determinedly as if they were certain of a positive outcome.

What if one is certain that there is more to individual experience than just what is expedient and useful, that human action is symbolic. How will the symbolic be explained? Can the symbolic be explained within the principles of cause and effect relationships? Can any theory of motivation explain it, or be expected to do so? Two persons reading the same book may acquire the same fund of information. A factual test of the content and even a test of their ability to analyze and organize information would reveal this to be the case. But does what they read mean the same to each? If they are asked to synthesize and evaluate and project outcomes the results may differ widely. Something changes their judgments, their imaginations and the possible trajectories of their subsequent actions. Should we try to explain this within some theory of reinforcement or cognitive dissonance or should we accommodate ourselves to the possible influence of the symbolic? Is the true uniqueness of a person explained by pragmatic theories or in the symbolic value of his actions? Our psychological theorists abstain from attempting to answer questions concerning the symbolic dimension of human action.

The horizons of life are not neatly bounded on the north, south, east and west by the conditions referred to in research either with animals or human beings. Man has a way of relating in the most unpredictable ways with the most fantastic situations. Frequently he arrives at a carefully reasoned response to some situation and, ignoring it, goes beyond the bounds of reason or probability. Should an explanation of such action be attempted by reference to drive reduction or the amount of incongruity between actual and aspirational levels? Or has man some kind of "inner choice" that can and does exert a guiding and perhaps determining influence on the decision reached and obtained. One conclusion is to accept the fact that human deeds are symbolic of human intentions and are not exhaustively translatable into the categories of instrumentalism.

CONCLUSIONS

Traditionally the dominant theory was extrinsic motivation, or reinforcement theory. This has been supported by a significant amount of research over many years, but it has been challenged because of its lack of comprehensiveness since it has no theoretical explanation for some forms of behavior. It is recognized that in some instances activity takes place without any primary or acquired drive of motivation. Examples are free play, manipulating objects and the search for new perceptual inputs in form, color and movement. The reinforcement theory does not adequately explain self-motivated behavior for its own sake regardless of the outcome. The place to which it relegates emotion and perception become increasingly incongruous with the research findings in these areas.

Some of the answers proposed by the reinforcement theory fell under severe criticism as other answers were found. For instance, its answer to the instigation question, or how motivation is stimulated, did not handle well the facts of set and attention. The transcortical reflex-analogous notion of connection between sensory input and motor output became less and less acceptable.

Dissatisfaction led to the exploration of other hypotheses. Research over the last two decades has provided a more substantial foundation for the theory of intrinsic motivation. Among the significant current conclusions are the following: (1) the existence of a direct feedback-loop in the brain through which the central processes can regulate receptor inputs; (2) the development of the idea of frontal and posterior sectors of intrinsic motivation, the frontal section of the brain possessing moderating intentions and plans and the posterior hierarchically arranged "storage" of a wide range of inputs; (3) that motivation is energized from the incongruity that exists between the actual and the envisioned standard; (4) that this incongruity in information processing provides a source of arousal that can both energize and stimulate responses. The amount of incongruity determines the nature of the results. Too much incongruity may greatly inhibit or prevent action; too little may not motivate.

Emotions are now perceived as directly involved in motivation. They have some effect not only on the subcortical levels but also on the perceptual and cognitive levels. They are considered by some as exerting both a directional and specific drive, and are becoming the focus of study by motivational theorists.

Originally, perception was associated only with the subcortical or lower levels of functioning. Now perception is considered to operate not only on the simple sensory level but also on the more complex cognitive levels. Perceptions are also linked to motives; that is, many perceptions are seen as motivating. Some perceptions are, of course, neutral, but some are motivationally strong. But motives in the form of emotional drives are considered to have a pervasive influence on all levels, including the total breadth of sensory-cognitive processes. The latest conclusions relate emotions, perception and motivation. The result is actually a perceptual-motivational theory of emotion.

IMPLICATIONS FOR THE COUNSELOR

Every counselor uses some theory of motivation. Unless he is going to operate blindly, he needs to know the assumptions basic to his counseling effort. If he is going to decrease his failures and increase his "success," he must have a better reason than a guess why he has failed or succeeded. It is not sufficient reason for a counselor to continue to use a theory because it is familiar to him and he is comfortable with it.

Much emphasis is currently placed on the counselor's adjusting his style to the unique character of his counselee. What this means is never clearly explained. Does it mean that a counselor who believes in reinforcement theory upon occasion shifts his position to that of the nondirective counselor relying on intrinsic motivation? It is reasonable to suppose that a counselor who believes in reinforcement theory might modify the degree to which he uses reinforcement with a given counselee but not that he would or could immediately become a counselor who believes in intrinsic motivation.

One authority on motivation gives evidence of the time he spent and struggle he found in moving from the extrinsic to the intrinsic motivational position. Is it reasonable, then, to expect the counselor to really change positions without struggle? Can he do it, or is he only simulating something of which he has little knowledge, and less belief in? Certainly the counselor can adjust his method within the boundaries of what he believes — that is, what he is. To do more than this is only pretense and is perceived as such by most counselees. First, then, the counselor should be informed, should wrestle with the theory of motivation that is to be his own. Secondly, he should explore and fully use the theory that expresses his approach to life, his belief. If convincing evidence presents itself that he should change, then out of necessity and respect for himself and for the theory he should study, understand and accept it before he begins to use it.

The counselor needs to be open-minded and flexible. But to

assume the *appearance* of flexibility confuses everyone, including the counselee. For the counselor to move from one position to its antithesis is not being flexible. It is closed-minded phenotypical change on the basis of expediency.

The theory of motivation on which the counselor relies is basic to all his effort. He should be aware not only of the similarities among theories but, more and more, of the differences among them. To be as well informed about a theory in which one does not believe as he is about the one in which he does believe is not an easy attitude or task. It is much easier to assume that the differences are minimal, then to consider them minor, and finally to presume that they no longer exist. Counselors may fall into this error, but the authorities on the theories themselves do not.

Authorities on motivation are apparently not interested in trying to elucidate similarities. Instead they pose questions and then examine the theories to determine how well the theory answers the question. If the theory does not provide a satisfactory answer, then both the nature of the doubt and the inadequacies of the answer are explored and stated. Such a method has much to commend it to the counselor. Each counselor, in terms of his understanding and his beliefs concerning the nature of man, would do well to formulate his own questions. Such an examination might reveal to him the fact that he is attempting to use methods that are not congruent with his beliefs about man. His methods produce results, but the results are incongruent with his aims in counseling. He may discover that his methods, based on the theory he is using, hold little promise of improving the adequacy of the counselee to handle life. He will undoubtedly realize that his assumptions concerning motivation are too significant to receive only casual consideration. He could become more intelligent concerning himself and the probable effects his particular theory or theories of motivation have on his counselees.

QUESTIONS

1. Explain the function of incongruity between the standard set by the individual and his actual performance.
2. How is behavioral change explained in the theory of extrinsic motivation?
3. From the philosophical viewpoint, why is the explanation of the function of incongruity not fully acceptable?

Richard C. Teevan and Robert C. Birney (eds.), *Theories of Motivation in Personality and Social Behavior* (New York: D. Van Nostrand Co., Inc., 1964).

The book contains selections from a wide range of system builders. One of its chief purposes is to illustrate the manner in which motivational questions are subject to concepts from several disparate points of view. They provide for the student a broad panorama of points of view, ranging from the conception of motivation as a set of prime movers to that of motivation as a set of derived behaviors.

John L. Fuller, *Motivation, A Biological Perspective* (New York: Random House, 1963).

The author encompasses the area of motivation and integrates the contributions of biology and psychology in relation to the usual problems in motivation. It is assumed that only indirectly, if at all, can many aspects of behavior be related to stimuli arising from tissue needs within the organism. One of the chief arguments of the book is that the physiological diversity of these needs entails a corresponding diversity of psychological consequences. The general position taken is that motives vary to the extent to which they are related to tissue need, to internal sensitizing agents such as hormones, to perception of the external world, and to individual experience. Each person is considered more or less unique in these respects.

Edward J. Murray, *Motivation and Emotion* (Englewood Cliffs, N.J.: Prentice-Hall, Inc., 1964).

The author views man as a complex biosocial organism. He explains his approach to the subject of motivation and emotion as "pluralistic and integrative." He considers this approach best because it avoids too great simplification, on the one hand, and too great certainty, on the other. His treatment of all the current theories is well balanced and emphasizes the inadequacies of the theoretical framework of human behavior. Through lucid writing, pictures and diagrams he demonstrates that the laboratory, field and clinical studies are all valid complementary sources of knowledge. He directs the reader to the continuing need for more research and study, and involves him in the never-ending struggle for understanding.

11

CHANGE IN BEHAVIOR

Many have expressed doubts that human behavior can be changed. Indeed, some consider any attempt to change behavior in an individual beyond adolescence a hopeless undertaking. When Winston Churchill in 1946 examined what had happened to an august Roman Empire and later to a Christian civilization, he asked, "Are we to sink through gradations of infinite suffering to primordial levels — or can we avoid our doom?"

It would appear that we in the nineteen sixties are taking a more positive view. We are more in accord with Nietzsche's affirmation that "Man is a recurring decimal." That is, you can never work him out. You may continue to divide, but each figure that you get, far from being the end, is simply a new beginning. We need to be open to new insights.

Our present optimism is partly an echo of our recognition of the desperate need for and faith in the ability to change. This recognition has led to several questionable and often conflicting results: (1) the tendency to consider the problem of change much too superficially, (2) the assumption that all change is of equal value as long as it is in a constructive direction, (3) the tendency to consider the reason for change in an individual unimportant, and (4) the view of change itself as a simple and understandable variable.

Change is considered to be a developmental, continuous process in response to both external and internal energizers. Change may be constructive or destructive from any one of a number of viewpoints — neurological, physiological, psychological, sociological, philosophical or religious.

A satisfactory definition of behavior is almost impossible to achieve. The problem frequently revolves around how to distinguish the behavior studied by *psychology* from that examined from other viewpoints, such as *physiology* and *neurology*. The approach suggested here is to consider behavior an organismic or integrated total response of the organism, but at the same time to emphasize the psychological or other components. In actuality, of course, such separations are not very meaningful, and present many dangers. The counselor frequently assumes he is dealing with all the factors of behavior when in reality he deals with only one or two kinds, e.g., psychological and sociological. He may, recognizing the complexity of behavior, place greater emphasis on the one in which he has most training and experience, but his conclusions will lack both balance and comprehensiveness. Until recently the sociopathic youth was studied from a psychological viewpoint. It is now recognized that he must also be understood from a neurological viewpoint.[1]

It is difficult to know positively that an individual has changed, because there is more than one kind of change. Counselors who have not given this fact much thought are surprised to discover that their friendly and cooperative counselee has not genuinely changed.

On the last day of school before summer vacation, Miss Randall, a ninth grade history teacher, sat with her elbows on the desk thinking of the year that was ending. She took pleasure in recalling that Eric Stoops had become such a good history student. With such interest she could already see him as a vital man occupying a prominent place in society. Later, as she walked down the hall, her eye fell on a strangely familiar notebook in the waste basket. She was right, it was Eric Stoops' history notebook. When she asked him about it the next day, he was a bit defensive. Finally he explained it this way: "Well, I made an 'A' grade, didn't I, and now I'm through with the course." This response was quite disillusioning to Miss Randall, but what Eric said revealed what had happened — or hadn't happened. The apparent change was not genuine change. It was a superficial, conforming kind of change on the basis of expediency. This kind of change is termed "phenotypical" change. It can, and often does, appear real, but it is really based upon expediency or opportunism, or occurs because there is practically no alternative. "Genotypical" change is genuine, the result of the individual's wrestling with experience when change and its direction are his to choose.

[1] Stanley Krippner, "Diagnostic and Educational Dimensions of the Sociopathic Child," Unpublished paper presented at the American Personnel and Guidance Association meeting, Washington, D.C., 1966.

THE PSYCHOLOGICAL EMPHASIS

Conditions Conducive to Change

Genuine change in behavior does not take place without *total involvement*. Psychologically, this means that the individual is involved on the cognitive, conative and motoric levels; that is, his involvement consists of his thinking, perception, meaning, feeling, and the action implied in carrying out the decisions. This parallels the thinking of Charles Sanders Peirce that in the psychology of the act is first, feeling, second, action and third, thought.[2] Samuel Beck concludes that "We cannot know without the intellect; we do not know until we experience with the emotions." [3] The need for total involvement is generally accepted. Philosophy would include in it the functioning of the will, and on occasion conscience, and religion would add self-transcendence.

A second accepted conclusion is that change takes place *within a framework*. When basically related perceptions change, the person changes. A change of any consequence requires a basic restructuring of values if it is to endure. Kipnis in her research demonstrates that to strengthen an individual's spelling, it is necessary to improve his self-concept as well as to work on his spelling.[4]

A third conclusion is that a new response is more likely to be integrated when it is perceived to bear some close relation to a previous situation that has proved satisfactory.

Charles, a bright fifth-grader, was aggressive in many ways. He pulled down and tore the other children's posters. He lay on the floor or on a table. He interrupted, frequently supplying excellent ideas. It was decided to place Charles alone with one of the teachers who worked with the group. After they had met several times and worked on a project, part of a whole that the class had planned, Charles was encouraged to ask another boy from the original group to work with him. After good relations had been established and had endured for a number of consecutive times, Charles was again

[2] Charles Sanders Peirce, "The Psychology of the Act," in *The Collected Papers*.

[3] Samuel Beck, "Emotional Experience as a Necessary Constituent in Knowing," in Martin L. Reymert (ed.), *Feelings and Emotions* (New York: McGraw-Hill Book Co., Inc., 1950), pp. 59–108.

[4] Dorothy M. Kipnis, "Changes in Self Concepts in Relation to Perceptions of Others," *Journal of Personality*, 1961, Vol. 29, pp. 449–465.

encouraged to invite in another boy. After he had formed good working relationships with a number of the boys and some girls, the idea was suggested that this small group rejoin the large group from which they had come. The total group, including Charles, now proceeded quite normally.

All theorists virtually agree that there are three stages in the change process if the change is to be maintained. The first stage has been called "unfreezing." This is the stage of disequilibrium. The second stage has been named "moving," and the third, "freezing." One stage does not necessarily ensure the next. Certain conditions must be met in each stage. It is necessary to analyze each situation in order to determine those conditions which are most likely to prove useful.

When Does the Counselee Change?

The individual is most likely to change when he experiences dissatisfaction within himself — that is, when he is in a state of disequilibrium. Or, as discussed in the preceding chapter on "Motivation," change is likely when there is neither too much nor too little incongruity between what he experiences as his actual self and what he desires to be. If there is too much incongruity he may become discouraged or withdraw from the prospect. If too little, he may not consider the desired change worth the effort.[5] The counselee who is uncomfortable enough to ask for help from a counselor is therefore more likely to benefit from counseling.

Disequilibrium may arise from many sources, from curiosity, from the wish to escape from boredom, from identification (wanting to be like someone), from genuine acceptance and love towards someone, or received from someone, from anxiety in many forms.

It is one of the paradoxes that genuine change does not take place unless the new set of values are freely chosen by the individual or group. Genuine change takes place when the individual is free to do otherwise.[6]

One of the boys in a group just before counseling began, said to

[5] J. Hunt, "Intrinsic Motivation and Its Role in Psychological Development," in David Levine (ed.), *Nebraska Symposium on Motivation* (Lincoln: University of Nebraska Press, 1965), pp. 189–283.
[6] Kurt Lewin and Paul Grabbe, "Conduct, Knowledge and Acceptance of New Values," *Journal of Social Issues,* 1945, Vol. 1, pp. 45–64.

the counselor, "Are you a Jew?" The counselor replied that he was of Jewish background. In the session the boy sat next to the counselor and drew a picture which he shoved over so that the counselor could not avoid seeing it. It was a picture of a man hanging from a cross, with blood dripping all around and fighter planes zooming in from above. The counselor accepted the picture without comment and continued the group counseling session. After the session the boy remained and offered to carry the counselor's brief case to his car.

Since the individual lives and has his being in several groups, he is less likely to change if by so doing he becomes less acceptable to the groups from which he receives emotional support. Many counselors seem to assume that the individual is more likely to change in individual counseling than in working with groups. However, experience in leadership training, changing food habits, work production, criminality, alcoholism, and prejudices all indicate that it is easier for some individuals to change when formed into a group than to change separately. The individual has more inducement to think outwardly in a group and inwardly in individual counseling. Such findings suggest that the counselors should give more attention to the possibilities of group counseling.

How Does Change Take Place?

There are two main streams of thought about the nature of change. The first is that change takes place primarily through some kind of reinforcement of cues as viewed by the counselor. The second is that change is the result of a choice freely made by the counselee. Those who support the first approach believe that elimination of the symptoms is crucial and that appropriate changes in the cognitive processes will follow it. They also believe that behavioral change will result from changes in the cognitive processes. Since change is thus considered to be involved chiefly with the intellectual processes, this tends to be a "rather impersonal, highly manipulative, ahistorical, symptom-reducing orientation." [7] Most therapists in this school of thought, with the possible exception of Wolfe,[8] place small importance on the interpersonal relationship in the process of change.

[7] Leonard D. Goodstein, "Behavior: Theoretical View of Counseling," in Buford Stefflre (ed.), *Theories of Counseling* (New York: McGraw-Hill Book Co., Inc., 1963), pp. 140–192.
[8] J. Wolfe, *Psychotherapy by Reciprocal Inhibition* (Stanford, Calif.: Stanford University Press, 1958).

The second stream of thought places importance on the total involvement and free choice of the individual. Its advocates assume that as the individual gains insight into himself and his behavior, he will choose to think and act in terms of his newly developing self-concept. In contrast to the first, which places primary emphasis on the cognitive, the second approach places emphasis on the integration of the emotional (values and valences), cognitive (thinking, perception and memory) and motoric, with special emphasis on the emotional.[9] Lewin and Grabbe discuss this second position in this manner: "The re-educative process affects the individual in three ways. It changes his cognitive structure, the way he sees the physical and social worlds, including all his facts, concepts, beliefs and expectations. It modifies his valences and values and these embrace both his attractions and aversions to groups and group standards, his feelings in regard to status differences, and his reactions to sources of approval or disapproval. And it affects motoric action, involving the degree of the individual's control over his physical and social movements." [10]

The first or *reinforcement approach* to changing behavior relies upon *extrinsic motivation* and the use of various methods applied by the change agent (the person who assumes direct responsibility for securing desirable change from his viewpoint in an individual or group).

The theory of *intrinsic motivation* (self-change) relies upon the individual's perception of the incongruity between the actual and the desirable. It assumes that he will progress toward a goal, which he will choose, and that he has the capability of examining and evaluating the related alternatives. Experience indicates that both methods can be relied upon to bring about change. Each theory should be questioned. One critical question is: What *kind* of change? The change may be phenotypical for some of the following reasons. (1) It is in conformance to the wishes of the change agent. (2) It is made for the purpose of gaining some temporary opportunistic goal. (3) It is effected through the repression of self-knowledge and identification with the change agent. (4) It is made because of the fear of doing otherwise. (5) It is made because the counselee has come to believe that he loses identity and meaning unless he accepts the prevailing viewpoint of authority.

Or it may be genotypical for some of the following reasons: (1) The counselee has examined and re-examined the issues and consulted various authorities (teachers, principal, parents, counse-

[9] Hunt, *op. cit.*
[10] Lewin and Grabbe, *op. cit.*, p. 56.

lor), and has arrived at his own conclusion. (2) The counselee respected the reactions of the counselor but did not feel impelled to be guided only by them. (3) The counselee, after thought and study, found himself in agreement with the position he perceived the counselor to have. (4) The counselee examined the ideas he gained in talking with the counselor but although they were logical and made good sense, he himself preferred to do otherwise.

A second question is: What is the *meaning* of the change to the one who changes? The same behavior may well have a different meaning to each person. For example, two counselors work with high school students — one because he views it as a good way to earn the money he needs, the other primarily because he views it as an opportunity to be of service in helping youth to live more satisfying lives. Two students, following counseling, remain in high school. One remains because he concludes that he cannot leave high school without criticism and rejection, the other, because he has found a goal toward which he wants to progress. Both do satisfactory work, but the meaning of life to each is greatly different. The counselor who cares is interested in the meaning of the change to the counselee.

THE PHILOSOPHICAL VIEWPOINT

The interest of philosophy in behavioral change has focused upon such topics as "inner choice," imagination, symbolism, love, will and conscience, all of which have been discussed in earlier chapters. Although these concepts are difficult to measure, they are nevertheless recognized as playing an important part in behavioral change.

The "Inner Choice"

The concept of the "inner choice" is a factor in the change of behavior that has long been recognized. It has been referred to in many ways, for example, "When he came to himself." The assumption is that something discrete exerts a commanding influence over the thinking and imagination of the individual and leads to changed action. This is sometimes referred to as the level of aspiration, the highest goal of the individual. In the theory of intrinsic motivation, it is the recognition of the incongruence between the actual state of the individual and his ideal self. The problem focuses upon the energization of this level of aspiration. Is it completely the result of learning experience, or is there also something innate? Science and philosophy come to a parting of the ways on this question. Both agree that the learning experiences should not be underestimated. Philosophy and religion would ask that an open mind be kept towards the possibility that something may be influential here that is not fully understood. This is a point of view that the counselor should not disregard. It could help him to maintain a more realistic expectancy concerning the counselee. It may help him to stay within the framework of a learner in his relationships, and generate an attitude more helpful with the complexity and unpredictability of human nature.

Imagination

Imagination is another variable worthy of consideration by the counselor. Psychologists and philosophers agree that imagination has an important function in the change of behavior. Analytical thought and feeling require imagination, which brings the future into the present and makes realization possible. Through it, we live vicariously in situations and exercise better judgment in our choices. Imaginative accomplishment adds a sense of possibility and provides attitudinal preparation for the task ahead. That imagination can serve in this fashion appears to agree with the findings of William James, who wrote, "The subjective difference between imagined and felt objects is less absolute than has been claimed, and the cortical processes which underlie imagination and sensation are not quite as discrete as one at first is tempted to suppose." [11] Imagination connects the field of sensation with the intellectual sphere, and supplies the means whereby future plans can be submitted to the scrutiny of the understanding.

"There is no human impulse or appetite, no desire or inclination, no striving or struggling after an ideal that is not accompanied or led by an image of the end to be accomplished, however vague this image may be, or whatever meaning may be inherent in it. Images are the impelling forces in all our actions. Our inner life is determined by images, produced by practical imagination." [12] For this reason a philosopher of distinction places imagination at the center of change in behavior. It should be recognized, of course, that imagination may produce images of defeat as well as images of courage.

The character of imagination differs among people. One may use

[11] William James, *Principles of Psychology* (New York: Holt, Rinehart & Winston, Inc., 1950), Vol. 2, p. 72.
[12] Richard Kroner, *The Religious Function of the Imagination* (New Haven: Yale University Press, 1941), pp. 7–9.

as his method reproductive imagination, which leads him to a method of interpretation that Jung has called reproductive.[13] This form of imagination and method focuses upon the past and the manifest content. Such a method is immediately visible, thoroughly intelligible, and for certain temperaments sufficiently satisfying to obviate any need for deeper understanding. Meanings so derived, however, are only sign meanings.

On the other hand, one may use productive imagination, which leads to a method of interpretation that is purposive. This does not ignore either the past or manifest content, but transcends them in a manner that permits them to point to other meanings in which they participate — i.e., permits symbolic meanings to arise.

To engage in the use of purposive or productive imagination is a challenging and threatening endeavor. Rokeach, in his Doodlebug Experiments,[14] found that those with relatively closed belief systems tried to solve the problem by the use of standard procedures — that is, by reproductive imagination. Those with an open belief system solved the problem by the use of productive imagination, which overcame the standard "sets" or old belief systems, making the generation of new systems possible.

Signs and Symbols

Signs and symbols have an important function in our lives. The nature of the goal and the change which ensues are functions of whether the person entertains a sign or a symbolic meaning in reaching out toward the new. This was in part the message of Nietzsche. He tried to arouse his fellow men to rise above the "sign" living of the times. He encouraged man to be a creator, to assert his humanness. He hoped for a new man beyond his nineteenth century, a man who would have the courage to shape the very symbols and meanings by which he would live.

The degree to which a person entertains the possibility of symbolic meaning is in part a function of his learning experience. It would appear that more attention in our teaching should be given to symbolic thinking. A college professor discussing the difficulty of decision-making used this kind of thinking as part of his illustration. He said to the students, "This great doctor spent a week in

[13] Carl Jung, *Psychological Types* (New York: Harcourt, Brace & World, Inc., 1923), p. 577.
[14] Milton Rokeach, *The Open and Closed Mind* (New York: Basic Books, Inc., 1960), Chapter 8.

the wilderness trying to decide what to do about his patient." When he paused, one student said, "Seems to me like a good excuse to take a vacation." Amid the suppressed laughter, another said, "Where did he go?" and a third added, "I know a good spot in Oregon." The meaning of life to these students and the inducements to change must be recognized as somewhat different than for those who, when the situation demands it, see meaning in terms of symbols, which add a depth to life that signs cannot offer. The more we perceive all aspects of life in terms of signs, the more superficial is our living. Our change in behavior is also superficial if it is in terms of "horizontal" meanings.

The inclination to think symbolically may be strengthened by an open belief system. Those with an open belief system are more able to include symbolic meaning in their consideration of change. For they are able to tolerate ambiguity, and this is one of the characteristics of those who recognize the symbol that points to, and participates in, that which cannot be fully understood. Those with closed belief systems may reject, distort, or ignore any indication that a situation may have intrinsic symbolic meaning.

Change Through Interaction

The interaction of imagination and sign or symbolic thinking influences change in behavior. When the person thinks with the use of signs, he makes use of reproductive imagination. He engages his imagination to visualize what has been and may be the outcomes of his thinking. This kind of thinking is unlikely to initiate the new, except perhaps incidentally. The power lawn-mower stops. The operator knows that the motor uses gas. His imagination proposes to him that the gas tank is empty. This is reproductive imagination. This is a kind of imagination which finds wide and useful application.

Some third grade girls and boys were asked if they could name a symbol. Their response was "a wedding ring." When asked why they thought that a wedding ring was a symbol, they said that it meant love, that the two people loved each other and that love was something about which there was always more. We could never know all about love. This kind of thinking and use of imagination is different. It is being willing to live with ideas instead of answers. It leads to developing thought and feeling. It holds the possibility of uniting the old and the new. The change in behavior that results is open-ended, with developing levels of aspiration and the expectancy of an unfolding universe.

A counselor complained recently of the unrealistic attitude of some of his counselees. "Imagine," he said, "John with an IQ of 120 and in his circumstances (father in lower income bracket) wanting to be a medical doctor." This may have been a situation in which the counselor was using reproductive imagination and "old sets." To John being a medical doctor could have been a symbol — a symbol of doing his part to reduce the misery of the world, concerning which he already had some understanding.

Love

Love has always been considered a strong change agent. Because of the love of or for another, many a person has changed his outlook on life. Our love for someone provides the condition in which change in the person loved has the optimum chance of taking place. Rogerian counselors believe that the counselor's love (deep understanding and acceptance) provides the climate in which constructive change can take place.

Love reduced to a sign loses its power to exert a meaningful and necessary depth influence in life. As a symbol, it is recognized as the most powerful influence conducive to constructive change in the individual. But since its power is so recognized, there is a strong inclination for counselors to simulate a kind of caring for the counselee. This transparent simulation may hamper more than it helps.

As indicated in earlier chapters, a comprehensive view of behavioral change from the philosophic viewpoint includes the place and function of the will and conscience. Regardless of how the counselor might describe or fail to describe their existence and functioning, he should not completely reject either as agents in the change process.

CONCLUSIONS

Change in behavior is a most important area of study for the counselor, and one of the most difficult to understand. Difficulties arise in meanings, assumptions, processes, evaluation and outcomes. Authorities agree in a few respects, but disagree in many. However, it may well be that the counselor who is a student in this area can lead us toward new insights.

Change may be phenotypical, having all the appearances of genuineness, but lacking any reorganization of values. It may also be genotypical, genuine change, which has resulted from a working through and reorganization of the individual's value system. Change may commence by being phenotypical, a matter of expediency or the perceived necessity of conforming to the demands of another. But the values and behavior resulting from such introjection may be re-examined and evaluated by the person at his own bidding and finally accepted on its own merits. At this point the individual engages in more integrative change.

Change, to be genuine, requires the involvement of the person on all levels of his being. This means at least on the cognitive, conative and motoric levels. If insights from philosophy are considered, the functioning of the will and conscience will have to be accepted as playing some not clearly defined part. Such total involvement is not easily attained, partly because it takes place within the person to be changed.

There is disagreement about how total involvement and resulting change come into being. It is agreed generally that some disequilibrium exists as an unsatisfied need. Extrinsic rewards or punishments are sometimes used as a means of need reduction. Educators, parents and others present to children the advantages of an education. This need on the part of the child having been established through introjection, either to satisfy those in authority over him or because he dimly recognizes some of the advantages of education, the child conforms to the wishes of the teachers. Many, then, are engaged in satisfying the need of their teachers and society in general. To ensure the continuance of this, they are placed in a competitive situation and rewarded through grades and honor rolls. It is disheartening to teachers that such a small number of youth, when left to make their own decision, choose to return to school in the evening to be assisted by teachers in their studies.

Those who use some method of reinforcement rely on identification and the reward system for the introjection of their ideas to have an effect. The rationale for this procedure is based on one or more of the following assumptions: (1) learning does take place; (2) the counselor or teacher knows what is best for the counselee or student; (3) the counselee or student is incapable or unfamiliar with the necessary sources. Controversy focuses on the quality of learning. Can we be sure that we know what is best for another? Can we assume that the learner is incapable unless he is provided many opportunities to demonstrate his capability and interest?

Those who rely on intrinsic motivation are skeptical of the kind of change produced by reinforcement or extrinsic motivational methods. They are inclined to view such change as phenotypical. Intrinsic motivation theorists believe that an individual genuinely changes only when he is free to do otherwise. These theorists view their function as setting a climate in which the individual experiences the meaning of this assumption. They assume that the individual is or can become aware of what he desires to be and attain. They also believe that once the individual recognizes the incongruence between what he actually is and what it is that he really desires to be, this recognition will stimulate its own motivation. The decision and the recompense is within the person who is more truly confronting reality.

A comprehensive attempt to discuss change in behavior should encompass consideration of such intangibles as will, conscience, imagination, symbols and love. Although these are commonly recognized as influential in behavioral change, their specific influence evades exact description. Love has long been recognized as the most dynamic, powerful relationship known to man. It is also the most difficult to understand and to attain as a guiding influence in one's life. Although to truly love requires a maturity that we move toward with great difficulty, we do so knowing that it is more than worth the struggle for all engaged.

Change in behavior is intricate and complex. It encompasses the whole individual and such understanding as we possess is dependent upon insights from many disciplines. The counselor would do well to cultivate a humble and studious approach in his endeavor to improve his knowledge and understanding of what is taking place within the counselee.

QUESTIONS

1. What are some of the problems of the counselor as he tries to determine whether or not the counselee has changed?
2. Why do the theorists who rely on extrinsic motivation differ in their concept of the conditions of change from those who rely on intrinisic motivation?
3. What must be the character of the involvement for genuine change to take place?
4. What is the function of imagination in change of behavior?

FOR FURTHER READING

Kenneth D. Benne and Muntyan Bozidar, *Human Relations in Curriculum Change* (New York: Dryden Press, 1951).

Change in curriculum is considered to be primarily dependent upon change in persons — that is, change in the teachers, students, parents, laymen and administrators. This book explores in depth the different kinds and aspects of change. The authors describe these as change in knowledge, in values, in activity, and in skills. Also involved are changes in the relationships among personnel which change in program requirements. If the change is comprehensive it requires new reciprocal relations among all those involved. The means, therefore, of influencing change in the relations of people are also studied. The approach to social change in this book of readings is that of the participant in change who is seeking dependable relationships. The value system incorporated in the readings is democratic, and it is assumed that these values are safeguarded in a process of change only when they are conscious and explicit.

Bill L. Kell and William J. Mueller, *Impact and Change* (New York: Appleton-Century-Crofts, Inc., 1966).

This book presents a theory of change in persons based upon the experiences of the counseling relationship. Its purpose is to communicate a viewpoint on how change takes place in such a manner that the reader may experience it himself. It reflects the authors' own processes of anxiety, discovery, further anxiety, renewed discovery or rediscovery, and the final tentative integration of their theory. The book is unusual in that the reader enters into the struggle of understanding the changes in the counselee as if he were the counselor himself.

Association for Supervision and Curriculum Development Yearbook Committee, Arthur W. Combs (chm.), *Perceiving, Behaving, Becoming* (Washington, D.C.: Association for Supervision and Curriculum Development, 1962).

This book asks the reader to put aside the conception of the norm as the healthy person. It probes instead for some ideas concerning what would be the characteristics of a person who has reached a high degree of self-actualization. The primary purpose is to explore the factors that enter into the development of a person who fulfills his human potential. Four outstanding authorities have contributed chapters of penetrating insight.

12

DECISION MAKING

A PSYCHOLOGICAL POINT OF VIEW

In any situation that requires a decision there are relevant and irrelevant factors. To consider only relevant factors requires evaluation and action based on the intrinsic elements in relation to the requirements of the situation. The use of irrelevant factors lowers the quality and usefulness of the decision. Irrelevant factors take many forms, such as anxiety and the need for acceptance. These are heightened by the pressures of reward and punishment that may be exerted by peers, parents, other authority figures, and cultural and institutional norms. Other factors also affect the quality of the decision. Some decision making requires a high degree of tolerance for ambiguity. Else Frenkel-Brunswik found that as a result of the early parent-child relationships there is wide variance in the ability of youth to tolerate ambiguity, and that this emotional and social ambivalence manifests itself in the cognitive spheres (thinking, perception and memory).[1] Postman and his associates concluded from their research that the individual sets up a perceptual defense against adverse stimuli.[2]

There is also required an ability to perceive and examine evidence that is incompatible with one's own viewpoint. Such evidence may be narrowed, distorted, or even rejected. As Allport[3] observed in

[1] Else Frenkel-Brunswik, "Intolerance of Ambiguity as an Emotional Perceptual Personality Variable," *Journal of Personality*, 1949, Vol. 18, pp. 108–143.

[2] L. Postman, J. Bruner and E. McGinis, "Personal Values as Selective Factors in Perception," *Journal of Abnormal and Social Psychology*, 1948, Vol. 48, pp. 142–154.

[3] Gordon W. Allport and Leo Postman, *The Psychology of Rumor* (New York: Holt, Rinehart & Winston, Inc., 1947).

his study of rumor, some details are obliterated and others falsified, since the force of the intellectual and emotional context leads to *the assimilation of ideas in accordance with the value system of the individual*. This, Maslow concludes, wards off threatening aspects of reality and at the same time provides the individual with a compensatory feeling that he understands it.[4]

Such behavioral descriptions suggest that the quality of thought is influenced by emotions. When important decisions have to be made, the hope is often expressed that the decision makers will be able to keep "open minds." When we wish to express ourselves favorably concerning the decision making of a colleague, we say, "John has an open mind on the subject." The chairman of a committee may suggest, "Let us take an open-minded approach to this matter." The administrator insists, "We must be open-minded about this." Such expressions indicate a belief that certain factors may lower the quality of thought and decision making.

It is also assumed that a discriminative difference exists between those who have relatively "open" minds and those who have relatively "closed" minds, that this difference is overt, recognizable in the performance and the outcome of the interrelationship of cognition and feeling. An individual with an open mind can be expected to differ in his thinking and procedure from one with a closed mind. The difference is apparent in the making of decisions.

The interaction between emotional and cognitive variables suggests a difference in critical thinking between those with relatively closed and those with relatively open belief systems. This was tested in a study by the author.[5] The sample was a total of 500 male and female freshman students from three church-related colleges and one large state university. Of these, the 150 with more closed belief systems and the 150 with more open belief systems were selected through the use of the Dogmatism Scale Form E. By means of a pilot study, 50 discriminating items were selected as a test of critical thinking. It was discovered that those who had relatively open belief systems were superior at the .01 level in critical thinking to those with relatively closed belief systems. It was concluded that those with closed belief systems have a higher percentage of errors in problems that require the study of several factors of criteria for decision and that call for the deferment of a conclusion until judicious

[4] A. H. Maslow, *Motivation and Personality* (New York: Harper & Row, Publishers, Inc., 1954).
[5] C. Gratton Kemp, "Effect of Dogmatism on Critical Thinking," *School Science and Mathematics*, April 1960.

consideration has been given to each factor. Apparently the highly dogmatic person has difficulty in tolerating ambiguities, and is thus impelled toward a "closure" before full consideration is given to each piece of contributing evidence. This sometimes results in the perceptual distortion of facts and in a conclusion that does not encompass examination of all elements of the problem. The degree of openness of the belief system, then, is directly related to the quality of decision making.

A DECISION-MAKING MODEL

The theory of the open and closed belief systems was developed and tested by Milton Rokeach. His work was based on the thinking of the nineteen forties and fifties, in much of which there was a focus on the measurement of *single* beliefs and attitudes. Rokeach studied belief systems and attitude systems. He explains the rationale for his approach in these words: "In our view much of man's social behavior can be better understood by relating such behavior to man's belief systems rather than to the elements of such systems." Therefore the focus of his research became "the organization of belief systems, the openness-closedness of a belief system accepting and rejecting a system, entertaining a system, synthesizing beliefs into a new system, changing a system, and loyalty to and defection from a system." [6]

Rokeach views this theory as making a needed contribution to the understanding of behavior. He considers Gestalt theory to have contributed to the extent that man has open belief systems, and psychoanalysis and behaviorism to the extent that man's belief systems are closed. But none of these theories help greatly in understanding the many people whose beliefs systems are neither open nor closed.

It is possible that Allport,[7] Fromm,[8] Maslow,[9] Rogers[10] and White[11] have placed too much emphasis on man's *cognitive needs*

[6] Milton Rokeach, *The Open and Closed Mind* (New York: Basic Books, Inc., 1960), pp. 18–19.
[7] Gordon W. Allport, *Becoming: Basic Considerations for a Psychology of Personality* (New Haven: Yale University Press, 1953), Section 4A.
[8] Erich Fromm, *Man for Himself* (New York: Holt, Rinehart & Winston, Inc., 1947).
[9] Maslow, *op. cit.*
[10] Carl Rogers, *Client-Centered Therapy* (Boston: Houghton Mifflin Company, 1951).
[11] R. W. White, "Motivation Reconsidered: The Concept of Competence," *Psychological Review,* 1959, Vol. 66, pp. 297–333.

and his tendencies toward growth, productiveness and self-actualization. Rokeach takes the position that man is "driven by both rational and rationalizing forces." He therefore assumes that "all belief-disbelief systems serve two powerful and conflicting sets of motives at the same time: the need for a cognitive framework to know and to understand, and the need to ward off threatening aspects of reality." [12] Such a position avoids the danger of overemphasis on the image of man as rational and self-actualizing.

Definition

A description of the model of decision making as viewed within the theory of the open and closed mind will begin with a definition. The extent to which a person's system is open or closed is "the extent to which the person can receive, evaluate, and act on relevant information received from the outside on its own intrinsic merits, unencumbered by irrelevant factors in the situation arising from within the person or from the outside." [13]

Some irrelevant factors that interfere with the realistic reception and examination of information are unrelated habits, beliefs and perceptual cues, irrational ego motives, power needs, the need for self-aggrandizement, and the need to allay anxiety. Another external factor is authority such as that exerted by parents, peers, teachers, counselors, principals or other authority figures, reference groups, social and institutional norms, and cultural norms.

People with open minds proceed differently from those with more closed minds. The more open the belief system the more one proceeds to *evaluate and act on information independently on the basis of its own merits,* in accord with the requirements of the situation. The open-minded person is also governed more by internal self-actualizing forces and less by irrational inner forces. Such a person has more psychic energy and more initiative in resisting external pressures to evaluate and act in accordance with another's wishes. He resists also the externally imposed reinforcements of rewards and punishments.

Donald went to elementary school in a New England village. His father had not been educated beyond high school, and had ambitions for his son to become a scientist. However, he significantly added, "You may not want to be a scientist, and of course you know that any honest work you do will be all right with me." Donald did

[12] Rokeach, *op. cit.*, p. 66.
[13] *Ibid.*

well in school; he was considered by his teachers one of the brightest boys in his group of 30 or 40. He attended high school in a much larger town, worked diligently and made good grades, but he was slightly disturbed to discover that he was not among the brightest in the class. His parents too, were perturbed. When he entered college, his father said, "Your mother and I still hope you'll be a scientist, but if it is not in the cards, that'll be all right."

At college he was competing with a much more select group and although he continued to work, at the end of his freshman year his grades were all B's and C's. At this point he went to a college counselor. After interviews and testing, he learned that his I.Q. was about 120 and that his interests strongly resembled those of a science teacher in elementary or high school. In discussing the situation he said, "My father always planned that I would be a scientist. I wasn't sure myself, and at times felt that there was something else I might do. Of course, my parents always left me a free hand to decide. They said as long as it was honest it would be O.K. I'd like to think more about this and come back. Right now, it seems to me that to plan to be a science teacher might be a good idea."

Donald made a realistic adjustment. When we examine his experience closely it is apparent that he respected and lived close to his feelings and desires. His home relationships were sufficiently permissive and understanding that the views of his parents as well as his own were available to his self-awareness.

The more closed the belief system, the less adequately the individual distinguishes between the information received about the world and the information received about the source. To the extent that he cannot and does not distinguish between the two kinds of information, he is not free to receive, evaluate and act on information in terms of the intrinsic requirements. The closed-minded person is less able to think for himself.

This was the case with John. For years the father had talked of his son John's becoming a medical doctor. John liked and admired his father. He introjected his father's ideas, and gradually came to think of them as his own. His intelligence was average compared with college students, but his experiences of increasing tension during examinations disturbed him. When he reflected upon his goal of becoming a medical doctor, it appeared to agree with his basic desire. He did not realize that he had never symbolized his own desire but had merely accepted that of his father. He considered this vocational aim in relation to the value placed on it by society and by his father.

He concluded that he should work harder and make better grades. However, his grades were predominantly C's and D's. This scholastic record intensified his attitude of inferiority. He felt inadequate in social groups and believed that he was disliked by others. He resented this and struck out verbally against his associates. If John had been more open-minded he would have examined the facts according to their intrinsic worth. He would have considered his grades, his I.Q., and his feeling concerning his efforts, and he would likely have made a realistic adjustment toward a wider acceptance of himself and others.[14]

Belief-Disbelief Systems

Each person has countless beliefs, and each belief has a counterpart in a set of disbeliefs. On the one hand, there is a system of beliefs that one accepts and, on the other, a series of systems that one rejects. The disbelief system is more than the mirror image of the belief system. For example, the client-centered counselor accepts one set of beliefs and rejects several others. "The belief system is conceived to represent all the beliefs, sets, expectancies or hypotheses, conscious and unconscious, that a person at a given time accepts as true of the world he lives in. The disbelief system is composed of a series of subsystems rather than merely a single one, and contains all the disbeliefs, sets, expectancies, conscious and unconscious, that to one degree or another, a person at a given time rejects as false." [15]

The framework in which the beliefs and disbeliefs are expressed is a system. However, the term "system" suggests a logical relationship among parts. The parts of this system *may be* related logically, but they are also related psychologically. The potential for relationship is there, but the relationship that exists is not dependent upon logic. In fact, the parts may be isolated and compartmentalized, which in a sense is a description of their relationship. This condition leads to incorrect predictions concerning behavior.

The belief-disbelief system is more than a scientific, religious or political system. Krech and Crutchfield [16] remind us that we commit

[14] C. Gratton Kemp, "The Open Mind and Mental Health," *Journal of Human Relations*, 1961, Vol. 9, pp. 430–432.
[15] Rokeach, *op. cit.*, p. 57.
[16] D. Krech and R. S. Crutchfield, *Theory and Problems of Social Psychology* (New York; McGraw-Hill Book Co., Inc., 1948).

the "logical error" to include each and every belief and disbelief of every sort the person may have built up about the physical and social universe he lives in. We mean it to represent each man's total framework for understanding his universe as best he can.

The belief-disbelief systems have other properties that vary from one person to another. At times we have noticed that a person may believe in one idea or principle and express disbelief in another that is intrinsically related to it. To the degree that the person is reluctant to recognize and accept the interrelatedness, we say that *the two beliefs are isolated from each other*. They are potentially in communication but, for this individual, not actually in communication.

Isolation expresses itself in various ways. There is the counselor who professes belief in client-centered counseling but, because it doesn't work for some, uses reinforcement practices; and there is the teacher who believes that each student should be treated as a unique individual but who grades on the curve. Such expressions of clearly contradictory beliefs are indications of isolation in the belief system.

Or consider the scientist who feels the validity of the structural principles of science threatened by those who hint that science is unable to explain some things. He insists on his position and refuses to see any similarities between his point of view and that of his adversary. There is also the counselor who insists that counseling and teaching are very different and refuses to accept any delineation of their similarities.

Such accentuations of difference are *attempts to evade a threat to the validity of one's own system*. The accentuation of differences and minimization of similarities between belief and disbelief systems is, from a structural viewpoint, one form of isolation.

Another method of keeping one's own system intact is to claim that an idea, proposal, plan, or method is *irrelevant* when, if judged by objective standards, it might well be relevant. How frequently a student with some creative imagination is made to feel that his contribution is irrelevant since it does not conform to the preconceived idea of the teacher's plans. Another indication of the open-closedness of the belief systems is the *amount of differentiation*. How well and to what extent is the person familiar with that which he believes or disbelieves? How comprehensive is his knowledge, how rich the detail regarding his total system? Or, specifically, an inquiry into amount of differentiation would focus on (1) the degree of differentiation of the belief system, (2) the disbelief system, and (3) each of the several disbelief subsystems. A third important consideration is the amount of knowledge one has concerning what he believes in and what he does not believe in. For example, so many of our citizens know so much more about democracy than they know about communism.

The theoretical model of the open and closed mind is organized along two dimensions: the *central-intermediate-peripheral dimension* and the *time-perspective dimension*.

In brief, the *central region* represents the "primitive" or early beliefs of the individual. These are all the beliefs the person has acquired about the nature of the physical world and the nature of the "self" and the "generalized other." The *intermediate region* represents the beliefs the person entertains about the nature of authority and authority figures with whom he is related and who shape his world. The *peripheral region* represents the beliefs derived from authority. These complete, so to speak, the details of the individual's total framework.

The time perspective dimension refers to the person's beliefs about the past, present and future and the manner in which they are related to one another.

Central-Intermediate-Peripheral Dimension of Beliefs • Each one of us has certain beliefs that are basic. They are formed in our early developing years. These are beliefs about our world whose validity we do not question and are not prepared to question. These beliefs have to do, first, with the nature of physical reality (form, sound, space, color, time) — the physical properties of the world and the world of numbers. We form early beliefs also about the social world — whether it is basically friendly or unfriendly, whether parents, teachers, counselors and other authority figures love us or hurt us, whether people in general are to be trusted or feared, and whether the future is to be eagerly welcomed or anticipated with apprehension. We form beliefs also about the self — about who we are, about our self-worth, about our autonomy or dependence on others.

These descriptions will serve to clarify what is meant by the central region and our primitive beliefs. Primitive beliefs can be looked at from another viewpoint. Among our many beliefs there

[17] Based upon Rokeach, *op. cit.*, pp. 140ff.

are those which we and a few others may hold. On the other hand, we assume that many of our beliefs are held by everyone. *Those beliefs concerning which we assume that virtually everyone else is in agreement with us are our primitive beliefs.*

Trueblood [18] clearly pictures for us how little we would know if we depended entirely upon first-hand knowledge. He describes first-hand knowledge as "extremely slight — a mere slit in the world expanse." We are therefore dependent upon authorities for the great bulk of our information. Authorities are the intermediaries to whom we turn to supplement that which each of us can obtain for himself.

The intermediate region represents our beliefs about authorities. An authority may be defined as any source to whom we look for information about the universe. All of us depend upon authorities. What distinguishes us is our ideas about the nature of authority and the use we make of authorities. Our reliance on authority, Fromm suggests, ranges from a rational, tentative reliance to extreme, arbitrary reliance. Harold Rugg used to tell his students that insights came where the disciplines crossed. For some with an arbitrary reliance on certain authorities the disciplines are never brought together.

Our beliefs about authority are of two kinds: beliefs about positive authority and beliefs about negative authority. The first guides us toward what is "true" about the world; the second suggests what is "false."

For those who place only tentative, rational reliance on authority the psychological distinction between positive and negative is not as great as that of those who have the need for arbitrary reliance. It should be noted that whereas in discussing the Central Region the interest is focused on the specific content of beliefs, the case is different with reference to the Intermediate Region. In the Intermediate Region the focus is on the formal content. Two counselors may believe in the reinforcement theory of motivation but disagree on the methods and conditions of use. This conception suggests that we look for similarities among persons in their orientations to authority even though they may adhere to different ones. Thus, theoretically, *why* one believes in authority is more indicative of his open-mindedness than the particular authority in which he believes.

We also have beliefs about people in general. *If authority is seen as absolute and final, extreme cognitive distinctions are made.*

[18] D. E. Trueblood, *The Logic of Belief* (New York: Harper & Row, Publishers, Inc., 1942).

Some persons are then believed to be faithful or unfaithful, loyal or subversive, honest or deceitful. Those who agree with us are accepted only so long as, and on the condition that, they agree. Those who perceive and cling to authority in this manner are somewhat incapable of both decision making and learning. Qualified acceptance lurking just beneath the conscious awareness of the counselor negatively influences the counseling "climate."

There is here, then, a possible intimate relationship between the way we accept and reject people and the way we accept and reject ideas from authorities. This becomes evident as we listen to the use of opinionated language. Such phrases as, "How can anyone be so stupid?" or "Any intelligent person knows . . ." impress upon us how frequently opinionated rejection or acceptance creep in.

The Peripheral Region serves as a filing system for beliefs and disbeliefs. It receives the new information that comes from the Central Region to the Intermediate Region and finally to the Peripheral Region. The specific content of the beliefs and disbeliefs will vary from one person to another. It is this specific content that we examine when we wish to ascertain and identify another's ideological position.

The major concern, however, is not the content but the *reason why* the belief or disbelief is held. Or, using the model, this concern is focused on the kind of interconnections among the peripheral beliefs and on their structural relations with those beliefs as represented in the Central and Intermediate Regions.

Information impinging upon the person from the outside is processed. The processing-coding activity is thinking. In accordance with the hypothesized model, the process of thinking commences with the screening of the information to ascertain its compatibility with the existing beliefs of the Central Region. This initial screening may lead to a rejection of the information, or a distortion or narrowing of it. The idea that a camera could take a picture now of something that took place in the past would generally be rejected because, regardless of the evidence or authority, we are not prepared to accept it since it violates our primitive beliefs.

Information that is to a large degree compatible with one's primitive beliefs is *now examined in relation to authority* (Intermediate Region). It may be compatible and accepted as is. It may not be compatible or acceptable for various reasons. It may not be accepted because it is in disagreement with one's authority. It may not be completely rejected, but narrowed and distorted. Narrowing and distortion takes place in one or more of several ways. We ourselves may avoid serious contact with the reinforcement theory because we feel it to be a threat to the validity of our ideology. We may selectively avoid contact with stimuli, people, events, or books because we do not wish to risk the threat to our present way of life. This in part explains the passivity of some members of an audience during a lecture.

Narrowing may be done for us. An institution may do the screening rather than the person involved. This may be done when books are removed from a reading list, when a school insists on a teacher's adherence to the course outline, when a counselor-educator mentions a theory in such a way that it is obvious that he has a low regard for it. The person himself may narrow or distort by being careful to expose himself to only one point of view in one discipline rather than several points of view in several disciplines.

From the foregoing, it can now be said that those with more closed belief systems are more inclined to reject, narrow and distort. Or they accept information only when it is, in large measure, in agreement with their authorities. Those with more open belief systems consult several authorities, avoid dealing with ideas on a dichotomized basis, tolerate the ambiguity that this involves, and arrive at their own conclusions, which they hold tentatively until complete information is available.

The Time-Perspective Dimension · Those with relatively closed belief systems experience difficulty in making use of information from a broad time perspective. Their decisions, therefore, tend to be based upon an insufficient comprehensiveness. The time perspective refers to the person's beliefs about the past, present and future. They are all represented within the belief-disbelief system, and the person sees them as related to each other. When the time perspective is narrow, the person overemphasizes or fixates on the past, present or future without appreciating the continuity and the connections that exist among them.

The tendency to take refuge in any one time span is increased by rapid cultural changes or severe changes in the individual's health and self-perception. The individual's perception of a high degree of threat in his world may cause him to live chiefly in the past, present or future. This reduces the probability of his living intelligently and wisely both now and in the future. Good decision making, which requires the careful examination of as many relevant factors as possible, is more likely if the person is able to and does encompass in his efforts relevant factors from a broad time perspective.

APPLICATION OF THE MODEL

Self-Perception and Decision Making

A study was made to compare the accuracy of the self-perception of the relatively open- and relatively closed-minded.[19] A total of 150 college students, ranging in age from 20 to 45 years, participated in the study. Each student was administered the Rokeach Dogmatism Scale, Form E,[20] and the Zuckerman Affect Adjective Check List for the Measurement of Anxiety,[21] the latter just prior to the midterm examination. Before the students received the results, the theory, norms and method of scoring for each instrument were explained and discussed. Each person was then requested to estimate his degree of open-mindedness and anxiety. All respondees remained anonymous; identification was by numbers drawn by lot. It was found that those with Open Belief Systems perceived themselves more closed and those with closed Belief Systems perceived themselves more open. Also, those more open-minded perceived the degrees of their anxiety quite accurately. Those with more closed minds perceived their degrees of anxiety inaccurately. Each group perceived itself as having the same degree of anxiety. Almost two thirds of the closed-minded overestimated, and almost one third underestimated, the degree of anxiety. The closed-minded, feeling more anxious, are under greater tension and threat in decision making. The perception of the closed-minded group may be too inaccurate to act as a guide to its performance.

Psychological Needs and Decision Making

Understanding the psychological needs of individuals is one means of comprehending why they respond differently under the same circumstances. To compare the manifest needs of each group, a study[22] was made using a random sample of 120 university students of both sexes, ranging from 20 to 51 years in age. Each student took

[19] C. Gratton Kemp, "Self-Perception in Relation to Open and Closed Belief Systems," *Journal of General Psychology*, 1964, Vol. 70, pp. 341–344.

[20] Rokeach, *op. cit.*, p. 33.

[21] M. Zuckerman, "An Affect Adjective List for the Measurement of Anxiety," *Journal of Consulting Psychology*, 1960, Vol. 24.

[22] C. Gratton Kemp, "Counseling Responses and Need Structures of High School Principals and Counselors," *Journal of Counseling Psychology*, 1962, Vol. 9, pp. 326–328.

the Dogmatism Scale Form E and the Edwards Personal Preference Schedule.[23] The students remained anonymous. Each chose his code number and received the results on coded cards. The general results were discussed with each group of approximately 20 to 25 students. In this manner the students became interested and involved in the undertaking. The results of the 30 with relatively closed minds (mean score 186.21) and the 30 with relatively open minds (mean score 108.63) were chosen for further study.

Significant degrees of difference (at the .01 to .001 level) in the manifest needs of the open and closed-minded are found in 8 of the 15 scales. The open-minded have a greater need for *autonomy, dominance, intraception* and *heterosexuality;* the closed-minded have a greater need for *abasement, succorance, nurturance,* and *endurance.*

In any given task, those with open and those with closed minds are seeking to satisfy different needs. Their perceptions of and attitudes toward the same task, reactions to directions and superiors, and performance could be expected to differ widely. Certain conditions such as explicit directions, encouragement, the completion of the task undertaken, and benevolent authoritarian leaders or supervisors are among the chief necessary conditions in order that the closed-minded may satisfy his needs.

On the other hand, opportunity to make independent decisions, to plan the method of work, to observe and try to understand others from their point of view, and to analyze his own motives and to engage in social activities is necessary in order that the open-minded may satisfy his needs.

The two groups are satisfying different sets of needs in their decision making. Decisions whose outcomes would provide more security, greater maintenance of the status-quo, and more approval from authority figures would be more acceptable to the closed-minded. On the other hand, those decisions which may offer a greater breadth of experience and more independence, and which encompass a wide range of facts and lead to broader and satisfying relationships with people are more attractive to those with open minds.

Perception of Authority and Decision Making

A study[24] was made to determine to what degree a counselor

[23] Allen L. Edwards, *Edwards Personal Preference Schedule* (New York: The Psychological Corporation, 1953).
[24] C. Gratton Kemp, "Influence of Dogmatism on the Training of Counselors," *Journal of Counseling Psychology,* 1962, Vol. 9, pp. 155–157.

trainer would influence the kinds of responses of trainees in counseling. Two counseling situations each in pre- and post-situations were used. In one experiment the trainees selected one response from five in each of ten carefully described situations. In the other context, a random sample of each trainee's responses in actual counseling situations was recorded and analyzed.

As a result of their training, both the relatively open- and relatively closed-minded groups became more permissive and supportive in the paper-and-pencil hypothetical situations. In the actual counseling situation, the group low in dogmatism (open belief system) did not change significantly in the character of their responses from the hypothetical to the actual situations. The group high in dogmatism (closed belief system) changed significantly in the character of their responses from the hypothetical to the actual situations. The direction of the change was toward fewer understanding and supportive responses and toward more evaluative, interpretative, and probing or diagnostic responses.

The open-minded, who could be expected to be more aware of their reactions to stimuli, who have less need to narrow and distort, and who normally consider ideas on their merits, are better integrated, experience less threat, have less anxiety, and are more permissive in their normal relationships. They respond this way and therefore are more understanding and supportive in their responses in the beginning. In the actual situation, which demands a somewhat immediate, less considered response than that which is possible in responding to situations on a page, their responses resemble those on the "test," since this is in accordance with their genotypical response repertoire.

The closed-minded are more inclined to review their responses in the light of the demands of the situation. Therefore, they adjust their thinking and responses to the degree that they feel is acceptable and in accordance with the perceived demands of the instructors and the environment. Since in this situation the instructor favored the client-centered principles, the closed-minded gave more permissive responses on the "test" to conform to the expectations of the environment as they perceived them. In their response to situations on a page they could reflect and select the most appropriate response in accordance with interpreted expectancy. However, in the actual situations there was not the opportunity to reflect. The situation demanded an immediate response. They therefore responded more in accord with their customary and genotypical attitudes, which were more directive.

The closed-minded were influenced in their decisions by their perception of the counselor (authority figure). The open-minded, who had more self knowledge and were more secure, could respond from their own genotypical framework, whereas the more closed-minded were engaged in "party-line" change.

Quality Performance in Decision Making

What does the efficient decision maker do well that the less efficient does not do, or does poorly? An answer to this question is the outcome of a study[25] designed primarily to analyze and if possible improve the quality of decisions of freshmen college students. A total of 80 freshman students, 40 in the control group and 40 in the experimental group, participated in the study. The two groups were matched in intelligence and in degree of open- and closed-mindedness. The Dogmatism Scale, Form E, and the Otis Test of Mental Ability, Form A, were administered to the total sample of 80 students. On the basis of these criteria two comparable groups of 40 each were established. Both groups also took the Watson-Glaser Critical Thinking Appraisal.

The control group and experimental group were each taught by the same instructor. The control group received no special help in solving critical thinking problems, but the experimental group was divided into five subgroups of eight each, with four high and four low in dogmatism in each subgroup. Each of these subgroups participated in ten one-hour meetings. Each meeting was used in solving critical thinking problems. The critical thinking problems were selected from the following forms: *Taxonomy of Educational Objectives, A Test of Problem Solving* (High School Edition), and *A Test of Critical Thinking,* Form G.

Reasons for correct and incorrect conclusions were discussed. These were recorded and those which were general to the five groups are listed below as factors which affected efficiency.

Factors that increased efficiency:

1. Synthesis and evaluation of process relationships.
2. Evaluation of conclusions for inclusiveness and basicity.
3. A flexible approach.
4. Adherence to the conditions given.
5. Analysis of data provided.

[25] C. Gratton Kemp, "Improvement of Critical Thinking in Relation to Open-Closed Belief Systems," *Journal of Experimental Education,* 1963, Vol. 31, pp. 321–323.

Factors that decreased efficiency:

1. Ignoring, distorting or omitting some of the given data.
2. Including additional words and/or ideas.
3. A rigid, often nonadaptive approach.
4. Failure to synthesize or a poor quality of synthesis.
5. Failure to evaluate conclusion or incompleteness of evaluation.

Pre- and post-testing of the control and experimental groups using The Watson-Glaser *Critical Thinking Appraisal* led to the following conclusions:

(1)   The experimental group did better than the control group at the five per cent level.

(2)   In the control group, there was no significant improvement in the performance of either the more open-minded group or the more closed-minded group.

(3)   In the experimental group the more closed-minded group improved but the improvement was not significant; the more open-minded performed significantly better at the one per cent level.

This study clarifies the factors involved in efficient decision making. It emphasizes what the good decision maker does that makes his decision more comprehensive and valid. It also suggests that a direct approach in small groups does little to improve the decisions of the emotionally grounded and threatened perceptions of the closed-minded.

Involvement

Involvement with a person or group differs with the material under discussion. There is not the threat to one's own value system and feelings if the topic is one of an ideational or academic nature. If this is true, the performance of a counselor could be expected to differ in discussing ideas and working with feelings. In the former situation his decisions might be quite adequate, but in the latter much less so because of the kind of involvement demanded. To test these assumptions a study[26] was made using reports of judges, student observers and student group leaders.

[26] C. Gratton Kemp, "Behaviors in Group Guidance (Socio Process) and Group Counseling (Psyche Process)," *Journal of Counseling Psychology*, 1963, Vol. 10, pp. 373–377.

A total of 90 graduate students in three sections participated in the study in regularly scheduled courses in group process. Each section of approximately 30 was divided into groups of six students on the basis of the scores on the Dogmatism Scale, Form E. Each six-student group met as a unit for a total of fifteen 50-minute periods.

Plans were made to use the first three meetings to become acquainted with and accustomed to observers (their peers) and judges in each group. For the following six meetings, a problem was chosen requiring a "socio process," and for the remaining six meetings it was planned to use the "psyche process" in discussing personal concerns. The socio process (group guidance) and psyche process (group counseling) as described by Coffey[27] were discussed. Descriptions of each process were formulated to act as a guide in determining progress. As a means of quantifying the degree and direction of change in the process, a rating scale was developed.

Three judges observed and rated the members and leaders of each of the subgroups. Through comparison and evaluation of ratings during the first three sessions, the judges' ratings (each with the other two) reached a correlation of .92. A student also observed and rated each group using the same criteria as the judges, and made notes regarding the progress of each group. Student observers and student leadership rotated from member to member. Each leader, following his session, made a written report on what took place with reference to the members and himself. Neither the judges nor the students knew the rationale for the establishment of the subgroups.

The comparisons made gave the following results. In group guidance there were no significant differences between those with open and closed minds in the number of group guidance and group counseling indices expressed by members and leaders. In group counseling there was a significant difference (.001 level) between the open and closed-minded members and leaders in the number of group counseling indices expressed.

A comparison was also made of the kinds of responses by those leaders with more open and those with more closed minds. In group guidance each group of leaders used all categories of responses with about the same frequency, with one exception: those with open minds reflected and clarified ideas more frequently. In group counseling, those with more closed minds felt the need for more structure. They also listened less frequently to get the covert meaning of responses

[27] H. S. Coffey, "Socio and Psyche Group Process: Integrative Concepts," *Journal of Social Issues,* 1952, Vol. 8, pp. 65–74.

and much less frequently accepted strong expressions of personal feeling of other members.

Since effective counseling requires unreserved involvement of the counselor, those who are unable to involve themselves because of closed mindedness are in a less favorable position to make the decisions necessary for successful outcomes.

Values and Decision Making

In certain church-related colleges a foundation assists undergraduates who will prepare to enter service organizations upon graduation. These students participate in a counseling and testing program, the results of which are used in part for employment purposes. Among the tests used are the Kuder Vocational Preference CH, the Strong Vocational Interest Blank, the Allport, Vernon, A Study of Values, and the Rokeach Dogmatism Scale, Form E.

In one situation a six-year follow up study[28] was made to examine the relationship between the values and vocational interests found in college students and the values and occupation which they held six years later. This was done in relation to the degree of the openness of the subjects' belief systems.

At graduation, each group (open and closed minds) had the same order of values: religious, social, political, economic, theoretical and aesthetic. Six years later there was a significant difference. The rank order of values for the "open" was: religious, social, theoretical, political, aesthetic, economic. For the "closed" it was: religious, political, economic, theoretical, social, and aesthetic. The open-minded had increased significantly the theoretical value and decreased in the economic value. The closed-minded had decreased significantly the value placed on the social.

A comparison of the high-ranking interests on the Strong and Kuder tests at the time of graduation indicates a close relationship between the number and kinds of interests on the two instruments for those with open minds. Those with closed minds had indicated more interests on the Strong but fewer on the Kuder. On the Kuder their interest was greatest in the social service and persuasive areas, which were more closely related to the kind of preparation for which they had been granted a scholarship.

A comparison of the kinds of employment held by those with

[28] C. Gratton Kemp, "Changes in Values in Relation to Open-Closed Systems," in Rokeach, *op. cit.*

open and closed minds six years later indicates that among those with open minds, 96 per cent were in social service occupations, as compared with 28 per cent of those with closed minds. The closed-minded also were in vocations offering more stability and security. They changed their decisions in accordance with the change in their value patterns.

As described earlier, the closed-minded make decisions on the basis of party-line thinking. They decide in terms of what their authorities have decided. They decide on the basis of security and expediency rather than examination of their own knowledge and the values that they themselves have chosen. Frequently we hear a counselor express regretfully that so many counselors cannot really care about the counselees since their attention is on gaining a promotion. Values that are phenotypical change easily on the basis of some advantage the value holder perceives in the change. The genotypical values of the open-minded change on the basis of a total working through the interrelatedness of the values independently held by the individual. The result is a genuine change in the value structure. The decision making of the closed-minded becomes seriously inefficient whenever his values are threatened and when the counselee "tunes in" on the problems that have been distorted or repressed rather than openly confronted.

A PHILOSOPHICAL POINT OF VIEW

Philosophy respects the carefully reasoned theory of decision making, for it is considered illustrative and useful. Philosophy would warn, on the other hand, that a place must necessarily be reserved for the unpredictable quality of decision making. Philosophy clings without apology to the idea of human freedom. It would insert into the system the possibility of a decision that, after the careful consideration of all perceivable cause and effect relationships, responded, "Nevertheless. . . ."

Again, philosophy would make room for the unpredictable effects resulting from the interplay of imagination and intuition. It respects those little understood variables that are connected causally with our experience and for which no data exists. Or, as stated by Eddington in 1928 in his Gifford lectures, "The future is a combination of the causal influences of the past together with unpredictable elements — unpredictable not merely because it is impracticable to obtain the data of prediction but because no data connected causally with our experience exist." [29]

If the matter of human freedom is taken seriously, the counselor conceivably will live more comfortably with decisions of the counselee that apparently have no discernible reason. He also might be helped to develop the necessary humility if he is to relate to such a mystery — the person. This mystery neither the counselor nor anyone else wishes either to rely upon completely or to remove entirely. Many a recovery cannot be fully explained without the use of the unpredictable variables. Somewhere along the way the person may have affirmed life and determined to live, and this made the difference required to change the outcome.

CONCLUSIONS

The laboratory worker is free to restrict himself to limited aspects of human nature, but the counselor must deal with the whole person. In doing so, he works with hypotheses, some proved and some probably unprovable. Many variables enter into the process of decision making, not only those of adequacy and security as discussed in the theory of the open and closed mind, but also many others. A few of these are the person's values, aspirations, feeling of responsibility, and love for the persons who will be affected by the decision, the personal advantages to be gained, self transcendence, and the will. Nevertheless it is vital that one be aware of what frame of reference he is using, for only by being aware of it will he be able to change it or himself as the facts may indicate he should do.

In keeping with this point of view one theory of decision making has been discussed in detail. This theory was presented because of its comprehensiveness and wide applicability, and because it is one to which reference is often made in speaking and writing. Also, it is a theory to which attention is directed in the National ACES Standards,[30] in which it is stated that the counselor "should have an open mind."

That the making of decisions is more than a so-called "mental" activity has been long accepted. It is now widely recognized that emotion influencing perception plays a significant part in every im-

[29] A. S. Eddington, *The Nature of the Physical World* (Cambridge: Cambridge University Press, 1928), pp. 294–295.
[30] "The Counselor: Professional Preparation and Role: A Statement of Policy," *Personnel and Guidance Journal*, 1964, Vol. 42, p. 537.

portant decision. Also accepted is the manner in which past experience and attitudes built upon this experience affect our decision making. The theory of the open and closed belief systems is built upon these assumptions. In effect it purports that we think as we do because of the kinds of persons we have become.

This theory re-emphasizes that the best decisions are those made by open minds. Those with relatively open minds are distinguished by their ability to make independent decisions based upon a wide range of relevant authorities and their ideas and the toleration of ambiguity during the process. Those with open minds, because of their openness to themselves and their ability to examine their beliefs and disbeliefs, unintimidated by the claims or pressures of others, are able to thread their way more accurately, confidently and serenely in this maze of complex eventualities, our world.

From this description it is clear that some persons, including counselors, have relatively closed minds. Research[31] indicates that authoritarian home conditions are conducive to the development of too great reliance on a single authority, the inability to tolerate ambiguity, and an apprehensive outlook on life. All of these conditions tend to develop a closed-minded approach to reality and to the making of decisions.

To encourage an open-minded approach in himself and in the counselee should be an aim of every counselor. The method of procedure must be discovered and explored. From a theoretical viewpoint the development and maintenance of the following conditions point in the right direction.

"1. A permissive and consistent environment of safety conducive to the toleration and examination of ambiguities.

2. Encouragement and assistance in the symbolization of visceral and sensory stimulus.

3. Experience in locating the center of evaluation within oneself.

4. Avoidance of the dichotomization of experience, recognizing that we discriminate among greater goods and lesser evils.

5. Concerted effort to make necessary conformity intelligent rather than automatic." [32]

[31] C. Gratton Kemp, "Open and Closed Systems in Relation to Anxiety and Childhood Experience," in Rokeach, op. cit.
[32] C. Gratton Kemp, "The Open Mind and Mental Health," Journal of Human Relations, 1961, Vol. 9, pp. 434–435.

QUESTIONS

1. Why does ambiguity frequently lower the quality of a decision?
2. Why may an individual avoid the full consideration of certain factors in decision making?
3. What are the characteristics of good decision making?
4. Why are some decisions illogical?

FOR FURTHER READING

Gordon W. Allport, *Becoming: Basic Considerations for a Psychology of Personality* (New Haven: Yale University Press, 1955)

Since this book is concerned in part with aspects of man's mind and the development of his personality, it is indirectly concerned with decision making. The author believes that psychology should be able to account for the organization and growth of the individual person, with all his decisions and reaching out toward his world. With this belief and purpose in mind, primary consideration is given to those psychological doctrines that advance our understanding of the human personality.

Carl R. Rogers, *On Becoming a Person* (Boston: Houghton Mifflin Co., 1961).

This is a collection of the author's writings over a period of ten years. These papers are all directed toward the problems and decisions faced by the individual who desires to become a more mature person. The book is intended for those from any walk of life who are concerned about the person and his becoming in a world that appears intent on ignoring or diminishing him. For the counselor, it provides a unique kind of basic knowledge and an indication of the skills he needs to develop. It is Rogers' belief that this knowledge, used preventively, will aid in the development of mature, non-defensive, understanding persons.

Milton Rokeach, *The Open and Closed Mind* (New York: Basic Books Inc., 1960).

This book is a systematic presentation of research concerned with the nature of belief systems, especially in relation to decision making. The investigations have been arranged under the following six headings: (1) the theory and measurement of belief systems; (2) the nature of general authoritarianism and general intolerance; (3) experimental cosmology: explorations into the relation between belief and the cognitive processes; (4) the study of disbelief systems; (5) the dynamics of belief systems; (6) personality, ideology and cognitive functioning. Decision making is viewed from many foci against the background of a broad perspective.

13

PERSON TO PERSON

Counseling is still referred to occasionally as a person-to-person relationship. Those who use this description rarely if ever give any indication of its meaning. The assumption seems to be that neither of the terms "person" or "person-to-person relationship" requires explanation. Yet questioning counselors concerning the significance of such a relationship reveals only a limited understanding and even less congruence. The lack of congruence is due to the varying interpretations of the similarities and differences between animal life and human life. The second disparity in viewpoint is the distinction, if any, between the connotation individual-to-individual or one-to-one relationship and person-to-person relationship. We now turn to these differences.

There is general agreement that plant life and animal life are separate. Plant life is a lower form of life. The plant lives as a unity. Its death means the destruction of that unity, and its components sink back into the inorganic world. The animal lives on a higher level and achieves a higher degree of separation from environment by means of a central nervous system. However, the actions of animals are governed by instincts, which imprison each animal. In the animal world it is the species rather than the individual animal that is really unique. Any one animal is only an expression of the endless repetition of the special life strategy of the species.

The difference between plant and animal life wins ready acceptance. However there is much disagreement about the distinction between animal and human life. Bugental emphasizes that a true psychology of human beings is a psychology of noninterchangeable units. "The past 50 years have seen a tremendous accumulation of data about people treated as interchangeable units." [1] Korzybski explains

[1] J. F. T. Bugental, "Humanistic Psychology: A New Breakthrough," *American Psychologist*, 1963, Vol. 18, pp. 563–567.

man's uniqueness as his ability to use the past, present and future in the planning and living of his life. He describes "Humanity" as the "Time-Binding Class of Life." [2]

The nature of man's uniqueness has been a continuing controversy for several centuries. Is uniqueness the result of heredity and environment? If so, how does the product in the human being differ from the product in the animal? Will there be a time when the person is completely known, or even known better than he is known today? In *Six Characters in Search of an Author,* Pirandello makes the point that the imaginary character Sancho Panza is more real than he is himself. That is, Sancho Panza is a finished product and therefore Pirandello views him as having an advantage over himself. Sancho Panza is all that Cervantes has said of him and nothing more. Can the same be said of each of us? Can we by any means whatsoever be fully described and contained? Or must we be content to conclude that within every man there remains even for himself something of an impenetrable mystery?

Is it just chance or coincidence that the description of counseling as a "person-to-person relationship" has now been replaced almost completely by "one-to-one relationship." Is this indicative of our perception of the human being? Is it an outcome of the empirical and materialistic trend? Why has the concept of the person been eclipsed? To the degree that we lose our sense of personhood and become a link in the chain of cause and effect relationships, our uniqueness is only a matter of color, size, aptitude, skill, temperament. When this takes place the word "person" should be replaced by the word "individual" as more appropriate in the description of you and me.

If our uniqueness consists only in our skills, aptitudes, appearance and performance, and if we no longer exercise our innate freedom — our "inner choice" — then it could be that we are no longer *persons,* either to ourselves or to others, but only individuals. Writers on the continent view our loss of personhood as a matter of concern. Stocker writes, "The confusion of modern man is owing to the fact that he has lost his sense of personhood." [3] As Spoerri views our impersonal civilization, he concludes that "We must pass through the Renais-

[2] Alfred Korzybski, "Time-Binding and the Concept of Culture," in M. F. Ashley Montagu, *Anthropology and Human Nature* (Boston: Porter Sargent Publisher, 1957), pp. 43–55.
[3] Arnold Stocker, *Desarai de l'homme Moderne* (Geneva Editions du Mont Blanc, Coll. Action et Pensée, 1946), p. 113.

sance again, but not as Monnier said, in the sense of the individual but rather that of the person." [4] What do those disciplines most concerned with the individual suggest to us?

A PSYCHOLOGICAL VIEWPOINT

Gordon Allport, writing in the thirties, favored the biophysical position as an acceptable principle for the definition of personality. He decided to use the definition of Warren and Carmichael: "Personality is the dynamic organization within the individual of those psychophysical systems that determine his unique adjustments to his environment." [5] This definition focuses on what lies behind specific acts and within the individual. Allport emphasized that the key word, adjustment, should be considered to include "a great amount of spontaneous, creative behavior toward the environment. Adjustment to the physical world as well as to the imagined or ideal world — both being factors in the 'behavioral environment' — involves mastery as well as passive adaptation." [6] He includes in his thinking the inner world of man as well as the outer. He views this definition as a convergence of the popular, biosocial and sociological with the philosophical, theological and religious — or, as he explains it, of the "outer," more superficial, definition and the "inner," metaphysical, definition.[7]

In the fifties Allport again expressed an interest in the unique adjustment of the individual. Under the heading, "The Dilemma of Uniqueness," he discusses personality as a "transitive" process, a continuous change or becoming, and this he designates as "our special concern." He considers each individual a violation of the species, "an idiom unto himself." [8]

Allport affirms the fact that psychology is interested in the person. But the methods of psychology are not able to capture what is "peculiarly Johnian." In explaining what psychology does to the

[4] Theophile Spoerri, "La Politique du Condedere," in *La Suisse forge son destin* (Neuchatel: Editions de la Baconniere, 1942).
[5] H. S. Warren and L. Carmichael, *Elements of Human Psychology* (Boston: Houghton Mifflin Company, 1930), p. 333.
[6] Gordon Allport, Personality, *A Psychological Interpretation* (New York: Holt, Rinehart & Winston, Inc., 1937).
[7] *Ibid.*, p. 50.
[8] Gordon Allport, *Becoming: Basic Considerations for a Psychology of Personality* (New Haven: Yale University Press, 1955), p. 19.

person, John, he describes the process, methods and instruments of clinical psychology. The inherent weakness he sees is that *derived informations do not intersect one another in John.* Therefore, "the result is that we usually view John's personality as a diagram drawn in a set of external co-ordinates, having no interrelations, no duration in time, no motion, no life, no variability, no uniqueness." [9]

Allport does not accept the reply "that science by its very nature is impotent in the face of the idiomatic process of becoming. If there is to be a science of personality at all it should do better than it has in the past with the feature of personality that is most outstanding — its manifest uniqueness of organization." [10] He views man's uniqueness as resident in his separateness from animals ("no other creature worries about his life cycle"), and he sees each man as unique from every other since he has "the capacity to vary his biological needs extensively and to add to them countless psychogenic needs." [11]

Allport makes a strong plea for a transcendence of the "limitations of a psychology of species" and the development of a "more adequate psychology of personal growth." [12] Is it too much to expect that this can and will be attained by the refinement and enlargement of present methodology? Will progress within the present conceptual psychological framework deal adequately and comprehensively with such an assertion as "no other creature worries about his life cycle."

It is exceedingly difficult for psychology to vary its approach. The present position inherits a viewpoint that has a history of more than a century. For over a hundred years psychology, medicine and sociology, to mention disciplines directly concerned with man, have treated him as a machine. By so doing they attempted to avoid assigning functions not fully understood to any mysterious central agency. Wundt thus boldly declared himself for "a psychology without a soul."

For example, medical science has viewed man as a complex ensemble of different machines — the digestive system, respiratory system, nervous system, and others. This attitude has been given emphasis by the addition of the chemico-industrial production of substances such as vitamins and hormones that were long considered characteristic of only living organisms.

[9] *Ibid.,* p. 20.
[10] *Ibid.,* p. 21.
[11] *Ibid.,* p. 22.
[12] *Ibid.,* p. 23.

Tournier points out that medicine has made the human machine more materialistic than the industrial machine.[13] In industry the engineer plans the arrangement of the parts in terms of what is desired. In the case of the human being, science assumes that the different organs and their chemico-physical functions accidently came together to form an organism. This position is the result of the rejection of all arguments stemming from design. Such a rejection increases the difficulty of dealing with the existence of human freedom.

However, some of the students of man do recognize a greater complexity. Claude Bernard, the brilliant founder of modern physiology, kept his attention focused on the whole man. He wrote that "the vital force directs the phenomenon which it does not produce; the physical agents produce phenomena which they do not direct." [14] De Rougemont, a French surgeon and professor at the University of Lyons, uses concepts that might seem to have little relevance to his work. He writes: "Life models the forms, it animates them; it does not construct, it creates. . . ." Later he continues this thought. "Life makes use of some materials and neglects others . . . it therefore exercises a choice. In this exact choosing there is evidently a memory and another intelligence at work." [15] Thus in his study of the life of the body he recognizes the need to use such concepts as creation, choice, memory and intelligence.

Many serving in psychology and medicine are becoming interested in the whole man, the person. They are recognizing the limitations of their specialized fields of effort in answering the quasi-scientific questions that they confront. They are encouraging one another and their students to look to other patterns of thought and other disciplines in an endeavor that each may understand, improve and advance the possibilities of his own and thereby enlarge their understanding of man in his uniqueness.

The counselor would do well to consider this approach. He also needs to seek understanding of the counselee beyond the now comprehended borders of the specific discipline in which he was trained. Rollo May cautions against a narrow preparation of the counselor.

[13] Paul Tournier, *The Whole Person in a Broken World* (New York: Harper & Row, Publishers, Inc., 1957), p. 183.
[14] Claude Bernard, *An Introduction to the Study of Experimental Medicine,* trans. by Henry Copley Greene (New York: The Colonial Press, 1900), p. 131.
[15] Jean de Rougemont, *Vie du corps et vie de l'esprit* (Lyons: Paul Derain, 1945), pp. 126–130.

He writes concerning the advice he gives to students: "I advise them to major in literature and the humanities rather than biology, psychological and pre-medical courses. . . . If the student concentrates on these before he grasps the symbols and myths in man's self-interpretation in our present historical literature, he will be outfitted with a method which will do everything except help him to grasp his real data." [16]

Science can increase our knowledge and understanding to the degree that we are willing to contain the uniqueness of man within the bounds of some form of measurement. Man as only the product of nature can be known by the use of our intelligence. This is so because "this order is intellectual and therefore intelligible because it answers the question of the intellect or because it is produced by the subordination of sense data to the unity of the understanding, which investigates and reasons about the natural phenomena." [17]

Beyond the world of science man is more than this. Man, the individual because of his discreteness, becomes man the person because of his uniqueness. To those who use a speculative or artistic approach another order is revealed. It is a deeper order, grasped by the intuition of the artist and of everyone who views it with the eyes and heart of the artist.

THE VIEWPOINT OF PHILOSOPHY

Philosophy has retained the belief of Aristotle that the language of nature is also the language of speculative thought. However, philosophy has recognized that the methods of science are efficient and reliable but partial. Science requires the subordination of all to the intellect, whose end is a mathematics of nature. This subordination has been opposed by philosophers as an abandonment of the pearl of great price.

Galileo recognized the partiality of the experimental approach and protested that this method would not lead to a knowledge of the "nature of things" as sought by the ancient systems. He warned that the mathematical method could not penetrate into the ultimate constitution and the ultimate fullness of things. In fact, it was to take the world farther away from Greek speculation, which saw it as a panorama of uttermost extremes, universality and individuality, ma-

[16] Rollo May, *Symbolism in Religion and Literature* (New York: George Braziller, 1960), p. 13.
[17] Richard Kroner, *Culture and Faith* (Chicago: University of Chicago Press, 1951), p. 98.

terial and spiritual. His philosophical successors did not all agree. Descartes, Spinoza, Leibniz and others encouraged a new metaphysics that was based upon the mathematical method. Only Hume and Kant reviewed and emphasized the insights of Galileo.

Kant confirmed that the intellect can help considerably in understanding nature, including man. However he thought that it should confine itself to the phenomenal (finite and fragmentary), and should not consider itself completely comprehensive and able to solve the absolute tasks of contemplation. His appreciation of the ability of the natural sciences is clear. He considered them capable of reaching an empirical truth by subordinating phenomena to the general unity, concepts, and principles of knowledge, and writing all the empirical data under general rules or laws. On the other hand, he emphasized that the natural sciences could never reach a speculative truth that "could rival the intuitive and imaginative work of art in uniting the extreme poles of experience, thereby presenting the 'thing-in-themselves.' " [18]

In a limited sense science reconciles particularity and generality. Such procedures as classification, for example, subordinate the particular to the general. If the investigator is content to ignore the uniqueness of the individual and investigate only quantitative relations, he can dominate the facts by symbols. These can be replaced by numbers in order to describe what is considered individual. This ignores that which is most meaningful, i.e. "the Johnian in John." This method does supply useful information, but the counselor finds it difficult to accept its limitations. It should be appreciated within the framework of its empirical restriction as stated by Galileo and interpreted by Kant. It is difficult for the counselor to learn and accept the fact that science eliminates the individuality of the ego more successfully and thoroughly than philosophy has done or is capable of doing.

It is this very difference between the approaches of philosophy and psychology that should receive more attention from counselors. Ignoring the uniqueness of the individual ego, it becomes easy to assume that the corruptions of the self-interest of the individual may disappear with the overcoming of the cultural lag. The scientific method then becomes an idol.

John Dewey was certain that the failures of the past and present were due to the fact that the scientific method "has not been tried at any time with use of all the resources which scientific material and

---

[18] Immanuel Kant, *Critique of Pure Reason,* trans. by J. M. D. Meiklejohn (New York: The Colonial Press, 1900), p. 246.

the experimental method put at our disposal." [19] His faith in science was based on his conviction that the same methods that were successful in the field of physical nature would succeed also in human relations. In his call for an "organized co-operative inquiry" he apparently does not recognize that due to the uniqueness of persons it is not possible to transcend conflicts of interest and achieve the intelligence that he attributes to this process. Such a conclusion is the result of discounting the speculative and intuitive insights; it fails to recognize the centrality of man's freedom to break and remake the antinomies of nature.

Philosophy and religion maintain a deep respect for all the sources of knowledge, including those that are not controlled by the intellect. This position is separate from that of science. Science ignores the truth inherent in individuality itself. Philosophy would emphasize that this world of ours is not a mechanism precisely because it is individual in all its manifestations.

Thus philosophy is at home with the problem of human freedom. Science has great difficulties with this concept. Some writers, referred to in an earlier chapter, have suggested that modern developments in science have opened the door to an understanding of freedom. Philosophy questions this since it considers freedom in its genuine and proper meaning to belong to the will and action of man as a self. Can modern statistical probability tell us anything about the will? It is improbable, since the selfhood of man is methodically excluded from the scientific world. The growing recognition by science of the limitation of causal necessity may encourage counselors to consider another approach to understanding the person.

Philosophy, then, uses different methods in its endeavor to understand the uniqueness of the person. It appreciates the contribution of science but considers that its own contribution is distinct and different from what science can offer. Philosophy relies upon artistic imagination and philosophic speculation, which in turn rely upon contemplation as the supreme capacity of man.

Philosophy at its best also recognizes its limitations. It recognizes that contemplation is unable to help the person to understand reality in a mystical sense. The articulation of the deeper mystical depth of the person requires the assistance of imagination. It is difficult at first to believe that imagination can be better trusted with this function than speculative metaphysics. Of course, it has long been common knowledge that imagination has a part in scientific hy-

[19] John Dewey, *Liberalism and Social Action* (New York: G. P. Putnam's Sons, 1935), p. 51.

196

potheses and discoveries. It is also accepted that poetry frequently attains to a truth about the person to which science has no access.

Although religious imagination (imagination concerned with the community of persons) is by no means infallible and is subject to illusions, these illusions are discoverable by religious feeling itself. This is clearly illustrated by the Greek criticism of Greek mythological religion. Heraclitus, Xenophanes, Socrates and Plato were able to reject the Homeric gods and to conceive of deity in a deeper, worthier fashion approaching Biblical revelation.

CONCLUSIONS

There are two procedures to be followed in gaining a knowledge of the person. Either one alone provides only partial understanding. One procedure is the objective and scientific, the other the subjective and intuitive. The counselor needs both approaches. The first supplies him with information. Information is intellectual and although very necessary, it is limited to understanding the individual — that is, his particularity and discreteness but not his personhood. Useful information is the contribution of sociology, anthropology and particularly psychology. Psychology has made great strides in understanding the individual insofar as he can be known through cause and effect relationships. Without this, our understanding of the person would be impossible. On the other hand, without the subjective and intuitive insights of philosophy the essence and mystery of the person would not have become a reality. The individual who rejects his potential for freedom and for making his inner self the object of consideration remains an object with particularity but not personhood.

We become persons not only because of the objective knowledge we integrate but also because of the attitude of mind in which the self deals with this knowledge and with its experience. This is not done without great effort, since one may reach mature years and not go beyond asking the pragmatic questions of society, answering these questions with the objective knowledge of science. In this scientific, materialistic world the discipline of meditation remains undeveloped.

The individual becomes a person partly through his relationships with others. But not all relationships develop his personhood. Many of his relationships are only relationships between individuals, relationships of "personages." This is the character of the great majority of our business, social, and even family relationships.

Underneath the façade of the personage is the person. The counselor works constantly with both. He recognizes and senses a double dialogue, and so does the counselee. One dialogue is "apparent and visible, formed of our words, our confidences, our looks and our gestures — an encounter of personages: the other inward and invisible — the encounter of our persons. The second could not have existed without the first; but the first has no value except as an expression of the second." [20]

Both the counselor and counselee are participators in a society that, in general, lacks the sense of personhood. They have been conditioned to treat one another optimally as individuals and minimally as objects. The "marketplace society" vividly described by Erich Fromm is a condition we have all experienced.

The most difficult part of life today is not its uncertainty, its false values, its competition. It is being treated as an object, manipulated as a tool, being ignored when no longer useful. McCracken, writing on lust, emphasizes that "the worst evil in fornication and prostitution is not the gratification, not the surrender of self-control, not the possibility of venereal disease, but the terrible impersonality, each treating the other as an object of desire; in the case of the prostitute, professional or amateur, as a means of gain." [21] "Getting along with others" requires only that we learn how to adjust, to associate, to present the appropriate personage to fit the particular occasion. Counselors discuss "roles," and sometimes the role playing becomes the significant part of the process.

Hearing the other as subject means hearing him as a person. Martin Buber, in his book *I and Thou,* awakens us to the fact that self-concern does not provide self-fulfillment. He shows us that we are interdependent in our quest to become persons. "We cannot really be unless our being is affirmed by others, and they will not affirm us in a manner that makes us sure of our own existence unless we affirm them in a manner that totally acknowledges them for themselves." [22]

This is the dimension that is not contained in the objective, scientific study of man. Science can help us to know man's condition. It is able to analyze his physical and psychical relations with his environment, but it can go no further. Only through religious feeling,

[20] Paul Tournier, *The Meaning of Persons* (New York: Harper & Row, Publishers, Inc., 1957), p. 131.
[21] Robert J. McCracken, *What Is Sin: What Is Virtue?* (New York: Harper & Row, Publishers, Inc., 1966), p. 49.
[22] Martin Buber, *I and Thou,* trans. by Ronald Gregor Smith (New York: Charles Scribner's Sons, 1958), p. 31.

imagination and sensitivity is it possible to enter into a person-to-person communion with the other. This attitude is helped but not ensured by training in the sciences including psychology.

The attitude is "dominated by this belief in the centrality of personal relations. . . . [It] sets the relationship of the self to other selves as the center of valuation and values everything else in relation to this. For such an attitude the main business of life consists in understanding, appreciating, and creating the full reality of personal relationship." [23]

IMPLICATIONS FOR THE COUNSELOR

Knowledge is necessary, but for the counselor it is not enough. With the well developed case study or series of taped interviews the counselor may at the end of the day still be in the world of *things.* This is not to say that it is not useful to synthesize all the information we can secure concerning the counselee. But, however successful, the synthesis will reveal only one side of his nature — his mechanisms. The counselor will find it necessary to add to this knowledge a different kind of understanding, the kind that comes from a person-to-person encounter in which each relinquishes the façade of his personage and puts himself at the service of the other. It is not enough to associate; we must communicate. The counselor who only associates may do much to help the outer individual; but the real person within, with his longings and misunderstandings, is not touched.

Without freedom man would possess no self. He would have individuality but not personhood, since he would not be a subject in contrast to objects. Counseling presupposes that the counselor has a self. To function adequately the counselor must be committed. He will not succeed unless he dedicates himself to the task. His dedication is the very nerve of morality, since in being dedicated he becomes a self; he brings into fruition to some degree his capacity for "inner choice." To become a self is to be a moral self, which presupposes a substantial degree of loyalty, of permanence in striving and willing, of endurance and steadfastness and consistency in acting and doing. In this way we experience the self as a self.

The counselor, in the development of this self, transcends the limits of his profession because such a development involves the inner motivation, the character and heart of man. The counselor expresses himself more deeply in this inner motivation than in a pragmatic, ex-

[23] John MacMurray, *The Structure of Religious Experience* (New Haven: Yale University Press, 1936), pp. 25–26.

pedient response to the demands of culture. One counselor may ask, "What will result if I do this?" But another may ask the prior question, "Is what I am thinking of doing right?" The counselor who is "free" does not depend upon the world. Such a counselor strives to become a person. He is concerned with himself in order that he may be more useful to the counselees. He is his own target and the scene of exertion and action and becomes an ego in a deeper sense, exercising both his freedom and his capacity for "inner choice." In fact it is in this very effort of reconciling the individualistic ego of discreteness and the universal ego of eternity that he gains his personhood.

Everything with which the counselor comes into contact assumes the tone quality of thing or of person. The difficulty is not only that our counselors need better training and longer and more intensive counseling practicums and internships, but that at the end of this they may still have a *thing* approach to those they have agreed to help.

It would be comforting if we could depend on experience to mould us into more imaginative, sensitive, caring counselors. If we really desire it, experience may help us to become persons. We may recognize that we are becoming able to discover the world of persons. But for many of us this will not be easy. One who has travelled the road would help us to understand in these words: "To become a person, to discover the world of persons, to acquire the sense of the person, to be more interested in people as persons than in their ideas, their party labels, their personage means a complete revolution, changing the climate of our lives." [24]

QUESTIONS

1. What is your conclusion concerning the person's uniqueness?
2. What methods does philosophy use in its endeavor to understand the uniqueness of the person?
3. Why should the counselor try to relate to others as a person?

FOR FURTHER READING

Paul Tournier, *The Meaning of Persons* (New York, Harper & Row, Publishers, Inc., 1957).

The author describes the many ways in which we avoid becoming persons and the ways in which we treat one another as objects.

[24] Tournier, *op. cit.*, p. 183.

He involves the reader in the consideration of what life really is when lived as a person. Finally, he confronts us with the necessity of choice and commitment if personhood is to be attained and if we in turn are to help others to attain it.

Erich Fromm, *Escape from Freedom* (New York: Holt, Rinehart & Winston, Inc., 1941).

This book illustrates well some of the results of treating one another as objects rather than as persons. The author makes clear that the reason for our predicament must be searched for in the dynamics of the psychological processes. The thesis of his book is that modern man, freed from the bonds of pre-individualistic society, has not gained freedom in the positive sense of the realization of his individual self. Despite the fact that he is independent, he is isolated, an object among objects, and therefore anxious with a feeling of powerlessness. He has communication but not communion.

C. Gratton Kemp, *Perspectives on the Group Process* (Boston: Houghton Mifflin Company, 1964).

This is a book of carefully chosen readings, with introductions to each part by the author, who also wrote the first section. The parts of the book are titled: (1) Issues in the Group Process; (2) The Group; (3) The Group Process; (4) Leadership; (5) The Group Member. The division into parts facilitates the purpose of the book in that it permits focusing on one constituent element at a time. The author views the group as a means of developing the conditions conducive to a person-to-person relationship, and group process as the method of furthering communication between and among persons.

Earl A. Loomis, *The Self in Pilgrimage* (New York: Harper & Row, Publishers, Inc., 1960).

This excellent book describes the development of the self concisely and with clarity. It then proceeds to explain incisively and illustrate the meaning of communication with others. Finally it examines the conditions that exist when the self is alienated or "in hell" and the self's experience when in communion with others. The author elucidates with an interesting style the full meaning of what is involved in a person-to-person relationship.

INDEX

Change in behavior (*cont'd*)
  genotypical, 153, 157–158, 162–163
  imagination in, 159–161
  "inner choice" concept, 158–159, 163–164
  through love, 162, 164
  meaning of, to the counselee, 158
  phenotypical, 153, 157, 162
  through reinforcement, 156, 157, 163
  stages, 155
  symbolic meaning in, 160–162
  total involvement in, 154, 157, 163
Christianity, source of individualism, 8
Classicism, 5–6
  revival of, *see* Renaissance
Clinebell, Howard J., Jr., 73
"Closed mind," *see* Belief systems, open and closed
Cofer, C. N., 145
Coffey, H. S., 182
Cognitive dissonance, 141–142
Combs, Arthur W., 165
Competition
  and anxiety, 93
  Russell on, 118
Conditioning, in counseling, 40–41
  operant, 108
Conscience
  immature, 28
  nature of, 26–27
  philosophical view, 26, 33–36
  product of acculturation, 26
  psychologists on, 26–29
  religious view, 26, 33–36
  socio-psychological view, 28–32
  transmoral, 33–36
Conscientiousness, 32
Counselee
  anxiety and guilt, 90
  counselor's beliefs about, 12–15
  decision and action, 43–44, 106
  interests, personal vs. community, 29–31
  self-commitment, 69–70
  value systems, 74–75
  will of, 43–49
Counselor
  belief about the nature of man, 12–15
  belief in the will of the counselee, 44–46

Counselor (*cont'd*)
  dedication, 199
  and modern values, 78
  motivational theory, 149–150
  as person, not "personage," 128–129, 199–200
  reactive behavior, 127–128
Cox, Harvey, 71, 72
Crutchfield, R. S., 171
Curriculum change, 164–165
Cybernetics, 140

Dale, Edgar, 116
Decision making
  and ambiguity, 166
  emotional variable, 167
  open and closed minded, *see* Belief systems, open and closed
  and perception of authority, 178–180
  and psychological needs, 177–178
  quality performance in, 180–181
  relevancy in, 166
  and self-perception, 177–178
  time perspective in, 176
  unpredictable quality of, 184–185
  and values, 183–184
Democratic theory of man, 136–137
Determinism, 22–23
Dewey, John, 20, 73, 195–196
Ding an sich, 22
Doane, B. K., 142
Dogmatism Scale, 167–168, 177–178, 180–183
Doniger, Simon, 16
Drive and drive-reduction, 137–138, 145
Durant, Will, 83

Eckhart, Meister, 102
Eddington, A. S., 185
Education
  search for meaning in, 119–120
  in the technical age, 68
  of the whole person, 119–120
Edwards, Allen L., 178n
Ego, Freud on, 88
Egotism, 20
Ellenberger, Henri F., 70
Emotion
  directional qualities, 145–146
  function of, 144–146, 148–149
  Pascal on, 83